TALENT

TECTONICS

STEVEN T. HUNT, PhD

TALENT

TECTONICS

NAVIGATING GLOBAL WORKFORCE SHIFTS, BUILDING RESILIENT ORGANIZATIONS, AND REIMAGINING THE EMPLOYEE EXPERIENCE

FOREWORD BY DAVE ULRICH, RENSIS LIKERT COLLEGIATE PROFESSOR OF BUSINESS ADMINISTRATION, UNIVERSITY OF MICHIGAN

WILEY

Published by John Wiley & Sons, Inc., Hoboken, New Jersey.
Published simultaneously in Canada.

For general information on our other products and services or for technical support,
please contact our Customer Care Department within the United States at
(800) 762-2974, outside the United States at (317) 572-3993 or fax (317) 572-4002.

Wiley publishes in a variety of print and electronic formats and by print-on-demand.
Some material included with standard print versions of this book may not be
included in e-books or in print-on-demand. If this book refers to media such as a
CD or DVD that is not included in the version you purchased, you may download
this material at http://booksupport.wiley.com. For more information about Wiley
products, visit www.wiley.com.

Library of Congress Cataloging-in-Publication Data is Available:

ISBN 9781119885184 (Hardback)
ISBN 9781119885207 (ePDF)
ISBN 9781119885191 (ePub)

Cover Design: Wiley
Cover Image: © Stephanie Schmidt

SKY10035150_071422

This book is dedicated broadly to previous generations who fought for the better working conditions we now have, current generations who are finding innovative ways to improve the employee experience, and future generations who will hopefully realize the dream of providing meaningful work to all people the world over. At a personal level the book is dedicated to my parents Earl (Buz) and Marylou Hunt, who improved millions of lives directly and indirectly through their work as cognitive and counseling psychologists; my children, Robert and Antonio, who are starting their own career journeys and who will always be high potential talent in the eyes of their father; and especially to my wife, Dr. Cynthia Caraballo-Hunt, whose work as a family medicine physician betters peoples' lives in profound ways, including my own most of all.

Contents

Foreword

Decades ago, in my first Organizational Behavior course, my then-teacher and now mentor advocated, "Organizations don't think, people do." This mantra became an obsessive quest for me to figure out how people come together to create organizations that so dramatically influence all parts of our lives (how we work, play, eat, dress, and worship). Years later, after lots of observations, research, and writing, I tweaked his mantra, "Organizations don't think, people do; but organizations shape how people think, act, and feel." Why does this maxim matter? Because, as Steve articulately points out in this impactful book, recent societal trends of digitalization and demographics are changing the ways employees respond to organizations and how organizations influence employees. With unprecedented physical, social, economic, political, and emotional uncertainties, it behooves business and HR leaders to respond to these changes in positive ways.

Steve's ideas help turn potential threats of uncertainty into opportunities for progress. He masterfully offers insights based on solid evidence and relevant experience coupled with diagnostic questions and useful tools. What I most like is that his blueprint for reimagining work navigates paradoxes that organizations must balance as they seek to support the goals of diverse stakeholders. He does not fall prey to the simplistic trap of moving from A to B, but he recognizes the evolution of ideas that suggests A and/ also B. Managing the paradox of both A and B requires more complex analysis that leads to more informed decisions. Some of these paradoxes include these actions:

Balancing past, present, and future. We do not leave the past behind but live with it today as we create a better tomorrow. Steve consistently puts "new" ideas into their historical context and shows the evolution of thinking that cumulatively creates a new future. This applies to psychological trends about why people work, gender equity, worker's rights, employee primacy, and digital evolution. Rather than denigrating the past, he consistently brings it forward into our present, then anticipates what is next.

Balancing the individual and the organization. A major insight I take from this book is the clever melding of how individuals (called workforces, employees, talent, people, competence) come together into organizations (called workplaces, teams, cultures, systems, capabilities) to enhance both. Because of people, organizations operate more effectively. Because of organizations, people have higher well-being. The seven workforce challenges Steve addresses in the book have implications for both how organizations operate, such as "how to get the right people into the right roles?" and how individuals function within organizations, such as "how do I move into a role that works best for me?" He talks about agility both as an organizational capability and as an individual competence. His recognition of both "human" and "organization" elements of the future of work adeptly characterizes the inevitable trade-offs that leaders must manage to build effective companies.

Balancing information as data and as guidance. With technology advances, all manner of information is ubiquitous at the touch of our fingers through internet search engines, webinars, consulting reports, and social media. It is obviously better to make decisions based on data than merely intuition. But information can also come in the form of more qualitative guidance based on experience. Guidance moves beyond data benchmarking (How do I compare to others?), best practices (Who is a good example?), and predictive analytics (Why are they effective?) to personal insight (How can I be more effective?). Steve's recommendations balance use of both structured information (data) and unstructured information (observation) to offer guidance that makes the knowledge he shares not simply informative, but productive.

Balancing inside/out and outside/in. Steve consistently connects what happens inside an organization (e.g., employee attitudes) to what happens outside the organization (e.g., customer attitudes). As I have studied, this virtual cycle of external context connecting to internal actions creates a virtual spiral to make progress in both organizations and society (see Figure F.1). The future of work is not just taking care of people but taking care of people *so that* customers feel taken care of and customers feel taken care of *because* of the people who care for them. Companies must attend to and improve the experience of all groups to be successful.

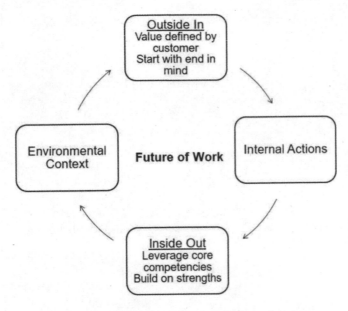

FIGURE F.1 Connecting environmental context and internal action.

You will discover your own insights from this wonderful book. Reflecting on the paradoxes and topics it addresses, my evolving mantra might be, "Organizations don't think, people do; but organizations shape how people think, act, and feel and by doing so improve personal, organizational, and societal outcomes that matter to all of us." Thanks for a wonderful book that makes a difference both for the future of work and for the future of society.

Dave Ulrich
Rensis Likert Professor, Ross School of Business,
University of Michigan
Partner, The RBL Group

Introduction: How We Managed People in the Past Will Not Work in the Future

Why Are We Still Using Management Methods Created During the Roman Empire?

Many roads and buildings in Europe can be traced to the Roman Empire. In some cases, people literally walk on stones placed more than 2,000 years ago. Many other inventions created by the Romans also continue to shape our lives. Some endured because they still work, such as crop rotation in farming. Others are still used because they are familiar, even if they are not very effective. Hierarchical organization structures and the associated "org charts" used by companies belong in this category (see Figure I.1). Org charts categorize workforces based on how they are connected via higher level leadership positions. If the person in the role of "Governor of Imperial Provinces" on the left of Figure I.1 had an issue with the "Administrator of Rome and Italy" on the right they would first go to their leader the "Amici Caesaris," who would talk to the "Proco. Imp. Maius," who would then communicate to the "Consilium Semestre," who would finally tell the "Admin of Rome and Italy." This top-down method for workforce management has been familiar to leaders since the Roman Empire, but it has significant limitations when applied to the modern workforce.

Hierarchical organizational structures were created to manage workforces during a time when work was largely defined by geography. Prior to the 21st century, where people physically lived heavily influenced the work they did and whom they worked with. Team members all worked in the same building with their immediate leaders. Org charts usually mirrored how the workforce was structured geographically.

The rise of the internet economy has created a split among people's location, roles, and work relationships. Teams are no longer constrained by geography. It is common for people to work in one city, report to a manager in another city, and collaborate with people across the world. Org charts might accurately reflect how a company reports financial numbers, but they contain little information about the roles, social interactions, and relationships

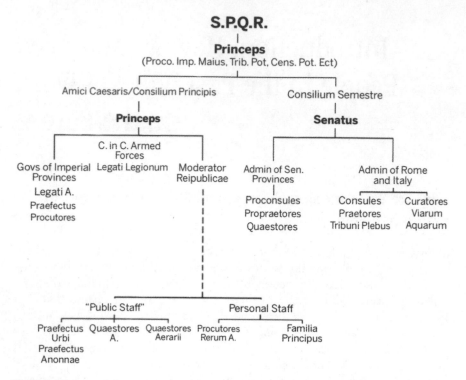

FIGURE I.1 Roman hierarchical organizational leadership structure.[1]

Source: The Government of the Roman Empire Under early Principate. (n.d.).
[Gif]. Fordham University. https://sourcebooks.fordham.edu/ancient/spqr-under
-augustus.gif

that drive profit and loss. Where an employee is placed on an org chart, it may tell little about what they do or who they work with. The continued use of org charts also reflects a top-down leadership style that is antithetical to the cross-functional nature of most modern organizations. It implies that decision-making authority resides in roles higher up the chart, which disempowers frontline employees to act quickly. Because org charts often provide little insight into what people actually do or how they work together, using org charts to guide workforce decisions can also result in inadvertently firing the wrong people and disrupting team relationships that are critical to a company's performance. I have known multiple companies that let employees go based on their positions on an org chart, only to discover these people were doing work that was critical to the company's performance. In several cases, they had to rehire the people as contractors at much higher pay rates with much lower levels of organizational commitment.

Innovations in technology have created tools that are far superior to org charts for capturing information about the employee roles, skills, and relationships that make a company function.[2] Relatively few companies have adopted these tools largely because it would require leaders to change how they make decisions. At some point, leaders will stop clinging to their love of org charts. When that day comes, employees will rejoice in seeing org charts jettisoned to join bronze swords, lead plumbing, and other things from the Romans that were once useful but are now at best inefficient and at worst harmful.

The purpose of this book is to help organizations build workforces for a future that is very different from the past. It discusses how the twin "talent tectonic" forces of digitalization and demographics are changing the nature and purpose of work. It explains the psychology of employee experience and why it is critical to building adaptable organizations that can thrive in a world of accelerating change and frequent skill shortages. It discusses how to integrate business strategy, psychology, and technology to create more nimble companies. And it explains why we must move beyond ineffective workforce management methods based on outdated technology such as hierarchical org charts.

This book discusses the future, but its focus is on the present, identifying things companies can do now to attract talent and create resilient organizations. It also talks about the one thing about work that is not changing: the psychology of the people who work in organizations and how employee experience influences their engagement, performance, and adaptability. This book looks at these topics from the perspective of an industrial-organizational psychologist who has helped thousands of companies around the world use technology to build effective workforces. Few people have viewed the future of work from this particular angle. The book is based on engagements with organizations spanning virtually every industry.[i] It also incorporates a range of research from industrial-organizational psychology, management science, socioeconomics, and related fields. The book is a product of extensive experience working at the intersection of people,

---

[i]Most stories and examples in this book are based on companies I have worked with over my career. I do not share names of companies for several reasons. First, not all the stories are positive. Second, I do not want people to evaluate an example based on the name of the company that did it. Just because a company has a strong public brand does not mean it has good workforce management methods. The company Enron was widely admired for years despite using abhorrent workforce management methods to create fraudulent financial results. Conversely many great workforce management methods are found in privately held organizations few people have heard of. Company names are not what matters. What matters is what we can learn from company practices.

technology, and work. My goal as an author is to draw on this experience to share business insights you may not have considered and practical psychological knowledge you may not have encountered. The book includes fairly extensive citations if you wish to dive more deeply into the science and data underlying many of these concepts and observations.

The book provides guidance on how to attract, retain, develop, engage, and manage people for a new world of work, keeping in mind there is no one best way to manage workforces. My career involves working with companies over multiple years and I have seen how workforce management techniques play out over time. Theoretically well-designed processes often fail in application. Methods that work in one company fail in others, and methods that worked in one company at one time may not work later based on changing technologies, leadership characteristics, and company resources. It is critical to determine what solutions are appropriate for an organization given its unique culture, business needs, and resource constraints. Each chapter in the book ends with a set of questions to discuss with company leaders, managers, and/or employees to determine what makes sense for the organizations you work with. A goal of this book is to help you understand why these questions matter, when they are important to discuss, and what to consider when answering them.

Content Overview

The book is meant to be read from front to back. However, each chapter stands on its own for readers who are interested in specific topics. The first three chapters address changes reshaping work and workforce management. The remaining chapters provide guidance on how to respond to these changes. The content of the chapters is summarized next.

Forces Reshaping Work and Workforces (Chapter 1). The phrase *talent tectonics* describes fundamental shifts reshaping work and organizations. The two biggest shifts are the accelerating pace of change caused by digitalization and the reshaping of labor markets caused by demographic changes in birth rates and life spans.

- **Digitalization.** As technological innovation expands into every facet of life it increases the speed of change. This affects multiple aspects of corporate life including company survival. The life span of companies is growing shorter while the acquisition rate of companies has steadily increased.[3] Companies are restructuring faster than ever before. Industries are being altered with changes in one industry creating changes in another. For example, the shift to electric cars is transforming the automotive industry but also has massive implications for the energy, transportation, mining, oil and gas, and manufacturing industries.[4] This level of change is also playing out at the level of individual jobs. Automation is eliminating long-standing tasks while creating new types of work.[5] Even enduring professions such as land surveying, which dates back to the ancient Egyptians, are being completely altered by inventions such as satellite and drone technology. Whatever a company or job looks like now, it will almost certainly be different in three years.

■ **Demographics.** People are living longer and having fewer children, and not just by a small amount. The life expectancy in the US has increased by 38 years since 1910.[6] The generation of workers currently entering the economy can expect to live about one-third longer than their great-grandparents. At the same time, the global birth rate has declined by 51% since 1950.[7] In many countries more people are leaving the labor market than entering it.[8] Barring catastrophic events such as wars, this has never happened in modern history. It is creating growing labor shortages and redefining job markets. Companies are already struggling to find skilled employees and filling job roles is predicted to become even more challenging.[9]

Similar to how movement of geological tectonic plates drives changes on the surface of the earth, these two talent tectonic shifts are creating visible changes in the nature of organizations and work. Companies can treat these shifts as threats to be managed or opportunities to be leveraged, but either way they must adapt to survive. This starts with understanding how these technological and socioeconomic forces are changing the nature of work, jobs, organizations, and careers.

Employee Experience and Workforce Adaptability (Chapter 2). The world of work is radically changing, with one critical exception: organizations will always employ people, and the fundamental psychology of people is relatively constant.[10] Despite popular assertions that generations are radically different from one another, studies dating back to the 1920s show that the nature of what people want from work does not change much over time.[11] The things that make us happy, engaged, and healthy at work are rooted in human psychological attributes that do not evolve as quickly as technology and societies. What does change is the ability of people to demand better employee experiences at work. To illustrate this concept, consider two historic talent tectonic shifts from the 20th century: the workers' rights movement and the women's suffrage movement.

■ Coal miners in the late 19th century did not know what black lung disease was, but they did know that working in the mines was killing them prematurely.[12] Coal companies did not pay much attention to how miners felt about their safety given the social values and labor markets at the time.

Miners were unable to demand change lest they lose their jobs and the ability to provide for their families. Miners did not get protection for black lung disease until the workers' rights movements of the early 20th century changed social values regarding the obligation of companies to protect the health and safety of employees. The workers' rights movement did not change miners' desire for a better work environment. What changed was their ability to demand healthier working conditions.

- In the early 20th century, social attitudes toward educating women radically shifted due to the women's suffrage movement.[13] This led to an increase in women achieving college degrees throughout the 20th century. The rise in women's education led to large numbers of women in the 1960s and 1970s launching careers in professions that had historically been limited to men. These women faced openly sexist behavior and blatant sexual discrimination in pay and promotions. Working women in the 1970s did not like this discrimination but many did not feel empowered to overtly challenge it. By the beginning of the 21st century more women were graduating from college than men in many countries. As more women entered the workforce, social attitudes continued to shift toward gender equity, and overt sexism and blatant discrimination were no longer tolerated. We have a lot of work to do to achieve full gender equity, but this is not a function of changing what working women want. Working women always wanted to be treated fairly and respectfully. What has and continues to change is their ability to demand they be treated as equals.[ii]

These examples illustrate how past talent tectonic forces have driven companies to create better working conditions and employee experiences. Chapter 2 explains why improving how employees experience work is critical to responding to the current talent tectonic forces of digitalization and demographics. It also discusses the different types of employee experiences that affect work, why they matter, and how they are shaped by employee expectations, perceptions, and interpretations.

Work Technology and Organizational Agility (Chapter 3). Work technology refers to solutions designed to build and manage workforces so they deliver the goals of the business. At the broadest level, this technology focuses on doing five basic things: enabling people decisions such as

---

[ii]This example reflects stories my mother shared as a professional woman who founded a company in 1972. Working women of her generation demonstrated amazing strength and determination overcoming sexist attitudes about the roles, capabilities, and value of women in the workplace.

hiring or compensation, creating work communities and teams, supporting employee development, ensuring security and compliance, and reducing time needed to complete administrative actions. Chapter 3 explains the role that different types of work technology play in creating more agile organizations. It focuses particularly on the value technology provides by enabling large companies to act more like small entrepreneurial organizations.

Perennial Workforce Challenges (Chapters 4 through 8). Chapters 4 through 8 examine the future of work from the perspective of seven perennial workforce challenges (see Table I.1). These challenges are called *perennial* because companies always have to address them, and they never go away. They include designing organizations, filling roles, ensuring employees have the skills to perform their work, engaging employees to achieve company goals, increasing efficiency of work, complying with laws and regulations, and building culturally effective companies. These challenges can also be viewed from an employee perspective such as finding career opportunities, learning new skills, accomplishing career goals, achieving success, and making effective use of time.

TABLE I.1 Perennial Workforce Challenges

Challenge	Company Perspective	Employee Perspective
	What companies must do: perennial challenges to building and managing workforces	
Designing organizations	How will we structure roles and pay people?	What career opportunities are in this company?
Filling positions	How can we get the right people into the right roles?	How can I move into new roles?
Developing capabilities	How can we build people's skills and abilities so they can effectively perform their roles?	How can I achieve my future career goals?
Engaging performance	How can we motivate and retain people to execute the company's strategy?	How can I get fulfillment from my current work?
	How companies do it: perennial challenges to creating highly effective workforces	
Increasing efficiency	Are we maximizing the time of our employees and the money invested in our workforce?	Is it easy to get things done?
Ensuring compliance	Are we fulfilling our legal and ethical obligations?	Am I being treated fairly?
Building culture	Are we supporting our core values?	Does the company align with my beliefs?

The seven perennial workforce challenges provide a sense of order in the fast-changing world of work. I like to compare them to the perennial challenges associated with throwing a great party because both have to do with creating positive experiences. For organizations it is about creating experiences that inspire employees to work collaboratively to achieve company goals. For parties, it is creating an environment that inspires guests to have fun. A perennial challenge to throwing a good party is figuring out what music will inspire people to dance. In the 1920s people solved this challenge by playing ragtime music on a Victrola. Now we download a playlist of current hits from the web. Similarly, people's expectations about work and the technology they expect to use in organizations has changed since the 1920s. But the basic challenges to building workforces and throwing parties have not changed because they are about psychological truths. Employees want to be appreciated at work and people want to dance at parties. What changes are the nature of people's expectations when it comes to doing these things and the available technology to meet these expectations. The perennial workforce challenges never change, but the relative importance of each challenge changes in response to company growth, business market conditions, and shifting labor markets. The methods used to address the challenges also change due to technological innovation. For example, the internet profoundly altered how companies fill roles, and remote work technology is radically changing how companies design organizations.

Chapters 4 to 8 examine these challenges from the perspective of their impact on employee experience and how technology is transforming the methods companies use to address them.

- **Designing Organizations to Provide Positive Employee Experiences (Chapter 4)** is about determining what jobs define the company, where they are located and how they are organized and compensated. In the past, companies approached organizational design mainly as a financial activity with employee experience an afterthought. More attention needs to be placed on the employee experience, recognizing that people do not join companies to fill department headcount requirements. They join because something about the organization appeals to them. The top issue on employees' minds when considering a job or going through a corporate restructuring is not "how will this help the company's financial portfolio." It is "how will this affect my job experience, career opportunities and work relationships?"
- **Filling Positions and the Experience of Moving into New Roles (Chapter 5)** is about finding and hiring people to perform different functions including transferring people internally based on business needs and career interests. In the past, companies assumed they could find talent when they needed it. This is no longer the case for many

jobs. Companies must look at hiring from an employee experience perspective, recognizing that people do not want to be qualified, selected, and onboarded. They want to discover opportunities, learn about roles, be welcomed into organizations, and develop new careers. This means filling roles based on what candidates want and not just what companies need.

- **Developing Capabilities and the Employee Experience of Learning (Chapter 6)** is about providing people with knowledge and skills to perform current work and take on future responsibilities. In the past, development programs focused on making incremental improvements to employee's existing capabilities through training. This approach worked when careers were more stable and linear. This view of career growth no longer makes sense in many industries.[14] It is not enough to train employees to be better at their current job if their current job is likely to radically change or disappear due to automation. Companies need a new approach that views development as enabling people to do things that are much different from what they did in the past.

- **Creating Engagement and Employee Experiences That Inspire Successful Performance (Chapter 7)** is about guiding, inspiring, supporting, and retaining employees to achieve the goals of the company. Companies must put considerable effort into engaging employees in a high-pressure world where people can easily change jobs if they are not fully supported in their roles. Another topic discussed in this chapter is team performance dynamics, recognizing that the performance of the people we work with has a major impact on our own experience of work, particularly when we are under pressure.

- **Increasing Efficiency, Ensuring Compliance and Security, and Building Culture (Chapter 8)** is about how companies can address the first four challenges in ways that optimize the time and money spent on workforce management activities; comply with employment regulations, laws, and contracts; address security and compliance risks; and support cultural values related to health and well-being, diversity and inclusion, and environmental sustainability. This chapter also discusses the importance of hybrid/remote work cultures. People do not want to work for companies that do not respect their time, privacy, safety, rights, and values. Nor do they want to work for companies that force them to relocate or commute to an office if they feel it is unnecessary to doing their job.

An important difference between the seven perennial challenges and the more traditional process view of human resources (HR) that focuses on things such as recruiting, training, or performance management is their inter-complementary nature. As the nature of work changes, the distinction between traditional HR processes is disappearing. For example, the design of a company's organization influences how it fills job roles and develops employee capabilities. Training is one method to develop employees, but staffing can be a more powerful tool for development if used in the right way. One of the most effective ways to get someone to learn how to do something is to put them in a job that requires knowing how to do it and then help them develop the capabilities and skills they need to succeed. An overarching theme in the future of work is moving away from narrow process-oriented views of workforce management toward methods that use a range of techniques to address broad workforce challenges.

Using Employee Data to Guide Business Decisions (Chapter 9). Companies are gaining access to unprecedented levels of data about the workforce. Companies have much to gain from leveraging this data to increase workforce efficiency, ensure compliance and better understand, influence, and predict employee behavior. Yet many companies make little use of this information or use it ineffectively. Benefitting from data requires developing methods to collect and analyze workforce data in an efficient, sustainable manner, giving the data meaning by framing them in the context of business problems, and managing concerns about data privacy and security.

Changing Employee Experience (Chapter 10). Talent tectonic shifts are forcing companies to solve old challenges in new ways. It can be difficult to get leaders to realize that the way the company solved perennial challenges in the past will not work now. Companies often persist in doing things the way they have always been done simply because they have always done it that way, using technology to incrementally improve existing work methods as opposed to making large-scale changes to improve employee experience. This chapter discusses common barriers to changing work practices including why leaders dislike changes, why managers struggle to support changes, and why employees resist them.

Employee Experience and the External Environment (Chapter 11). The experiences that people have at work are influenced by the experiences they have outside of work. This chapter discusses societal issues that shape and often constrain the ability to reimagine the nature of employee experience, noting how many of our current views about work are still rooted in social norms and work technology constraints from the 20th century.

Where Do We Go from Here? (Chapter 12). The book concludes with general thoughts about how work will evolve over the coming years and the role companies play in shaping the future of employee experience.

The Vocabulary Used in This Book

When it comes to talking about work, words matter. For example, I know companies who refer to employees as partners, associates, champions, athletes, team members, cast members, or crew members and are adamant that their employees be referred to by these names. There are valid reasons why companies rename or redefine common terms. But it creates confusion when working across companies. For this reason, here are definitions for some commonly used terms in this book.

- **Organization:** a group of people who collaborate to achieve common goals by sharing common resources. The terms *company* and *organization* are used interchangeably, though not all organizations are commercial companies (e.g., government or nonprofit organizations).
- **Employee:** a person who receives financial compensation from an organization for work they perform on the organization's behalf. This includes contract workers as well as direct employees. The terms employees, workers, and people are used fairly interchangeably.
- **Candidate:** a person who may have the potential to become an employee. An applicant is a candidate who has expressed interest in a certain job role.
- **Manager:** a person who has responsibility for guiding the work of employees. Many managers oversee staffing and compensation decisions, but not all do.
- **Leader:** a person responsible for setting the strategic direction of a company or group. Most leaders are also managers.
- **Digitalization:** the application of technology in a way that transforms, augments, automates, or otherwise noticeably changes some aspect of work and life.
- **Rating:** assessing and placing people in different categories based on qualifications, potential, performance, or some other attribute relevant to work. Rating requires categorization but it does not require using numerical labels, ranking people against each other, or evaluating people as better or worse individuals.
- **Talent:** the capabilities employees possess that enable them to achieve business-related objectives including knowledge, skills, abilities, values, motives, and attitudes. Skilled employees are also sometimes referred to as *talent*.
- **Workforce:** used to refer to all the employees working for a company including senior leaders and contractors, as well as to refer to the labor force available in a broader society.

- **Workforce management:** methods, actions, and processes focused on helping organizations create effective workforces. Other terms used for this include *human resources, human capital management,* or *human experience management.*

I strive to use these and other words in a consistent manner throughout the book. I also try to avoid marketing jargon, trendy terms, and other phrases that often sound good but mean little.

Applying These Concepts to the World You Live and Work In

The nature of work is being transformed by the talent tectonic forces of digitalization and demographics. Companies must get far better at attracting, developing, and engaging employees to deal with a world characterized by accelerating change and growing skill shortages. This requires using technology to rethink how companies design organizations, fill roles, develop capabilities, engage performance, increase efficiency, ensure compliance, and build cultures. Companies that succeed in the future may not have the biggest market share, strongest brand reputation, or most charismatic leaders. But they will have highly capable and adaptable workforces.

Going through the following steps and questions with leaders you work with will help connect concepts in this book to specific challenges they are facing.

Step 1: Talk with Business Leaders About the Company's Operational Strategy

- What goals must the company achieve to meet commitments and expectations of its financial shareholders, external customers, and/or constituents?
- How does the company plan to drive profit and growth over the coming years? What does it plan to do in the future that it is not currently doing today? Three years is usually good time frame for answering these questions, although the ideal length can vary depending on the nature of the company.
- What challenges will the company have to overcome to be successful?

Step 2: Explore the Implications This Strategy Has on the Company's Workforce

- What kinds of employees will the company need to hire in the future? How are they different from the kinds of employees hired in the past in terms of skills, location, interests, and other characteristics?

- What things will current employees have to do in the future that are different from what they are doing now?
- What types of employees must the company attract or retain to successfully execute its business strategy?

Step 3: Review the Seven Perennial Workforce Challenges

- Which perennial workforce challenges will be most critical for the company over the coming years?
- What must the company change about its current workforce management methods to create and sustain the type of workforce it will need to meet its future business goals?
- What aspects of the company's current employee experience must be changed to create the work environment needed to attract and support the kind of talent it needs to succeed?

CHAPTER 1

Forces Reshaping Work and Workforces

We Do Not Have to Sit Together to Work Together

During spring 2020, millions of employees shifted from working in offices to working remotely from home to protect people during the COVID-19 pandemic. Company leaders soon learned, often to their surprise, that the shift to remote work often increased employee engagement, productivity, and sense of belonging.[1] These benefits happened even though the move to remote work was done to protect health, not to improve employee experience. Employees missed in-person interactions and access to workspaces outside of their homes but welcomed greater control over their time and not having to commute to work every day. As one customer I work with shared after adopting remote work, "we don't want to go back to normal. We want to go forward to better." And better meant permanently embracing some hybrid mixture of remote and on-site work.

The fact companies shifted to remote work in a matter of weeks means the technology to support remote work was widely available before the pandemic. In fact, many people had been working remotely for decades. However few companies embraced the concept of remote work prior to the pandemic. The positive reaction of employees showed that had remote work been supported before the pandemic, many people would have embraced it much earlier. People disliked commuting to work every day. But prior to the pandemic they were not given an alternative, even though it was technologically possible to work remotely. The pandemic forced companies to rethink long-standing assumptions about work, especially the belief that employees need to be in an office to do a good job. It forced company leaders to accept that in a digitalized world we do not have to sit together to work together.

The phrase *talent tectonics* describes underlying shifts reshaping work and organizations much like underlying geographic tectonic plates reshape the surface of the earth. Using this analogy of talent tectonics, the shift to remote work in 2020 can be likened to an earthquake. It was a sudden change in the visible nature of work that was made possible because of underlying advancements in technology that had been happening over decades. People in the 20th century did not want to commute to work every day, but they had no choice given existing technology. With the advent of the internet in the 1990s, the concept of remote work became more viable. For 30+ years, remote work technology steadily improved, but few companies took advantage of it. In 2019, less than 5% of work was done remotely. This shot up to over 60% in 2020 and then dropped back to about 30% in 2021.[2] Remote work was a possibility before 2020, but what was needed was some triggering event to change people's attitudes. Sadly, it took a pandemic to get companies to rethink assumptions about the importance of having employees commute to office buildings every day. Once this triggering event occurred, the change happened extremely quickly and forever altered the landscape of work.

The biggest talent tectonic forces currently affecting work are digitalization and demographics. Figure 1.1 summarizes how these tectonic forces are changing work using the concept of "fault lines." In geology, fault lines are where we visibly see or experience forces caused by the movement of tectonic plates through mountain ranges, coast lines, volcanoes, and earthquakes. Fault lines in talent tectonics are visible changes to the nature of work and organizations.

The most visible impact of digitalization on companies is an accelerating rate of change. Business markets, customer preferences, supply chain operations, and every other aspect of business is being transformed by technology. Digitalization is also changing the nature of jobs and work. Automation is eliminating some jobs and simultaneously creating new kinds of work. The work people are being asked to do is different from what people did in the past. This is increasing demand for employees who possess or can quickly learn new skills. In many cases, this means specialized technical skills or exceptional service or creative skills. But it can also increase the importance of relatively common skills. For example, people with good typing skills have an advantage when working in virtual teams presumably because it involves greater use of electronic communications technology such as chat and e-mail.[3]

The most visible impacts of demographics on companies are changes in the labor market. The median age of the workforce has been rising for

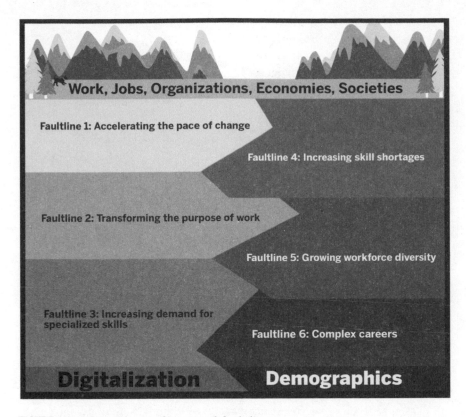

FIGURE 1.1 Talent tectonic forces and fault lines.

decades. Many countries have reached a point where, for the first time in history, more workers are aging out of the labor market than entering it. Figure 1.2 shows the projected 2025 age pyramids for the world's 10 largest economies.[4] Each image shows the percentage of men and women in the country at different ages. Of these countries, India is the only one that is not seeing the size of its working age population shrink, or at least not as severely. Companies in these countries must adapt to a new reality in which fewer young people are entering the labor market relative to the number of older people leaving it. A direct impact of declining birth rates is increased shortages of people willing to do the work companies want at the wages companies want to pay. Workforce shortages also enable employees to have more influence over the work they do. When there are more job openings than qualified candidates to fill them, candidates are able to demand jobs tailored to their unique interests.

The workforce is also becoming more diverse due to variations in birth rates across demographic groups coupled with the growing role of immigrant labor.[5] Many less economically developed countries in Africa

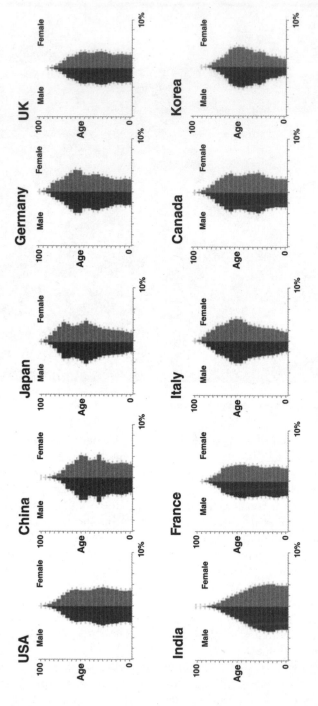

FIGURE 1.2 Age pyramids of the 10 largest economies in 2025.

and elsewhere have far higher birth rates compared to the countries in Figure 1.2. These countries have smaller job markets and higher unemployment, and immigration from these countries is often used to address the aging of the workforce in other countries. Companies will increasingly have to recruit talent from much more diverse domestic and international labor markets than those used in the past.

The talent tectonic forces of digitalization and demographics have been slowly changing the nature of economies and societies for decades. What is new are the increasingly visible impacts they are having on the nature of work. Digitalization is changing what companies need people to do and demographics are changing the characteristics of the people available to do it. These changes require companies to rethink how employees are managed and how jobs and organizations are designed. Companies must put what employees want on equal footing with what companies need. And societies must challenge long-standing assumptions about the nature of education, work, unemployment, and retirement if they want a population capable of competing in the 21st century global labor market. We cannot know exactly how these talent tectonic forces will change work, but we can make an educated guess by taking a deeper look at the major impacts of digitalization and demographics.

The Impacts of Digitalization

Thousands of statistics illustrate how rapidly technology is expanding into every aspect of work and life. Here are just a few:[6]

- There are about 1.35 million tech startups around the world.
- We generate 2.5 quintillion bytes of data daily.
- People check their mobile phones about 150 times daily.
- Every second, 127 new devices are connected to the internet.
- 3.9 billion people were active in social media platforms in 2021.
- There were 81,000 searches on Google every second in 2020.

These statistics are based on a web search done on November 1, 2021. By the time you read this, most of them will be considerably larger.

Technology has become so prevalent in our lives that it is creating new medical and psychological syndromes (e.g., smartphone pinky, compulsive phone checking).[7] There is a $40 billion+ category of technology solutions to manage stresses caused largely by use of technology![8] If there was a sign indicating how digital technology had taken over our lives, it is when smartphone manufacturers added applications that encouraged users to switch off their smartphones. Twenty years ago, who would have predicted technology companies would build features designed to decrease the use of their products?

The growth of digitalization is affecting every aspect of our lives from how we meet our partners, buy our homes, and raise our children to how we decide where to go for dinner and what movies to watch. It is fundamentally changing how companies design, market, sell, manufacture, and distribute products and services. It is altering the geopolitical landscape, how governments are elected, how wars are fought, and the actions we take to protect the planet we live on. Digitalization is also affecting the nature of work and organizations in three profound ways: accelerating the pace of change, transforming the purpose of work, and increasing the demand for specialized skills.

Talent Tectonic Faultline 1: Accelerating the Pace of Change

In 1963 a business professor observed that when it comes to companies "it is not the strongest that survives; but the one that is able best to adapt and adjust to the changing environment."[9] This observation is even truer now. A recent study of top-performing businesses found most share a common characteristic, but it is not size or depth of resources. It is the ability to alter their strategy and quickly adapt to a changing business market.[10] Digitalization has weakened the connection between company size and company success. In the past, companies that had large market shares and material resources could use these to overcome challenges. Strength of size enabled them to weather changes better than smaller competitors. Size still provides strengths, but it is not as valuable as it once was. In a digital world, the success of companies is more about an organization's adaptability than its existing assets. This is great news for smaller companies seeking to grow into big ones, but it is a threat for established companies where size and entrenched habits create inertia and bureaucracy that hinders change. The life span of organizations is shrinking as companies that once dominated their industries lose market share, get acquired, or go under entirely. The median age of the top S&P 500 companies decreased by 61% between 2000 and 2017. The median age across all S&P 500 companies in 2027 is predicted to be a mere 12 years.[11] This means about 50% of the 500 largest companies in the US will be younger than many children in primary school.

This pace of change does not just affect companies. It also affects people working in them. The stress of constant change is reflected in increasing mental health, burnout, and well-being issues.[12] A growing source of anxiety among employees is fear of losing their job due to changes in the economy or nature of work. People are as concerned about losing their job to another person due to outsourcing as they are to losing it due to automation.[13] Somewhat counterintuitively, the labor market disruption caused by digitalization has not yet changed the frequency with which people change jobs. Despite a common belief that "kids these days quit jobs more," in many countries the employees born in the 1980s and 1990s are on track to have roughly the same number of job transitions as employees born in the 1950s and 1960s.[14] What is different is the nature of these job changes. In the past, after a certain age people tended to keep working in the same industry. That will not be the case in a world where industries are being radically transformed by technology. Many employees know that whatever they are doing now they probably won't be doing the same thing five years from now. That things will change is certain. What is not certain is whether these changes will make their lives better.

Talent Tectonic Faultline 2: Transforming the Purpose of Work

The last major transformation in work caused by technology occurred in the 18th and 19th centuries during the industrial age. Technological innovation, fueled by the development of steam and electrical power, changed the focus of work from farming to manufacturing. These new technologies drastically reduced the time and labor needed to produce food and materials. The use of technology in the industrial age changed how organizations, cities, and entire societies operated. For example, at the start of the 19th century about 70% of US workers lived on farms. By the start of the 20th century fewer than 5% did.[15]

Figure 1.3 shows how the nature of work in the United States changed during and after the industrial revolution from agricultural and manufacturing work toward service work.[16] The same general shift shown in this figure is happening around the world, although the timing varies across countries. For the past 50+ years we have been moving from a somewhat manufacturing-oriented economy to one where the majority of workers

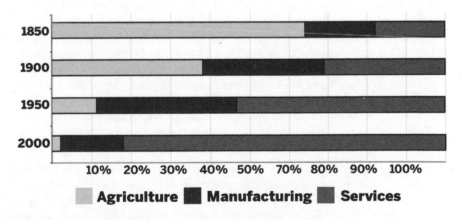

FIGURE 1.3 Shifts in the nature of work since 1850.

perform knowledge- and service-oriented jobs.[17] The kinds of service jobs
have also changed. Up through the mid-20th century most service work
involved relatively low-paying jobs such as housekeepers or clerks. Now,
many service jobs are specialized, high-paying professions such as health
care providers or business consultants. In 1949 the most common service
jobs in the US were food service and restaurant worker, followed by janitor,
servant, cook, and security guard.[18] The most common service jobs in 2021
still includes food service workers but it also includes registered nurses.[19]
This shift to more knowledge-oriented service jobs is a result of technology
changing the nature of work but in much different ways than that of the
industrial age.

Economists refer to the transitions in Figure 1.3 as shifting between
agricultural and manufacturing to service economies. In each transition the
focus of work changed toward producing different types of goods and services. A psychologist's view is slightly different. Instead of viewing each era
in terms of things workers are producing for society, one can view them
in terms of the societal needs that workers are addressing. Up until the
18th century, the main purpose of work was to fulfill lower-order survival
needs. People worked so societies had food to live. During the industrial
age, the purpose of work shifted from the need to stay alive to the desire
to live comfortably. Technology enabled more people to shift from spending time providing food to creating things that make living easier and more
comfortable. Technology is now making it possible to shift work toward an
even higher order need: creating experiences and relationships to make life
happy and fulfilling. We are still a long way from ensuring all people have
the basic needs of food and shelter, but we are far closer to it than we were
100 years ago.[20] Consequently, societies are starting to devote more of work
toward a new purpose: providing things that do not just keep people alive
and comfortable but that make them feel enriched and fulfilled.[i]

Adequate food and comfortable living conditions are necessary for a
happy and fulfilling life, but they do not make life happy and fulfilling. It
is psychologically unhealthy to seek happiness solely through consuming
food and acquiring material possessions. What makes us truly happy are
the experiences we have in life and the people we experience them with.[21]
Technology is enabling us to focus more work resources on providing
people with meaningful and happy lives. This does not mean work focused

---

[i]Tragically, vast numbers of people die each year due to starvation and poor living
conditions despite humanity having adequate material resources to feed and house
everyone on the planet. It is possible that we may already have the technological
capability to give everyone the opportunity to live a fulfilling life, but it is a major
challenge to actually do it.

on creating food and making things that provide shelter and comfort is disappearing. We need farmers and manufacturers, but fewer people are needed to do work related to farming and manufacturing due to technology. Consequently, an increasing percentage of work is shifting to creating experiences that make people feel good. This includes activities such as interacting with friends and family, improving our mental and physical health and well-being, going on trips, watching entertainment events, playing games, and others that provide positive experiences and foster healthy relationships.

Technology is not eliminating work. It is altering the purpose of work from "growing food and making things" to "providing services and experiences." This shift in the purpose of work is also changing the capabilities and conditions employees need to effectively perform their jobs. The industrial era of the 20th century characterized work as a transactional contract between employees and companies that emphasized paying employees based on time spent at work or production of tangible things. Cynically, employees were expected to "show up, shut up, and make stuff." Anyone who thinks the world of work is becoming worse because of technology does not know much about what work was like 100 years ago. A lot of jobs in the industrial era were miserable. They involved repetitive, physically exhausting work in unpleasant, dangerous environments. Employees were expected to follow specific rules and were discouraged from being creative.[22] The stressful "command and control" style of management common in the industrial age literally shortened people's life span.[23] How employees felt didn't matter as long as they created what they were paid to make. Employees did this work only because they had to. Happily, technology has made it possible to automate most of this work, so now no one has to do it.

In the 21st century, employees are increasingly employed to generate ideas, build relationships, solve problems, and deliver services to others. It is hard to be creative, caring, or collaborative if you feel stressed, exhausted, or mistreated.[24] There is a big difference between telling employees to "rivet iron plates for eight hours" or "load 16 tons of coal" compared to asking them to "show these customers we care about them" or "find ways to build our market share." How employees feel internally matters more now because the purpose of work has changed. Work is becoming physically easier but mentally more difficult. There is a concept in psychology called *emotional labor* that defines the experience of acting differently from how we feel internally.[25] Acting happy when we feel sad is not just difficult. It is stressful and often unhealthy. Companies cannot be successful in the future if they try to coerce employees to do work purely through tying tasks to external rewards such as compensation. Employees have to sincerely enjoy their work to be good at it. To be successful in this new era, work should not be thought of as a transactional contract built on requirements.

It should be viewed as a supportive partnership based on shared trust and mutual goals.[26] To do this companies must demonstrate they are trustworthy and show they care about creating positive work experiences for employees. This does not mean work should be easy or stress-free. To the contrary, we enjoy our work the most when it challenges us to fully apply and develop our capabilities.[27] But work should not feel like a prison of measured time. Work should be something that people find meaningful and fulfilling.

Talent Tectonic Faultline 3: Increasing Demand for Specialized Skills

Digitalization changes jobs by automating repetitive tasks and augmenting human activities. An example of automation is using robots to move packages in a warehouse, so a person does not have to do it. An example of augmentation is using artificial intelligence to scan X-ray images to help radiologists more quickly find and diagnose tumors. Technology supports people by performing tasks that people did in the past or by enabling things that people want to do in the future.[ii] As technology applications become more powerful, they enable automating and augmenting increasingly complex activities to the point that they often seem "intelligent." But they are not actually intelligent in the human sense.[iii] Technology as complex as self-driving cars is amazingly impressive, but at its core it is still automating and augmenting tasks that were either previously performed by humans or envisioned by humans as being something worth doing.

[ii]Technology can also have unintended consequences creating things that we did not want from messing up our sleep through blue light to potentially exterminating our species through pollution.

[iii]The term artificial intelligence (AI) gained widespread use in the 1960s to describe mathematical algorithms and computer programming techniques designed to model psychological theories of human learning and decision-making. My father Earl Hunt did early work in AI and explained that "we discovered that computers aren't very good at mimicking how the human brain actually works. But they are good at solving complex problems that the human brain could never solve. And they do it by acting like computers, not by acting like people." The computer science of AI quickly diverged from the psychological science of human intelligence, and most modern applications of AI have little in common with how people actually think or learn. Calling these complex mathematical models *artificial intelligence* is like calling Lifesaver candies *artificial fruit*. There may be surface similarities between the organic version and the artificial version, but they are not at all the same.

Technology does not replace the need for people. But it does change what people need to do. When technology is applied to an existing job, it tends to create two new types of jobs:

- Technical jobs focused on developing, maintaining, and using the technology. These jobs tend to be associated with operations, engineering, maintenance, analytics, and programming.
- Service jobs to engage or support customers who receive the products and experiences associated with the technology. This creates new jobs associated with marketing, sales, and customer support.

A good example of how digitalization changes the nature of work is the way online shopping technology is changing retail jobs. The events of 2020 massively accelerated online shopping. As one retail CIO put it, "we achieved our five-year online growth plan in five weeks." But online shopping did not replace physical stores the way many people thought it would. It turns out that the presence of physical stores influences online purchases. One retail company found that opening a store led to a 30% increase in online purchases from the local community. People become more attached to brands that have physical store locations, certain items such as perishable groceries are better purchased in-person than online, and physical stores play a critical role in the supply chain supporting curbside pick-up and home delivery.

Online shopping is not eliminating the need for physical stores, but it is changing their function. The main purpose of stores used to be making it easy for customers to find and purchase products. Customers increasingly use the internet for this type of transactional shopping. The purpose of stores is becoming more about entertaining, educating, and engaging customers often to sell products online. For example, customers may go to a store to try on clothes and get advice from a fashion consultant or talk about hiking equipment with an expert in outdoor activities. In these examples, the job of store employees is to create a compelling social experience that attracts customers and influences both their in-store and online shopping behaviors.

The digitalization of shopping is changing the nature of retail jobs. In-store employees are now being asked to switch between fulfilling online orders and assisting in-store customers. This includes helping in-store customers make online purchases and answering questions about online services that support in-store products (e.g., maintenance programs). Store staff members must be skilled at demonstrating, inspiring, and instructing customers on the value that comes from using company products. This requires a higher level of expertise than what was historically required for many frontline retail jobs. The employee is not just helping customers find and purchase products in the store. They are building the company brand to influence future online product purchases. The shift to online shopping is also creating highly specialized technical jobs that integrate in-store layouts, online shopping platforms, and mobile technology to create new kinds of customer experiences (e.g., using smartphones so customers can see what products will look like in their own home). Many of these jobs require skills that did not even exist five years ago.

As the retail example shows, the more digitalization transforms work, the more companies need people with specialized skills to operate technology or provide experiences that connect customers to the company. Digitalization is not eliminating the need for work; it is changing the type of work we do. Similar examples can be found in every industry ranging from mining[28] to health care.[29] Digitalization eliminates some jobs while creating new ones. The pace at which jobs are changing due to digitalization varies across countries, but this general trend is the same around the world.[30] Companies will always need employees, but what they will need employees to do will require new and increasingly specialized skills. This includes people who are highly skilled at integrating different areas of specialization.[31] As has been said, the future will be like the past but different.

The Impacts of Demographics

Historically, demographic shifts in the labor force were mainly a result of immigration and population changes caused by wars, persecution, famine, or disease. For example, the migration of people from Asia and Europe to North America in the 19th and 20th centuries was driven by opportunities found in the growing US economy. Many immigrants were fleeing adverse if not horrific social conditions. But the reason they went to North America instead of somewhere else was primarily economic. It was a place they could find work and build a better life for their families. These shifts occurred in a relatively short amount of time and their impact was immediately visible in society. By contrast, the major demographic shifts currently reshaping labor markets are driven by changes in birth rates and life spans. These modern shifts are like plate tectonic shifts in the sense that they happen so slowly that we do not notice them until something occurs that makes us suddenly realize the world has changed. We feel the effects of plate tectonic shifts when we experience earthquakes and volcanoes. We feel the effects of modern demographic shifts when we experience labor market crises and social unrest.

The demographic shifts affecting the modern labor market are a result of more than 100 years of steady change. Starting in the 19th century, birth rates in many countries started to decline. This was due to changing economic conditions and social norms including an increase in women's education levels.[32] At the same time, people's life spans began increasing as medical and living conditions improved. These trends were temporarily interrupted by World Wars I and II and the subsequent "baby boom" but accelerated again starting in the 1960s. These trends are moderated by a country's culture and economy, but in almost every part of the world birth rates have been declining and life spans have been increasing. As a result, many countries are entering a phase in which more people are leaving the labor force then entering it.

The most visible impact of this demographic shift is the increasing age of the workforce. By 2024, roughly 25% of the US workforce will be over 55. In comparison, in 1994 only about 10% of US workers were over 55.[33] The US is growing much older, but not as fast as many other developed countries. Countries aging more quickly than the US include Japan, South Korea, Italy, Germany, and Russia. If current trends continue, China's workforce will be older than the US by 2040. Regardless of who is aging faster, almost every country is seeing a trend toward having relatively fewer people under the age of 20 compared to the number over the age of 50. Historically, the number of people over 65 in most countries never exceeded 4%. Now it is over 15% in many countries and continuing to increase. The median age in developed countries in 1950 was 29. Now it is over 40.[34] In 2018, for the first time in history, the number of people on the planet over the age of 65 was larger than the number of children under the age of 5.[35]

The second visible impact of this shift is relatively fewer people in the labor market. Economic growth created by digitalization increases demand for employees to fill new positions even while population growth declines. For example, the US job market is projected to grow by 11.9 million jobs between now and 2030.[36] Over the same period 42.1 million people in the US will reach the traditional retirement age of 65, and 43.5 million will reach the age of 25, which is roughly about when people finish school and start working full-time. In sum, the US society will add 11.9 million jobs but gain only 1.4 million people (based on subtracting 42.1 million labor market exits from 43.5 million labor market entrants).[iv] Historically, companies could count on a growing supply of youthful labor entering the job market to fill new job roles. This is no longer the case. Companies are now hiring from a smaller labor pool. The size of this labor pool will go up and down based on recessions, but the overall trend is a mathematical certainty barring some massive change in global economics. As more people age out of the labor market relative to those entering it, companies will be looking for talent in a smaller pool of labor compared to the growing size of the job market.

[iv]These equations are extremely simplistic and do not account for the range of variables that affect labor markets, particularly labor market participation rates because not everyone works. The basic point is countries are adding fewer people to their society relative to the number of jobs being created in their economy.

Many changes caused by these demographic shifts are positive. For example, smaller populations tend to reduce environmental impact on the planet. However, cities may struggle to maintain their infrastructure in the face of shrinking populations and declining tax bases.[37] Regardless of whether the changes are viewed as opportunities or threats, they will affect the nature of work and organizations in three ways: increasing skill shortages, growing workforce diversity, and reshaping career paths.

Talent Tectonic Faultline 4: Increasing Skill Shortages

The long-term impact of a shrinking workforce is a shortage of people available to work. But the more noticeable near-term impact is a shortage of people with the specific skills companies need. This is a result of the collision between the talent tectonic forces of digitalization and demographics. Digitalization creates demand for people with increasingly specialized skills. Demographic shifts reduce the relative number of people in the workforce with those skills. It is important to note that most countries do not have a people shortage so much as a "people with the skills we need" shortage. Digitalization also increases demand to help people learn new skills. Many skills that companies will need in the future have yet to be created, and some of the fastest-growing occupations barely existed 10 years ago (e.g., solar photovoltaic installers).[38]

Digitalization creates greater demand for "hard" technical skills and "soft" interpersonal and social skills. Many interpersonal and social skills can be effectively acquired through experience rather than formal education. But the most business-limiting skills shortages are likely to involve technical skills. As a hiring manager once told me, "People skills are great, but I need someone who can fix this machine." Our ability to acquire technical skills is enabled and constrained by our current knowledge. Learning cognitively demanding skills, such as writing, math, or computer programming, physically changes the neurological pathways in our brains.[39] This may make it easier for us to learn other advanced technical skills. For example, consider the difference between teaching someone to read English who already knows how to read in another language, compared to teaching a person who has never learned to read at all. These hard skills can be acquired while working, but they require giving people large amounts of dedicated time and resources to learn them.

The degree to which societies support people's ongoing education will have a growing impact on the ability of companies in those societies to find the talent needed for skilled roles.[40] This is not just about training people for existing jobs. It is about equipping people with the knowledge needed to learn new skills to perform future jobs that do not yet exist. This includes making sure employees have access to educational resources necessary to keep pace with the changing nature of their jobs and if necessary are able to learn to perform entirely new types of work. In many cases, this will require providing development resources beyond what companies can reasonably support internally. Some good examples are the private-public partnership projects underway to reskill workers in the automotive industry to transition to build electric cars instead of combustion engine automobiles.[41]

Another factor that will affect the ability of companies to find skilled workers is economic incentives. This is particularly relevant for service positions that require specialized nontechnical skills, for example, health care roles such as home and assisted living aids or hospitality workers in guest service roles. Anyone who has worked in these jobs or who has experienced the difference between receiving good and bad service should appreciate the skills they require. These skills include organizational planning, problem solving, active listening, emotional empathy, and attention to detail. The more we automate the transactional aspects of service jobs, the more complex the interpersonal component becomes. Consider the move to mobile self-check in at hotels. In many hotels it is now possible to check in to your room entirely through phone apps without ever talking to a person at the front desk. The only time a guest talks to the front desk clerk is when something goes wrong or when they want advice. The front desk job is no longer about routinely checking people in; it is about solving problems, calming down frustrated guests, and offering ideas to improve the guest's visit. This requires a much higher level of set of interpersonal, advisory, and problem resolution skills.

From an economic perspective, higher skilled jobs should be higher paying jobs because fewer workers have the qualifications to perform them. Unfortunately, many countries have historically underpaid service workers for reasons that have nothing to do with the skills these jobs require. In the past, the monetary value of work was often based more on who did it than what they were doing. Consider this quote from the 1910 US census: "Certain occupations which, technically, are skilled occupations were classified as semiskilled because [they were largely performed by] women."[42] This statement implies that if jobs are performed by women then they must be less skilled. Throughout history one can find examples in which societies downplayed the value of service jobs primarily performed by women and minorities as way to implicitly justify paying lower wages to the people in these jobs.

When given the choice, people are naturally attracted to occupations that they believe will provide them with good jobs that enable them to support their desired lifestyle, including supporting their family. In the past, many service jobs were not viewed as good jobs given their low wages, even if the jobs performed essential roles in our society.[43] There are signs this is starting to change due to the growing shortage of labor caused by the decreasing number of workers entering the labor market. The change is also being driven by the demanding nature of these jobs caused by digitaliza-tion.[44] As these jobs become more complex, there is greater financial value in retaining employees who have the skills to perform them. The challenge facing companies that employ service workers is how to rethink financial models to handle what are likely to be much higher workforce costs. This starts with abandoning past mindsets that treated these workers as though they were unskilled and therefore easily replaceable.

Skill shortages can be viewed as a threat or an opportunity depending on one's perspective. Skill shortages are a threat if companies and local governments cannot effectively collaborate to help people acquire the skills needed in an increasingly digitalized world of work, or if companies are unable or unwilling to recognize the value of skilled employees by paying them appropriately and providing them with better work experiences. How-ever, skill shortages are an opportunity to provide people with financially rewarding jobs that encourage continuous growth and self-development. These are the sorts of jobs that create happy and prosperous societies.[45]

Talent Tectonic Faultline 5: Growing Workforce Diversity

A direct result of declining birth rates and aging workforces is increased age diversity in the workforce. Organizations with higher levels of age diversity tend to be more successful.[46] But to take advantage of age diversity, compa-nies must address ageism and dispel stereotypes about the impact of age on work.[47] For example, based on empirical evidence, which one of these is true?

Relative to younger employees, older employees tend to be (choose one or more):

- Less motivated
- Less interested in training
- More resistant to change
- Less trusting
- Less productive
- Slower at learning new technology

All of these are false except "less interested in training." Older employ-ees tend to be skeptical about the value of training, which can make them less interested in participating in training programs. The others are false but common stereotypical ageist beliefs that have no basis in empirical fact.[48]

This book will discuss many ways companies can engage people at all ages and stages of their careers. But one thing every company can do immediately is stop actively promoting ageist thinking by using stereotype-laden terms such as gen Z, millennial, gen X and baby boomer. One does not need a PhD in psychology to understand the dangers of labeling and making sweeping generalizations about people based on their demographic characteristics. If you must talk about age, then use clearly descriptive terms such as "people over 40" or "people under 20." Instead of calling out differences between generations, focus on things that unite us regardless of when we were born. Recognize that interests often associated with youth such as career development and improving the world remain important as we age, even if we express our interests differently.[49] When it comes to work, the year people were born is not what matters most. What matters most is what people have done since they were born and what they strive to do with the years they have left.

Another result of declining birth rates is greater emphasis on attracting, engaging, and developing people from diverse backgrounds regardless of gender, race and ethnicity, or ability status. This is not just about equity and inclusion, although that should be reason enough. It is about business necessity. To fill jobs in a scarce labor market, companies must use all available and qualified talent whatever their demographic characteristics or disability status. Immigrant workers will also play a larger role in organizations than they have in the past.[50] Many countries already have programs to bring in employees from other countries to perform jobs at all skill levels. Companies in these countries cannot function without these "guest workers."[51] Reliance on foreign-born labor is likely to become far more common in many societies that historically discouraged immigration.

There is social and economic value in having a more diverse and inclusive world of work. Diverse workforces increase team creativity and create stronger connections between companies and increasingly diverse customer populations.[52] Providing work to historically disenfranchised local communities or to immigrants who lack job opportunities in their home countries also helps address problems of global poverty. At the same, there are significant challenges to creating diverse workforces and building inclusive cultures. Despite years of effort and investment, companies continue to struggle to achieve demographic equity, diversity, and inclusion.[53] Subsequent chapters in this book look at the challenge of diversity and inclusion from a variety of angles, highlighting ways to make future diversity efforts more successful than those of the past.

Talent Tectonic Faultline 6: Complex Careers

Demographic changes to the labor market are changing how employees and companies think about careers. Companies are increasingly facing situations where they cannot find candidates with the skills they need who are willing to work at pay levels the company can afford. In these situations, companies must change their staffing approach. Instead of hiring people based on existing skills and qualifications, companies need to hire people based on what they can learn to do as opposed to what they already know. In some cases, this may lead to employees making radical changes to their career trajectory by moving into entirely new industries or professions. Employees also have increasing ability to influence how their jobs are designed. This includes their job goals, where the job is located (on-site or remote), whether it involves part-time or contract work, and other features that enable employees to support their work and nonwork interests.[54] Hiring will be less about companies asking employees, "Can you do this job?" and more about employees and companies asking, "What can we do together?" As a recent MBA graduate put it, "I am not applying for jobs that I'm qualified for because I already know how to do them. I am applying for jobs that I am not qualified for because those are the ones where I will learn the most."

An aging labor market will also encourage rethinking the concept of retirement. Age-based retirement was created in the late 1800s in part to encourage older workers to leave the workforce so it would create jobs for younger people. This was the first time that societies suggested that people not work after they reach a certain age.[55] Prior to about 1870, retirement pensions were primarily awarded based on the physical ability to work. Workers did not retire because they were old; they retired because they were no longer able to be productive. It was not until the 20th century that people started planning their careers based on the assumption that they would just stop working at a specific age, such as 65. Our current model of retirement implies that people past an arbitrary age should no longer be contributing members of the workforce. This is not good for companies or for people.

People want to change the nature of the work they do as they get older. But encouraging people to stop working entirely is unhealthy. People do not do well when they have nothing to do. My wife, who is a family medicine doctor, told me that when patients say they are about to retire it is often treated as a health risk. As she put it, "it is important to have a reason to get up in the morning." This does not mean she wants patients to stay in their jobs. But she does encourage patients to rethink what it means to retire. The goal of retirement is not to stop working. The goal is to transition the time spent working and use it to do something new that they find joyful and fulfilling. It is unhealthy and unproductive to put employees "out to pasture" as though they were elderly farm animals. Most employees do not want to stop working completely. One study found that only about 25% of employees plan to stop working entirely when they reach 65.[56] This is good news. It makes no sense to discard highly experienced workers in an economy facing a growing shortage of specialized skills. Over the coming years we should expect to see fewer people retiring from work entirely. Instead, we will see people transition to new models of working that fit their professional interests and financial needs as they move through their 60s, 70s, 80s, 90s, and even beyond. This is likely to include greater use of contract-based work where people choose to work when they want to instead of working full-time set schedules. One retail company I know had an employee still working for them at the age of 102 simply because they enjoyed their job and liked getting out of the house.

Embracing the move to more flexible job models and dynamic career paths requires getting away from the transactional work models of the 20th century in which companies set job requirements and employees tried to meet them. It requires moving toward collaborative models in which employees and companies work together to create jobs that align what employees want to do, what employees are able to do or learn, and what companies need to get done.

Applying These Concepts to the World You Live In

The world of work is being transformed by talent tectonic forces of digitalization and demographics. Digitalization is accelerating the pace of change, transforming the purpose of work, and creating a need for highly specialized skills. It is interacting with demographic forces to generate skill shortages, increase workforce diversity, and reshape the nature of careers. So, what can companies do about it? The answer is: a lot! Innovations in work technology combined with insights gained from psychology provide countless ways to rethink work and create employee experiences that attract, develop, and engage talent. This includes making work accessible, enjoyable, and meaningful for all people regardless of their current skill level and demographic characteristics. This chapter explained the major challenges companies face regarding the future of work. The rest of the book is about the solutions.

Exploring the following questions can help with thinking about the concepts from this chapter in the context of the company or companies you work with.

Digitalization

- How is technology being used in your company or industry to automate or augment work? What aspects of work do you expect to see technology transform in the near future? How will this change the skill profiles need to perform this work?
- What attitudes do employees in your company have about the future of work? Are they excited about opportunities to grow their

skills or concerned about potential job loss? What could you do to help employees manage future job and career changes?

- What is the core mission and purpose of your company? How is this reflected in the way jobs are defined, staffed, and managed?
- Look at the job postings from the past three years in your company. Do they include tasks or skills that did not exist 10 years ago? What skills will be critical for the success of the company over the next three years? Who has these skills or how will they be developed?

Demographics

- What is the age distribution of employees in your workforce? How many are close to retirement eligibility? How many would work longer if given the right options?
- What are the population trends in the communities that you primarily hire from? What is the ratio of new entrants into the labor markets that you hire from versus people exiting those markets?
- How do you ensure your company is creating an attractive and inclusive culture for diverse employees and candidates? How do you measure diversity and inclusion in your organization? Do you have a good representation of ethnicity and gender across the organization including at the leadership level?
- What are the hardest roles to fill in your company? What makes them difficult to fill? How could you change the job or qualification requirements to expand the number of eligible candidates? Could you use contractors or part-time roles to help staff these jobs?

CHAPTER 2

The Employee Experience and Workforce Adaptability

Surviving a World of Volatility, Uncertainty, Complexity, Ambiguity, and Ice

The term VUCA stands for "volatility, uncertainty, complexity, and ambiguity." It was created to describe the sociopolitical situation in Russia and other eastern European nations during the collapse of the Soviet Union in the late 1980s.[1] It is often used to describe the chaotic nature of the modern world as though this sort of environment is new, but there are many examples throughout history of people facing VUCA situations. For example, many people's ancestors migrated across oceans in the 19th century to start new lives on different continents. They crossed mountain ranges in wagons without roads and built homes in the wilderness with no electricity or other modern forms of technology. Imagine the VUCA they faced.

History demonstrates that people are good at adapting to the challenges of a VUCA environment provided certain conditions exist. These conditions are largely about how they mentally experience the situation they are in. An exceptional illustration is the story of Ernest Shackleton's expedition to cross Antarctica in 1914. After their ship became trapped and crushed by ice, they drifted for 15 months until the ice flow broke up. Part of the crew crossed 800 miles of stormy open ocean in a small open boat to seek aid. The members of Shackleton's expedition spent 20 months in a freezing, extremely hostile environment, yet all 27 members survived. Shackleton knew that "in this environment his greatest enemies were high levels of

anxiety and disengagement, as well as a slow-burning pessimism."[2]
He used language and actions such as giving his own mittens to
a colleague to demonstrate commitment to everyone's safety and
health. He stressed the most important purpose of the mission was to
get everyone home alive. He worked to make sure the men believed
survival was possible, so they would not lose hope. He organized
activities and celebrated holidays to build camaraderie and lift peo-
ple's spirits. He also emphasized the importance of small kindnesses
like saying "please" and "thank you" to ensure people felt appreci-
ated by their colleagues. Shackleton and his men relied on excep-
tional sailing and navigation skills to overcome their challenges, but
how they psychologically experienced this extreme VUCA situation
was fundamental to their survival.

People are the one constant in any organization. Companies can exist
without actual products, services, or profits. This is the initial state of many
startup companies. But a company without people is just a legal document.
An organization is, at its core, an organization of people. People are also
the most effective resource that companies have for dealing with change,
provided they are the right people, in terms of skills and capabilities, and
they work together in the right way. Working together the right way comes
from creating the right employee experiences. Shackleton's crew consisted
of the right people in terms of skills, but their survival was a result of experiencing adversarial changes in a way that transformed them into a confident,
resilient, and supportive team.

This chapter discusses the role that employee experience plays in
building adaptable workforces that can survive and thrive in a world being
reshaped by the talent tectonic forces of digitalization and demographics.
It begins with a discussion of the unique role that people play as the one
constant in a world of change. It explains the three kinds of experience that
affect how people experience work, and why these are critical for building
an adaptable workforce. It then looks at factors that affect how companies
understand, shape, and manage employee experience. The chapter concludes with a discussion of employee experience from the perspective of
four key stakeholder groups within an organization: employees, managers,
leaders, and support functions.

People: A Constant Resource in a Changing World

People often talk about companies needing to pivot in response to change.
Figure skaters and dancers know that pivoting requires having a stable
point to pivot from. In a similar fashion, creating an adaptive company
requires understanding the stable components of the organization that are

FIGURE 2.1 Elements that drive organizational performance.

not changing. These stable resources are the ones companies need to master to navigate change, and the most constant and valuable of these resources are the people in the organization.

Figure 2.1 illustrates the three things that determine the performance of an organization:

- **People:** the individuals in the workforce who carry out activities to support the organization's mission and strategy. This includes full- and part-time employees as well as contractors.
- **Resources:** tools, materials, technology, finances, and other assets that can be accessed by the workforce to achieve company objectives.
- **Environment:** the business market or social setting where the organization is situated. This includes external stakeholders that influence the organization's success such as customers, business partners, and government agencies.

An organization is successful when the people in its workforce use the resources available to them to capitalize on opportunities and overcome challenges in its environment. Resources can swiftly change due to technological innovations, supply chain shortages, or access to financial capital. The environment can be altered due to changes in consumer preferences, government regulations, and other economic, social, or environmental events. The one factor in organizations that does not change much is the psychology of the people in its workforce. An organization can change the size and composition of its workforce through staffing and change the attitudes and skills of its workforce through management and development. But the fundamental psychological attributes and processes that influence people's motivation, performance, development, and well-being at work stay relatively constant over time.[3] We cannot be certain what the future of work will look like, but we can be certain organizations will always involve groups of people working together using shared resources to accomplish shared or complementary goals. Even if the structures of organizations radically change, organizations will still consist of people cooperating to achieve mutually beneficial outcomes. This makes the psychology of people one of the few things that does not change within companies. It also makes understanding employee psychology critical to building resilient and adaptable organizations.

People's behavior is a function of what they can do, what they want to do, and what they believe they are able to do. This is determined by various abilities, traits, needs, and aptitudes that are remarkably stable from one generation to the next. The abilities, motivations, and personality traits that guided people's actions in our great-grandparents' generations are very similar to those found in the generations of people currently working. This is one of the reasons why stories told in Shakespearian plays written more than 400 years ago still feel relevant today. What people can do and want to do does not change that much. This might seem counter to statements frequently made in the popular press that suggest employees belonging to different generations are radically different from one another. These statements tend to be both ageist and wrong. Longitudinal research on generational differences and employee attitudes suggests that what people fundamentally want from a job has not changed much over the years.[4] These studies analyzed job interest data collected from millions of students and recent graduates during different decades dating back to the 1920s. They found that, at a basic level, what people want from work has not changed much from one generation to the next. Regardless of when they were born, most employees want jobs that provide some sense of meaning, challenge and career growth, fair compensation, pleasant and safe working conditions, a reasonable level of work-life balance, and some degree of stability. What does change a lot due to socioeconomic and technological shifts are people's beliefs about their ability to get these things and how they go about getting them.

People often confuse differences in labor market realities with changes in generational attitudes. For example, skilled college graduates entering the labor market in the 2020s have access to far more job opportunities than college graduates did in the 1980s. This means job candidates graduating now can demand more from employers. Graduates in the 1980s wanted many of the same things that graduates want now, but they could not get them given the labor market at that time. One of the most influential business books in 1950s, *The Organization Man*, spoke of people being stuck in meaningless, unfulfilling jobs because they did not have the opportunity to pursue their true career passions.[5] If our grandparents and great-grandparents had job search technology like Google and LinkedIn, how different their careers might have been! It is also common to attribute changes caused by life situations with generational differences. People do change as they age, but these changes have little to do with what generation they belong to. For example, what employees want from work changes as they gain career experience.[6] Early career employees are usually more interested in development and advancement than more tenured employees. This is true regardless of age. The career interests of a 40-year-old finishing college after raising children are likely to be more similar to their 20-year-old classmates than their 40-year-old spouse with 18 years of job tenure. The main reason generations have different career interests is because younger employees are more likely to be in earlier career stages. Another major factor is changes in nonwork obligations, such as raising children and paying for home mortgages. Employees' willingness to take financial risks and switch jobs tends to change as they age because family responsibilities and financial situations often change as they grow older.[7]

There are two areas that do change significantly from one generation to the next: expectations about use of technology and attitudes toward social values.[8] How we grow up shapes what we expect when we start working. For example, people born after 2000 are the first employees who have had access to mobile smartphone technology since they were very young. This affects their expectations for how people can and should communicate. They are more likely to expect their employer to use mobile communication technology because it is how they conduct their lives outside of work.[9] People born after 2000 also grew up in a time when women are as educated and active in the workforce as men. As a result, they may hold different social beliefs about the role of women in the workplace compared to previous generations that grew up in a time when fewer women went to college and worked. One reason younger employees may be more vocal about workplace change is because they want to work in a world that mirrors the technology and social values they experienced growing up. Older employees might take solace by saying things at work are better than they used to be, but if you are young then there is no "used to be"; there is only the way it should be now.

Although there are differences between generations in terms of social values and technology expectations, the basic things people want from work are remarkably constant regardless of age or era.[10] Similarly, the things that make people successful in their jobs do not vary much with age. This includes the widespread myth that young people are better at learning technology.[11] Older people may be less interested in using a new form of technology, but that does not mean they are less capable of learning how to use it. In sum, people are the most constant and valuable resource organizations have for managing change, but only if the company is able to hire the people with the right skills and capabilities and manage them in the right way. This requires understanding the basic psychology of people as it relates to how they view work and how they respond to change, and then using this knowledge to create employee experiences that support the creation of engaged and adaptable workforces.

The Employee Experience and Workforce Adaptability

The success of an organization hinges on building a workforce capable of executing the company's strategy, including adapting to changes when necessary. Regardless of a company's industry or geography, changes are bound to occur that will require it to rethink its strategic direction or operational approach. These could be a result of economics, technology, regulations, labor markets, consumer preferences, or other factors. Companies may be unable to forecast when these changes will happen, but once they start, companies must quickly adapt. A critical part of adaptation is getting employees to do things in the future that are different from what they did in the past, even if it means abandoning practices and activities that had once made the company successful. I am often asked, "How can we train employees to be adaptable?" My response is that this is the wrong question. People are born adaptable. The competitive advantage of humans as a species is our ability to adapt to changing environments. It is called learning. The question is not how to teach people to adapt but how to create employee experiences that unlock people's innate adaptive ability.

Historically, companies focused on staffing jobs and managing people to maximize their productivity. People are most productive when they are doing things they already know how to do. Management methods built on productivity emphasize efficiency and performance. They focus on providing people with clear job direction, educating them with targeted learning activities, and motivating them through tangible rewards. These methods work when the goal is to maximize productivity in doing repetitive tasks in familiar work environments.[12] But they often fail when the goal is to maximize people's ability to adapt to new environments and master constantly changing activities. Managing for adaptability requires understanding the psychological factors that influence how people respond to change. This starts with dispelling the myth that people fear change. People do not fear change. What they fear is poorly managed change. They also fear change that leads to losing valuable resources or being forced to do things they do not want to do. But change in the right conditions for the right reasons is exhilarating. It is the feeling of developing new capabilities, overcoming challenges, and achieving meaningful goals. If you hear a leader blame a failed strategy on employees' supposed fear of change, what you are really hearing is a leader who does not know how to inspire employees to adapt.

Companies may not be able to control the change employees experience, but they can influence how employees experience change. When faced with significant change people adopt either a survival or growth mindset. When employees adopt a survival mindset, they become skeptical, cautious, and protective. They experience change in terms of potential loss and work to resist it or minimize its impact. When employees adopt a growth mindset, they approach change with a sense of commitment, engagement, and confidence.[13] They may recognize risks associated with the change, but view the change primarily based on the opportunities it provides to achieve new things and develop new capabilities. Whether employees adopt a survival versus growth mindset is influenced by whether their experience of work meets two basic, innate psychological needs: a sense of achievement and a sense of confidence.

A sense of achievement is about tying work to something that is meaningful to employees. People are born with an innate desire to accomplish meaningful goals. We like doing things that give us a feeling of accomplishment. This is reflected in things as basic as an infant's desire to crawl across the floor.[14] Why do babies work so hard to learn to walk and speak? Because it instinctively feels good to achieve something that provides a sense of personal agency and accomplishment. The feeling that work is meaningful gives employees a sense of achievement and purpose to their efforts. This creates energy and desire to persist in the face of challenges. When work taps into this innate desire to accomplish meaningful goals, employees are more committed to finding ways to be successful in the face of change. For work to be meaningful, employees must have ownership over activities that they perceive as making a difference in something they care about. At one level, this may be tied to having a sense of job security and the ability to make enough money to provide for their families. But for most people, it is also about doing work that has social meaning[15] (e.g., helping others) or doing work that enables them to achieve goals that align with their own sense of self-identity and self-actualization[16] (e.g., fulfilling career goals). A key part of managing for adaptability is ensuring employees see a connection between their work and something that matters to them beyond simply punching a clock and getting a paycheck.

A sense of confidence comes from employees believing they have the capability to be successful. When employees lose confidence in the face of change, they give up, withdraw, or fall into despair. Confidence comes in part from employees feeling they have the knowledge, skills and resources needed to be successful. Another often more important factor that influences confidence is the people employees work with. Employees are far more confident and committed when they feel a sense of belongingness and support from those around them. An important part of managing for adaptability is creating connections and supportive relationships among employees who are facing similar challenges or have shared goals.

As the pace of change accelerates, companies must create employee experiences that lead to adapting growth mindsets in the face of challenges. This requires connecting jobs to activities and goals employees find meaningful and ensuring their work provides a sense of agency and achievement. It is also about making sure employees feel confident that they have the resources and knowledge to overcome obstacles and achieve their goals and belong to a community of people who value them and want them to succeed.

Creating Effective Employee Experiences

To be successful in a fast-moving world, companies need to create workforces that are productive and agile. Employees must execute on strategic goals while simultaneously finding ways to adapt to unforeseen challenges and changes. This requires creating employee experiences that attract the right talent, engage high levels of performance, support employee development and adaptability, and foster a growth mindset. This comes from actively managing three different kinds of employee experiences (see Figure 2.2):

- **Fulfillment experience: does my job provide the things I want from work?** This is tied to concepts in psychology called *intrinsic and extrinsic motivation*[17] that influence whether work provides a sense of achievement. Employee fulfillment can come in the form of extrinsic, external factors resulting from work, such as making money or having resources to provide for their families. It can also be tied to intrinsic, internal factors, such as the opportunity to do work they enjoy, helping them fulfill professional career goals, or enabling them to contribute toward achieving some higher-level purpose related to improving society or the planet. Employees' experience of fulfillment depends on all these factors to some degree, but the importance of each factor varies across individuals.
- **Task experience: is it easy to get things done?** This is about providing employees with tools, knowledge, and resources to accomplish their goals at work. At the most basic level, task experience influences our confidence that we can be successful. This is tied to a concept in psychology called *self-efficacy*, the belief that we can achieve our goals

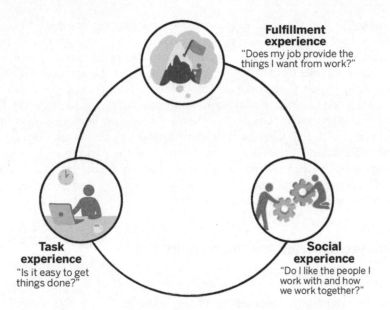

FIGURE 2.2 Types of employee experience.

through effort.[18] Positive task experiences make employees feel efficient and productive. Poor task experiences create frustration and a sense that the company does not appreciate the value of employees' time or skills.[19] If you have ever cursed in frustration at your smartphone or computer, you know how a bad task experience feels. Extremely bad task experiences can lead an employee to quit or stay on the job but give up trying.

■ **Social experience: do I like the people I work with and how we work together?** This is about creating supportive and inclusive cultures and teams. It is tied to concepts in psychology called *belongingness* and *need for affiliation*, which reflect the importance of feeling part of a group that values and cares for us.[20] Good social experiences make employees feel welcomed, appreciated, and supported. Bad social experiences make employees feel isolated, alienated, overlooked, and annoyed. Humans are social animals and do not do well if they feel isolated, excluded, or alone. This is particularly true when people are under pressure or in situations in which there is a risk of failure.[21]

Any experience at work can be viewed from three perspectives: does it help employees accomplish what they want to do, is it making efficient use of their time, and do they feel supported by others when they are doing it. Ideally the answer is yes to all three, but in reality employees make trade offs between them. It is easier to do a relatively unfulfilling job if we work with people we enjoy. We are willing to overcome bad task experiences if we believe in the purpose of our work. However, if any one of these experiences falls below a certain level for an extended amount of time, then jobs become unpleasant, stressful, and intolerable.[i] In addition, the more stress we are under the more critical these experiences become. These three types of employee experience also affect a company's ability to attract and retain talent. People are more likely to apply and remain in positions that allow them to do work they find meaningful that fulfills both the internal and external things they want from a job. A major factor affecting retention is the people we work with and the sense of belongingness we feel toward the company. Last, although people are unlikely to join a company simply because it is easy to get things done, they will quit a company if it does not provide the tools and resources they need to succeed.

Employee Experience Management and Business Performance

Employee experience management is about shaping the experiences employees have at work to create more productive and adaptable organizations. More specifically, it is about managing "the beliefs, feelings, attitudes, and behaviors resulting from one's job experiences."[22] The experiences employees have at work play a critical role in their ability to cope with stress, manage change, and deliver and maintain high levels of creativity, service, and performance.[23] Growing skills shortages also make providing employees with a rewarding and compelling employee experiences critical to attracting, engaging, developing, and retaining talent.

Managing employee experience involves understanding the links among company actions, employee experiences, and business results (see Figure 2.3). Company actions do not directly affect business outcomes. Company actions change the workplace, these changes affect how employees experience work, which in turn leads employees to change their behavior, which affects business outcomes. For example, if a company changes its

---

[i] I use the analogy of going on a hike to explain these three experiences. Task experience is like having boots that fit. A hike will not be good because your boots fit, but if your boots do not fit then the hike will be frustrating and could be miserable. Social experience is about whom you are hiking with. Do you all get along, enjoy each other's conversation, and walk at the same general pace? Fulfillment experience is about where you are hiking. Are you hiking through a beautiful valley to a lake you have always wanted to see, walking around a boring suburban neighborhood, or trudging through a mosquito-infested swamp? Whether a hike is good or bad depends on all three of these things. But if any one of them falls below a certain level, the hike will be terrible.

FIGURE 2.3 How employee experience influences business outcomes.

pay structure, the immediate impact is a change in the employee experience working for the company. Employees may feel the new pay structure makes their work more or less fulfilling and meaningful. In some cases, they may not notice the change at all. Then, depending on how employees feel about this new experience, they might decide to work harder, less hard, or quit entirely. This will affect their accomplishments, which in turn affect business operations.

Employee experience management involves balancing employee interests and company goals. It is rooted in simple truth: employees do not do things because the company wants them to do them; employees do things because they want to do them. This truth was often overlooked in the past when workforce management processes were mainly built on company needs. Employee experience was treated as an afterthought and discussed only when the company tried to create "what's in it for me" (WIIFM) arguments to persuade employees to adopt the process. When these WIIFM arguments failed, methods were used to force compliance such as withholding compensation until employees completed a required form or action. Effective employee experience management requires looking at company and employee needs simultaneously. This is not about putting employee needs above company needs. It is about putting them on the same level. The best employee experiences happen when the company is successful. Working for a company in financial trouble is rarely fun. Companies that do not put adequate emphasis on goals such as profitability and growth will eventually go under, which is not good for the company or its employees. The best employee experiences happen when there is an optimal balance between what employees want and what the company needs to achieve.

Understanding and Improving Employee Experiences

The key to creating successful, agile organizations lies in recognizing that the company cannot achieve what it needs to if it does not consider what employees want. This requires understanding the experiences employees are having and how they compare to their expectations. This is achieved by asking and listening to employees about their work experiences. One way to do this is to simply talk with employees on a regular basis. Every company should do this, but there is a limit to what can be learned about employee experience solely through conversations. This is why companies use different technologies to collect employee experience data such as surveying candidates' attitudes filling out job applications, getting online feedback from employees on the value of a training course, using natural language parsing technology to measure the sentiment expressed by employees in online job communities, using wearable technologies to track how the physical layout of an office influences employee interactions and collaboration, and leveraging pulse surveys combined with advanced qualitative and quantitative analytical tools to measure employee attitudes.

Employee experience data enable companies to get inside the heads of employees to understand what is and is not working well. Traditional workforce data such as headcount, turnover, course completion, and qualifications metrics provide insight into who is in the organization, what they know, and what they are doing. But it does not tell us *why* employees are doing different things or how they feel about the things they are doing. By contrast, experience management data provide insight into how employees feel about things they are doing and experiencing at work, and why they feel this way. The value of experience management data might be compared to having the sound turned on when watching a movie. You can see what the actors are doing in a movie with the sound turned off, but it is hard to determine what is driving the actors' actions when you cannot hear them express their thoughts and feelings. In this sense, experience management data turn the sound on for business leaders seeking to understand their workforce. It provides companies with insight into the underlying attitudes of employees, the factors that influence these attitudes, and how these attitudes affect employee behavior and business outcomes.

Employee experience management involves using experience management data to shape positive employee experiences to create more effective organizations. It is about understanding and managing three things: (1) the expectations employees have prior to the experience: what employees think should happen at work; (2) the work environments that shape experience: what actually happens at work; and (3) the interpretations employees draw from the experience: how employees feel about what happened at work and how they choose to respond as a result. To illustrate these concepts, consider the following examples of managing employee experience.

- **Establishing expectations.** Based on analyzing experience survey data, a financial services company learned that many employees felt the work demands in the organization were excessive. Employees who were dissatisfied with work-life balance were also more likely to quit. When shown these results, the CEO agreed that the company expected more from employees than most organizations but noted that it also shared more of its financial rewards with employees than most companies. Rather than change a culture that had made the company successful, the company changed the hiring process to give employees a realistic preview of what it was like to work there. It hired employees who expected and wanted the experience of working in a company that was highly demanding but that also provided very high levels of financial rewards.

- **Changing environments.** A technology company was struggling to retain salespeople, so it conducted a study to understand what they disliked about their job experiences. Salespeople enjoyed the process of selling the technology but disliked having to perform post-sales activities that focused on customer support issues. They believed these support activities were important, but they went into sales because they like selling new solutions, which is very different from maintaining solutions after they have been sold. To create a better experience for the sales force, the company created and staffed a new function focused specifically on post-sales customer support.
- **Influencing interpretations.** A consumer goods company found itself the target of union-organizing activities. The company was surprised because it offered compensation and benefits that matched or exceeded what employees would receive as union members. What they learned was many employees did not understand the value of these benefits. Employees were paid fairly, but they did not feel like they were. The company put communication methods in place to explain the competitive nature of their pay and benefits packages. The company also encouraged employees to voice concerns about compensation and other issues to company leaders. When employees better understood how they were paid and felt they were being listened to about their needs, the union-organizing activities stopped.

All the companies in these examples improved employee experience, but only one changed the work experience itself. The other two focused on shaping expectations and perceptions of work experiences.

Addressing the Subjective Nature of the Employee Experience

A challenge to managing employee experience is the subjective nature of experience itself. Two employees can have the exact same work experience and perceive it differently based on their expectations or interpretations. Experiences that matter a lot to some people may be of little consequence to others, and experiences some people view positively can be viewed negatively by others. For example, next time you are on an airplane, strike up a conversation with the person sitting next to you about whether passengers should bring pets onto planes. Some people think having a dog next to their feet greatly improves the travel experience, some think it makes it worse, and others do not care much one way or the other. The subjective nature of experience raises several important questions. What experiences matter the most to people? Where should the company focus efforts to improve the employee experience? What is the best way to balance the competing needs of a diverse workforce consisting of people who may not all want the same thing? There is no simple way to answer these questions, but the following four strategies can help:

- **Do not waste people's time.** If there is one universally disliked experience, it is spending time on tasks that we feel are unimportant, overly difficult, or inefficient. Collect experience data to find activities that are despised by employees as taking too much of their time. Then look for ways to simplify, automate, or eliminate the activity.
- **Use technology to identify employee experience issues.** It is impossible for company leaders to fully understand what employee experience is like in the organization without using surveys or some other technology solution to measure employee attitudes and perceptions. The experiences leaders have at work are not the same as their employees, and many employees will not candidly share their experiences with leaders particularly if the things bothering them have no simple solution. In large companies there is also no way a leader can efficiently gather experience data from across the entire organization. Whatever data they gather from one group of employees may not reflect the experiences of others elsewhere in the company. Having technology-enabled processes for measuring and interpreting experience data is critical to identify what employee experiences are having the biggest impact on the company, whether for good or bad.
- **Avoid managing based on "average" experiences.** Different employees can have very different experiences of work, even if they are in the same job in the same location working for the same manager. This was strongly demonstrated when companies shifted to remote work in 2020. Average employee engagement scores went up during this period with most people welcoming the ability to work remotely. But engagement went way down for employees who did not have good home office environments or who struggled with being physically isolated away from their colleagues. It is important to remember there is no such thing as an average employee.[24] Every employee responds to work experiences in a different way depending on their past history,

personality, job objectives, and life situation. In addition, the most memorable work experiences for some employees could be things that other employees never experience at all. For example, a study found that employee experiences related to health care coverage are very important for employees in the United States, where health care is tied to employment but are relatively unimportant to employees in other parts of the world.[25] The top five most memorable "moments that matter" in the study were experiencing discrimination, taking maternity or paternity leave, relocating for work, being passed over for a promotion, and establishing a flexible work arrangement. Many employees will never experience any of these things, and it is unlikely they'd show up in the top 10 experience concerns of a company. But they are experiences companies should be aware of when they happen.

- **Recognize that some employees' opinions may matter more than others.** The goal of employee experience management is not to make everyone's job easy and fun. It is to create a work environment in which employees are engaged, committed, productive, and impactful. Some employees are more productive than others, and the things valued by these productive employees may be different from their less productive colleagues. For example, highly committed employees tend to value access to training or technology that makes them more effective in their jobs. Less committed employees may emphasize things like office perks that make their job environment more pleasant. Showing preference to some employees' interests over others can make certain employees feel less valued and must be done with caution. But no company has unlimited resources to devote to improving the employee experience. It is important to invest resources where they will have the greatest ROI on company performance.

A final note about measuring and managing employee experience. Do not ask people's opinion about their employee experiences if you are unable or unwilling to act on what they say. Employees can accept that not all their work experiences will be ideal, but they strongly dislike being asked for their input if what they say does not seem to matter.

The Employee Experience and Organizational Stakeholders

An old saying goes, "work is not supposed to be fun, that's why it is called work." This saying was accepted as a reality by many people in the past. People did not work to have great employee experiences, they worked to get money and other things they valued. Historically, many activities associated with work were not particularly enjoyable and some were physically dangerous. As long as employees got paid, they expected to endure unpleasant employee experiences to some degree. The talent tectonic forces of digitalization and demographics are reshaping this view of work. Part of this has to do with attracting and retaining talent. Skills shortages make it possible for people to demand good employee experiences or go to another employer. The other even more critical reason is because the activities associated with work are changing. If companies want people to be creative, collaborative, adaptable, resilient, caring, and empathetic then they need to create work environments that make people feel confident, efficient, supported, included, and appreciated. As we will discuss in subsequent chapters, this requires changing how companies address the seven perennial workforce challenges outlined in Chapter 1 associated with designing organizations, staffing roles, developing capabilities, engaging employees, increasing efficiency, ensuring compliance, and building culture. But it also requires changing the capabilities and mindsets of the four major stakeholder groups within an organization: leaders, managers, employees, and support functions.

Leaders

Many leaders view employee experience similarly to concepts such as job satisfaction or employee engagement. They know it influences employee retention and other performance indicators commonly used by HR, but they do not think of it as a key driver of business growth and profitability. This is the wrong way to think about employee experience. It is not something separate from business operations; it is a critical part of business operations. Leaders should ideally give the same attention to employee experience that is given to other operational areas. This might be likened to the change in leadership mindset toward customer satisfaction that occurred in the 1980s and 1990s. There was a time when companies did not pay much attention to customer satisfaction. Leaders measured whether customers bought their products, but they rarely measured how customers felt after the products had been purchased. In the 1980s companies started to recognize the impact customer satisfaction had on brand loyalty, future purchasing decisions, and company profitability. This led companies to start including customer satisfaction metrics as the key indicators of company performance that are discussed during board meetings and shared as part of the company's annual report.[26]

A similar change in leadership mindset is needed toward employee experience. Achieving this change requires using data to make leaders aware of the impact employee experience has on business performance.

This involves collecting and analyzing experience data to show how corporate actions affect employees and how this subsequently affects profit and growth. This data makes it possible for leaders to constructively discuss employee experience alongside sales, productivity, and operating metrics. Employee experience data expand the language of business leadership to include discussions of employee feelings, beliefs, and attitudes in conversations about how to improve profit margins, revenue growth, and operating costs.

Managers

Managers play a pivotal role in supporting employee experience through the influence they have on employees' sense of appreciation, support, and recognition. Employees want to work for companies that care about their success and well-being. The challenge is that a company cannot actually care for a person. Only a person can care for another person, and the "face" of the company to an employee is often their manager. The role of manager becomes even more important and more difficult when companies are undergoing change. Increasing levels of change create greater levels of uncertainty, uncertainty creates a sense of insecurity, and insecurity creates stress. Stressed-out employees are unhealthy employees, and unhealthy employees are not fully effective employees.[27] The less effective employees are, the more stressed they become, which can lead to a viciously declining cycle. Part of managing for adaptability is helping employees manage and control the stress inherent in a rapidly changing world. This starts with creating a supportive environment in which managers display a sense of empathy and understanding toward both the work and nonwork challenges employees are facing.[28] It is also about actively listening to employees and taking action to address their concerns.

Many managers are woefully unequipped to take on the challenge of supporting employees in a rapidly changing world. This is rarely the fault of the manager. They are often people who were given the position of manager because of their technical skills. They may have received little or no training on how to create supportive work environments. The good news is managers can be taught how to be supportive. And technology solutions are available that can help them effectively listen and act on the concerns of their employees. It is up to companies to provide these resources to their managers, and then support and reward them to improve the employee experience of their teams. Companies should also keep in mind that managers are employees, too. The way leaders manage the people who report to them has a direct influence on how these people manage their own teams.[29]

Employees

Employees are the primary focus of experience management efforts, but they also play a key role in these efforts. First, they must be willing to provide constructive feedback on what they like and dislike about their experiences at work. This requires creating a "psychologically safe" environment where people feel comfortable sharing their feelings and opinions.[30] Second, they should adopt a collaborative and supportive attitude toward the company's efforts to improve their work experiences. This entails viewing work in terms of a partnership based on mutual goals, not a competition for resources where employees strive to improve their experiences with little concern about how it affects the company. Third, employees should be accountable for how they affect the experiences of their colleagues. One of the primary factors that influences our job satisfaction is how we are treated by our coworkers.[31] Employees must share in the commitment to do what they can to make a better experience for everyone in the company. This includes their manager, who, as we noted, is an employee too.

Support Functions

People in HR, information technology, and finance support functions all play a critical role in a company's efforts to improve employee experience. HR professionals are typically the ones tasked to guide employee experience efforts. This requires building expertise to understand the factors that influence employees experience, how to measure employee experience, and how to improve it. They should view themselves as coaches and consultants to help leaders, managers, and employees identify and address employee experience concerns. They should also actively partner with their IT colleagues to implement technology solutions to better measure, understand, or improve employee experience. IT professionals should ensure the technology used by the organization enhances the employee experience. This is about providing technology that is easy to access and simple to use. This may include taking advantage of the convenience provided by mobile and cloud-based technology solutions or using robotic process automation to eliminate time employees spend on administrative or repetitive activities. Finance professionals should partner with HR and IT to determine the financial return associated with positive employee experiences. This involves collaborating with their colleagues to use experience management data to guide decisions about job design, staffing levels, reward structures, development programs, and other activities that influence employee experience but also have cost implications for the company.

Applying These Concepts to the World You Live In

Employee experience is a critical component in the creation of agile organizations capable of thriving in a world of accelerating change and chronic talent shortages. Throughout this book we will be looking at the role that employee experience plays in a variety of situations, including how jobs are designed, how candidates are hired, how employees are coached, and how employee data are used. Employee experience is certainly not all that matters when it comes to building effective workforces, but it matters a lot more than many people realize. Exploring the following questions can help with thinking about these concepts in the context of the company or companies you work with.

Understanding the Employee Experience

- What data do the company have that measure the employee experience? How is this information used? What actions have been taken based on this information? Has this information been used to understand how the employee experience affects business performance and talent retention?
- How do employees know that leaders are listening to them? What methods do you use to gather employee input? How does the company demonstrate to employees they heard them and are acting on their input?
- What are the moments that matter most for employee experience in your company? Are these the same across the entire organization?
- How is the motivation, confidence, and engagement of employees affected by the different types of employee experience? What does the company do well and where does it struggle with regard to?

  - **Fulfillment experiences:** does work enable employees to achieve things that are important to them?
  - **Task experiences:** do employees have easy access to the tools and resources needed to achieve their goals?
  - **Social experiences:** do employees feel supported, appreciated, and included by their coworkers?

Shaping and Improving the Employee Experience

- How do leaders think about the employee experience? Do they discuss the employee experience when talking about business operations and results? Or is it viewed mainly as an "HR topic"?

- What role do managers play in improving the employee experience in the organization? Where are they struggling? What knowledge or resources might help them create more supportive work environments?
- What experiences at work create the most frustration, stress, or anxiety for employees? How could the company improve these through leadership and manager actions, new resource investment, workforce training and development, or job redesign?
- What employee experiences make the company a great place to work? How can the company strengthen and build on these in the future?
- Are some employee populations struggling with unique needs regarding their experiences at work? Do people in certain jobs or from certain backgrounds find it more difficult to work in the company? How can the company support them in a way that also feels inclusive to other employees?

CHAPTER 3

Work Technology and Organizational Agility

When Giants Fall

The company Nokia was the dominant leader in mobile technology in 2007, controlling 41% of the mobile handset market and 51% of the emerging smartphone market.[1] Nokia was over twice as large as its nearest competitor and had global brand recognition as one of the most innovative companies in its industry. Over the next six years, Nokia suffered massive losses in market share attributed to an inability to adapt to new directions in smartphone design and functionality. Nokia ultimately sold its mobile phone business to Microsoft in 2013. Although Nokia still exists, the company once synonymous with mobile phones is now remembered in the same way as the old film company Kodak: an example of how quickly companies can go from market leader to a memory of what once was. When reflecting on its rapid fall, Jorma Ollila, former CEO of Nokia, commented that "we knew what was happening, but our mistake was not being able to turn that into action."[2]

Bill Gates, the founder and former CEO of Microsoft, wrote in 1996 that "we overestimate the change that will occur in the next two years and underestimate the change that will occur in the next ten. Don't let yourself be lulled into inaction."[3] In 2014, one year after acquiring Nokia, Gates stepped down and Satya Nadella became CEO of Microsoft, where he was challenged to reinvigorate the company's growth in the fast-expanding app and cloud-based technology market. Over the next five years, Microsoft went through one of the most successful business transformations in recent history.[4] When talking about the change, Nadella spoke about shifting the company from a culture of "know-it-alls," where people competed against each other to win, to a culture of "learn-it-alls," where people worked together to be successful. A critical part of this effort involved implementing technology solutions that enabled Microsoft to change how it managed employees to create a more learning-oriented culture.[5]

As digitalization accelerates the pace of change, companies must constantly adapt their practices and strategies in response to shifting markets, technological innovation, and changing regulations. As the story of Nokia shows, organizations that cannot change fast enough can cease to exist. The agility of organizations hinges on the ability of people in the company to adapt. As discussed in the previous chapter, this is heavily influenced by employee experiences at work. The ability of employees to effectively change direction depends on having insight to make good strategic decisions, skills and resources to execute the strategy, and confidence and motivation to act. As the story of Microsoft demonstrates, this comes from having both the right culture and the right technology.

This chapter explores how innovations in work technology are enabling companies to become more agile. It looks at barriers that limit organizational agility in large companies, discusses how technology helps overcome these barriers, and identifies cultural attributes needed to use technology to create an agile, adaptable workforce. It describes capabilities enabled by emerging technologies and why these capabilities matter for improving employee experience and creating more agile organizations. The overall purpose of this book is to help companies reshape the experience of work for a future that is much different from the past. This will not happen by making incremental improvements to existing work methods. It requires using technology to fundamentally shift how companies build and support their workforces. Do not think about technology solutions solely based on how they are being used now. Think about them in terms of how they could be used in the future.

Our understanding of technology limits and enables our imagination about work. We do not seriously consider actions if we think they are unrealistic. But the reason we create technology is to accomplish things that are difficult to do without it. As technology progresses, actions that were impossible or difficult become easier. Consequently, knowing what technology can do expands our vision of what is possible, which fuels our creativity. For example, shift scheduling is one of the biggest challenges to hiring workers in many warehouse, retail, and production positions. Historically companies set shift schedules based on business needs and then told employees when they had to work. Telling employees when to work without giving them much input into the decision is a formula for bad employee experiences. Scheduling conflicts are a common reason for employees quitting and candidates turning down job offers. In recent years, technology has emerged that enables employees to set their own schedules. It uses complicated algorithms that enable employees to negotiate and trade shifts with each other while ensuring the company has adequate staffing throughout the week. This enables companies to reimagine the experience of shift work from "work when we tell you" to "let's collaborate to find the best way to work together." This level of transformation would never have been explored by someone whose understanding of technology was limited to traditional scheduling spreadsheets. They would have dismissed the idea of employees setting their schedules as impossibly complicated and unsustainable. Understanding the sorts of work tasks and human behaviors that are being automated or augmented through technology frees our mind to consider what's possible at a transformational level well beyond incremental improvements to existing methods. It is folly to write about specific technology features given how fast technology solutions change, but we can learn a lot by exploring how technology is evolving in general.

Most of the technology discussed in this chapter is associated with the field of HR, but the chapter avoids the language typically used to place HR technology into process-based categories such as "staffing solutions," "learning solutions," or "compensation solutions." The names used to describe technology solutions are intentionally different from those commonly used by HR technology vendors for two reasons. First, the names technology vendors give to their solutions change over time. People in the HR technology field joke that the purpose of product marketing is to come up with new names for old things. For example, training solutions became learning solutions, which turned into development solutions and are now being called reskilling solutions. Second, current names used to describe HR technology reflect work processes currently found in companies. These models reflect the nature of work as it is now, which is not how it will be in the future. HR technology is becoming far less about automating processes and more about improving experiences and enabling decisions. At some point we may stop thinking about it as HR technology at all. It will just be technology that helps us get stuff done at work, which is why this book uses the phrase *work technology* rather than *HR technology*.

Many discussions of technology start by explaining what different types of solutions do. But we don't use technology because of what *it* does, we use it for what it enables *us* to do. And the main reason companies need work technology in the post-internet age is to build more engaging, agile, and adaptable organizations. For this reason, the chapter begins by examining what makes companies agile and why much of this is lost as companies grow larger. This provides insight into the behaviors and actions technology must augment or automate to enable large companies to act like a small, highly agile entrepreneurial organizations. This is followed by an overview of the kinds of work technologies available to achieve this goal, including how they can be linked to business operations technologies to increase organizational agility. The chapter concludes with a discussion of the cultural traits that must surround technology if it is to increase agility and how this relates to aspects of employee experience.

What It Means to Act Like a Small, Agile Entrepreneurial Company

Leaders of large companies often talk about wanting to act like entrepreneurial startup organizations.[6] They want the urgency, creativity, responsiveness, and flexibility associated with small, growth-oriented companies. When it comes to agility, four things differentiate the employee experience working in small entrepreneurial companies from that found in large organizations. Compared to large companies, small companies tend to have a stronger collective sense of purpose, greater urgency and openness to change, tighter communities where everyone knows everyone else, and cultures that value employees based primarily on the impact they have on company success.

Collective Sense of Purpose

Most organizations trace their roots back to a few people coming together around an idea. When these organizations were founded, the only thing they had was people. They did not yet have any profit, probably had very few resources, and may not even have had a well-defined strategy. The organization consisted solely of people with a shared vision to do something and a desire to make it a reality. The employee experience in these companies was defined by a clear focus on a common purpose. Everyone in the organization knew what the company was trying to achieve and why it matters. This strong collective sense of purpose is hard to maintain as companies grow, add multiple divisions, and spread across different regions and locations.

Urgency and Openness to Change

People in small startups have a sense of urgency driven both by opportunity and threat. The opportunity is the chance to be "first to market" and build something successful. The threat is knowing the company has limited time to acquire customers and start building revenue. Grow or die is a reality in most startups. Maintaining status quo is not an option. This urgency fuels an openness to change. The purpose of the company is clear, but there is a high level of flexibility shown toward how the purpose is achieved. All strategies are viewed as temporary methods that will shift over time to address changing conditions. Frequent iterations and modifications are expected and normal. The act of adapting is viewed as a critical factor in driving opportunity. The goal of these companies is not to continue doing things that they have already done. It is to build on accomplishments to achieve new successes. Large companies tend to lose this sense of urgency because the stakes of success and failure are less noticeable. There is little risk of the company going under due to a poor quarter or even a poor year. As a result, people often start to grow comfortable with the way things are, taking an attitude of "why change what isn't broken?"

Everyone Knows Everyone Else

When you have a small group of people urgently working to achieve shared goals, it does not take long for everyone to meet everybody else. Many startup organizations begin with everyone in the company literally sitting in the same shared office. The companies may have leadership structures and defined roles, but these structures do not hinder collaboration between people based on job titles. The employee experience is one of "we're all in this together." Because everyone knows each other, they know what others are capable of beyond their formal title. This leads to people getting opportunities and exposure to a variety of things outside their normal job description. Consider this story from a startup where I worked. We had a major meeting with a Japanese company and the sales leader discovered the people he was presenting to had limited fluency in English. Fortunately, we knew one of our engineers lived in Japan as a child, so he helped deliver the presentation in Japanese. This is an example of the power of truly knowing your colleagues and organizing work based on what people can contribute instead of assigning work based on formal roles. It is hard to know people at this intimate level when the company's workforce consists of hundreds or thousands of people across different locations.

Influence Is Gained Through Impact

People with high levels of performance are quickly recognized in small entrepreneurial companies and moved into roles of increasing influence and responsibility. Conversely, people who do not make meaningful contributions are quickly identified. I was working in a startup when I first heard the phrase "He's all hat and no cattle" from a colleague who grew up in west Texas. He was describing a leader we hired who had excellent credentials but never seemed to get anything done. Shortly after my friend made this observation, our CEO ask this leader to seek opportunities elsewhere. Reputations are built quickly in small companies. If you are a person who makes a difference people will hear about it. Similarly, if you are not responsive, cooperative, and productive people will quickly know that, too. The way people gain influence in small companies is by having an impact on the company's growth and profitability. People who create successful products, increase sales, improve customer satisfaction, reduce costs, or increase operational efficiency quickly get noticed. They are given roles in which they can have even greater impact, regardless of what their current role may be. Terms such as *career ladder* or *chain of leadership* do not mean much in a small company. What matters is the ability to have an impact on things that affect the company's growth and survival.

In large companies it is hard to see the impact one person has on overall company performance. Because employees in large companies have limited ability to show how they affect business outcomes, they often shift toward demonstrating they are relevant to company operations. If you ask people in these companies what they do, the answer is often less about what they achieve and more about what they support. This can make it difficult to figure out the exact function of many roles in large companies.[i] This does not mean these roles are not important, but it is much harder to connect the contributions of people in these roles to tangible and specific business outcomes. People tend to gain influence in a large company by moving into formal leadership roles, which can lead to a lot of politics in staffing decisions. This inevitably changes the culture of the organization. People start to focus less on accomplishing things that tangibly affect business outcomes and more on managing the impressions they make on others.

A challenge facing large companies is how to retain the elements of the employee experience that enable the agility of small entrepreneurial organizations. This starts to become difficult after a company's workforce grows beyond a certain size. In my experience, the change starts to happen at about 250 people, when the CEO is unlikely to personally know or even recognize every employee.[ii] How can a large company build a collective sense of purpose across multiple divisions, maintain a sense of urgency

---

[i] This could be said about the role I am in now with its grandiose but somewhat meaningless title *chief expert*.

[ii] I have long believed organizational culture tends to change when the workforce expands past about 250 people. What I did not know until doing research for this book is the 250-person number also aligns with neurological research on social networks (see https://en.wikipedia.org/wiki/Dunbar%27s_number).

and openness to change over multiple years, enable everyone knowing everyone else across thousands of people, and identify individuals who are having the most impact within a complex organizational structure? There are certain things about how people work in small companies that simply cannot be replicated in large organizations. But large organizations can create many of the employee experiences associated with small companies through fully leveraging the capabilities of work technology.

What Needs to Be Automated and Augmented to Create More Agile Organizations

Before exploring the kinds of work technology that enable large companies to act like agile, small entrepreneurial companies, it is important to clarify what we need this technology to do. The five activities large companies need help with to create more agile, adaptable workforces are people decisions, creating communities, individual self-management, security and compliance, and saving time.

People Decisions

Decisions about employees make or break the success of organizations. The most significant are decisions about which people to put into different roles (e.g., hiring, promotions, team assignments, etc.). The decision of which employee to place into a particular role impacts on how the role is performed and also communicates to other employees what attributes the company values, rewards, or tolerates. For example, promoting someone who achieves results through belittling others sends a strong message about company values to everyone who has worked with that person.[7] Decisions about where to invest compensation and development resources, although not as influential as staffing decisions, also have a major impact on employee performance, motivation, and retention.[8]

People decisions can be broadly divided into external staffing decisions and internal talent decisions. External staffing decisions are about how many people to bring into the company, whether to employ them full-time or as contractors, and who specifically to hire. As companies grow, it becomes difficult to figure out where it makes sense to add headcount. If two departments say they need to add 100 people, but the company can only afford to hire 50 new employees, how should these staff be allocated? And when people are added to the organization, how can the company ensure it is hiring the right people? What companies need is technology that can evaluate the business impact of adding (or not adding) headcount and ensure quality of hires across the organization.

Internal talent decisions include assigning employees to roles or teams, making promotions, transfers, and terminations, and investing compensation and development resources. Large organizations face two major challenges in this area. The first is about matching people to opportunities. How can the company ensure the right people are on the right teams? When does it make sense to transfer people internally? How can the company match people in one part of the company to opportunities in another area? The second is about evaluating the contributions and capabilities of people to guide decisions about who to reward, develop, or move into new positions. Which employees are making the greatest contributions? Which have the interest and potential to take on greater levels of responsibility? Are any employees hindering the success of others through inaction or counterproductive behavior? What companies need is technology to help match employees to opportunities within the company, facilitate internal talent movement to maximize the impact people have on the company's performance, and enable leaders to make better talent decisions through accurately assessing the performance, potential, and capabilities of existing employees.

Creating Communities

A company is an organization of people coming together to achieve mutual or complementary goals using shared resources. Effective organizations are composed of effective groups, teams, and communities sharing information and supporting one another tactically and emotionally. The problem facing large companies is how to create, maintain, support, and change these communities over time.[9] Traditional methods for structuring teams, groups, and departments used spreadsheets and hierarchical reporting structures that provided little information about how people actually work together in a digitalized, virtual world. Just because two people report to the same manager does not mean they actively work together or even work on the same things. What companies need is technology that can help leaders measure how people in the company work together and provide insights into how the formal structure of the organization affects the people relationships that drive company performance.

Another challenge is maintaining the performance levels of communities as they grow. As teams become larger, the relative productivity of each additional member starts to decrease.[10] This is due in part to the complexity associated with coordinating activity across greater numbers of people. It also reflects the communication challenge of keeping members aware of things relative to their role without overwhelming or distracting them with superfluous information. What companies need is technology that enables community members to effectively share information and coordinate activities in an efficient manner across large numbers of people.

Self-Management

The phrase *self-management* incorporates both self-development and performance improvement. It is about employees' motivation and ability to build their capabilities and achieve results. People in small companies understand that if they don't figure out how to get something done then it probably won't get done it all. And if it doesn't happen then the company may cease to exist. This drives employees to learn what they need to know to accomplish their goals. As companies grow, this sense of urgency tends to decrease as the relationship between an individual's actions and overall company performance becomes unclear. The consequences of not doing something become less immediate. If someone in a small company does not do their job everyone notices. If someone in a large company does not do their job it may only be noticed by those who work directly with them. And even then, no one may really care.

Psychologists use the term *social loafing* to describe the tendency for people to work less hard in large groups and organizations.[11] People are born with two complementary psychological needs: the need to achieve meaningful goals and the need to conserve energy and resources. The first motivates us to get things done, and the second guards us against working too hard and burning ourselves out.[iii] Taking a break from work also plays an important role in self-reflection, enabling us to think about the future to ensure we are focusing our time effectively on things that truly matter to us.[12] The problem in large groups is people get stuck in a more passive, reactive mode toward work because to some degree they can "hide in a crowd." This is not necessarily because they are not motivated or committed to the company. It can simply be because they do not feel their individual contributions matter that much. Or that they do not realize what they should be doing differently. What companies need is technology that makes it clear to people in a large group why their individual contributions matter and how they can increase their effectiveness; that keeps people engaged by increasing awareness of the difference they are personally making for the company, its customers, and their colleagues; and that provides them with supportive feedback and constructive resources they can use to improve their level of impact.

[iii] The psychological conflict between these two needs was humorously explained in a cartoon extolling the virtues of procrastination: "Hard work often pays off over time, but laziness always pays off now."

Security and Compliance

The bigger a company becomes the greater its security and compliance risk. Larger companies are more likely to be targeted by criminals due to their visibility and depth of resources. The broader scope of operations associated with large companies often makes them subject to greater regulatory compliance than small companies. The more employees a company has the more likely it is that one of them will inadvertently do something that violates legal regulations or endangers the security and safety of themselves and their colleagues.[13] Security and compliance violations do not just create tangible damage, they also raise concerns among employees about working for an unethical or unsafe company. However, employees dislike being forced to spend time following extensive security and compliance protocols. Security and compliance are important, but they are not what makes a company successful. A challenge facing large companies is how to maintain security and compliance without making the experience of work seem overly rule-bound and bureaucratic. What companies need is technology that automates many of the activities associated with security and compliance and reduces the amount of time employees have to spend thinking about it.

Saving Time

One of the common complaints about working in a big company is how long it takes to get things done. In a small company, it is possible to get every stakeholder together and go from discussion to decision to action in a single conversation. This is not feasible in large companies where the stakeholders may be in different departments, locations, and time zones. Things happen slowly in large companies because actions have to be coordinated across multiple groups. Operations must agree the action makes sense, finance has to ensure adequate funds exist to support it, information technology must ensure it can be supported with existing systems, legal may need to ensure it meets regulations, and so forth. A friend working for a global company once told me, "Every single person in this company could agree that we should do something immediately and it would still take six months." Large companies also spend a lot of time on routine activities. For example, if a company hires only a few people a year, then time spent scheduling candidate interviews is manageable. This ceases to be true when a company is hiring hundreds of people each month. What companies need is technology that facilitates communication and decision-making across groups, makes it easier for people to find resources and gain permissions required for different actions, and automatically performs routine administrative functions. This technology reduces the time required to get things done and frees up employees' time to focus on more valued-added activities.

Large organizations face a dilemma in a digitalized world marked by an accelerating pace of change. On the positive side, the capabilities of larger companies provide them with more power and resilience than smaller companies. They have a depth of resources to overcome challenges and bounce back from setbacks. However, they lack the agility and efficiency of smaller, more entrepreneurial organizations. This lack of agility can also make it difficult to attract talent who don't want to work for what they see as a big, slow-moving, impersonal, bureaucratic organization. The question is whether big companies can use their depth of resources to create employee experiences that mimic what it is like to work in entrepreneurial startup organizations? Technology cannot solve this dilemma completely, but it can help large companies act and feel more like small, agile ones. And it is this agile ability to change that increasingly makes the difference to company success.[14]

How Work Technology Is Transforming Workforce Management

There is no single technology solution that addresses all the challenges that make large companies slower and less agile than smaller companies. It requires using a combination of technologies to rethink how to make people decisions, create communities, support self-management, ensure security and compliance, and save time. Using work technology to support workforce agility might be likened to how a chef uses different ingredients to create meals to fit the palates of different customers. It is about knowing what ingredients are available, understanding their properties, and being adept at using them in combination to address different needs.

Table 3.1 lists types of work technology that are transforming how companies build and manage workforces and how they relate to different challenges that prevent large companies from acting like small, agile organizations. The technologies are grouped into three categories: orchestration, collaboration, and general applications. Orchestration solutions help ensure companies have the right people in the right jobs supported by the right resources. They focus on putting people in different positions, paying them appropriately, and providing them with necessary knowledge and tools. Collaboration solutions support communication and coordination between people. They focus on clarifying roles, supporting ongoing coaching and development, sharing information, and supporting teamwork. General application technologies can be used to support different aspects of orchestration and collaboration. This includes things such as assessing talent potential, measuring employee experience, or

TABLE 3.1 Types of Work Technology

	People Decisions	Creating Communities	Self-Improvement	Security and Compliance	Saving Time
Orchestration Solutions					
Workforce design	X	X			
Recruiting management	X				X
Opportunity matching	X		X		X
Talent sourcing	X	X			X
Job transitions and onboarding		X	X	X	X
Compensation and benefits management	X	X	X	X	X
Contractor management	X	X		X	X
Work scheduling	X	X		X	X
Certification management				X	X
Talent decisions	X	X	X	X	X
Facilities and system access		X		X	X
Collaboration Solutions					
Work experience platforms		X			X
Learning experience platforms		X	X		X
Team management		X			X
Electronic communication		X			X
Collaboration spaces		X			
General Application Solutions					
Electronic profiles	X				
Talent assessments	X				
Experience measurement			X		
Virtual reality		X	X		

TABLE 3.1 (*Continued*)

	People Decisions	Creating Communities	Self-Improvement	Security and Compliance	Saving Time
Robotic process automation					X
Interoperable data management	X				
Mobile enabled					X
Single sign-on				X	X
Wearables and biometrics			X		
Relationship analysis		X			
Chatbots					X
Machine learning	X				

analyzing workforce data. The differences in orchestration, collaboration, and general application can be explained using the analogy of a musical symphony. Orchestration is determining what musical parts should be played by which musicians and ensuring each one has the instruments and skills to perform their parts. Collaboration is about the actual performance, ensuring the musicians can hear each other and are keeping the right tempo and volume to create the right sound. General applications are about doing things that support both orchestration and collaboration, such as digitalizing music sheets so they can be accessed with mobile devices. A successful performance starts with effective orchestration. It finishes with effective collaboration.

Most of the solutions in Table 3.1 address several of the barriers that limit organizational agility. No single solution can eliminate a barrier, but they can reduce its impact. For example, opportunity matching solutions enable companies to transfer employees to job openings based on their interests and capabilities. This leads to better people decisions and saving time. In comparison, work experience solutions can be used to build connections between employees with common work interests. This helps with creating communities. The following are brief descriptions of each of these technology solutions. It would be impossible to fully explain what all of these solutions do in a single book. The intention is just to provide enough insight to understand how each technology enables companies to reimagine different aspects of work at a general level.

Workforce Orchestration Technology Solutions

These technologies enable companies to more effectively design and staff organizations, decide how to invest resources such as compensation and benefits, pay employees and fulfill employment contract obligations, and ensure employees meet relevant qualifications to perform their roles.

Workforce Design and Analytics

These solutions integrate financial, operations, and human resource data to guide decisions related to organizational design, headcount allocation, and compensation structures. The power of these systems lies in their ability to incorporate data from multiple sources and interpret it using sophisticated mathematical and visual analytics tools. The more advanced solutions provide insight into the impact workforce design has on business outcomes and employee work relationships and experiences.

Recruiting Management

These solutions support the logistics associated with hiring new employees. The core focus of these solutions is to make it easy for managers to staff roles by automating administrative tasks tied to opening requisitions, recruiting and interviewing candidates, and enrolling new employees. Most of these solutions incorporate or link to features associated with opportunity matching, talent sourcing, and job transitions and onboarding.

Opportunity Matching

These solutions match job opportunities to people based on their interests and capabilities. These solutions can support external hiring and internal talent transfer, as well as job sharing, part-time, temporary, and contractor job assignments. The solutions may support both formal job transfers and informal team assignments. Many of these solutions use complex machine learning algorithms to evaluate people's fit with different opportunities. This makes it easier for companies to fill positions while also supporting employee career growth.

Talent Sourcing

These solutions help find and attract job candidates. This is done through a combination of methods including solutions that search for candidates based on online information, tools to support targeted placement of job ads and recruiting marketing materials, and tools to create and maintain candidate communities such as alumni networks and career interest groups.

Job Transitions and Onboarding

These solutions support activities associated with moving people into new jobs or positions. This includes tactical activities such as completing forms, enrolling in payroll, and providing work training and equipment. It may also include cultural aspects such as meeting new people, clarifying job roles and expectations, and becoming part of the work community. These solutions can support external hires or internal job transfers.

Compensation, Payroll, and Benefits Management

These solutions support designing and administering compensation, benefits, and rewards programs. This includes supporting payroll operations and benefits administration, legal and regulatory compliance associated with pay plans, and complex commission-based pay structures. They help ensure companies fulfill the financial aspects of employment contracts. Automating the operational complexity of pay and benefits administration processes also enables companies to create more tailored and effective reward systems.

Contractor Management

These solutions support the operational and regulatory needs associated with contract employment relationships. This includes matching contractors to roles, onboarding contractors into positions, handling the administration of contractor pay, and complying with contract work regulations. This technology enables companies to effectively use contractors as a critical part of the organization's workforce.

Work Scheduling

These solutions support shift scheduling common to many operational, manufacturing, and service jobs. This includes designing shift schedules, collaborating with employees to cover different shifts, and tracking hours worked to support pay and other operational activities. These solutions may include tools giving employees control over setting schedules, analytics systems that integrate operational and employee experience data to set staffing levels for different shifts, and methods to ensure compliance with scheduling requirements and regulations.

Certification Management

These solutions ensure employees have the necessary qualifications required to perform jobs. Many of these solutions include links to training and other resources employees can use to become certified or maintain their certification status. These solutions may be linked to scheduling and facilities management solutions to ensure work shifts and locations are staffed with people possessing the necessary qualifications and security access. This may include assessing health requirements such as vaccinations or scanning visual images to ensure employees are wearing appropriate equipment such as safety glasses.

Talent Management Decisions

These solutions help companies make decisions related to compensation, development, promotions, transfers, team membership, and role assignments. These solutions work by providing decision frameworks that integrate data about employee accomplishments, behaviors, interests, and capabilities and present it in a way that supports accurate decision-making.

Facilities and System Access

These solutions manage and track access to online systems and physical work offices and facilities. These solutions are used to maintain security and ensure regulatory compliance. They can also provide data showing how facilities are being used and that provide insight into how the design of offices and work sites influences employee experiences.

Workforce Collaboration Technology Solutions

The following technologies enable employees to effectively work together to execute business strategies, achieve individual and team goals, and develop and improve performance and capabilities.

Work Experience Platforms

These solutions incorporate technology solutions employees use at work into a single platform or portal, enabling employees to more easily access tools and information needed to perform their jobs. They shape the experience of work through how the solutions are displayed and the user experiences they create. They often include features to create online communities consisting of employees in similar jobs or groups.

Learning Experience Platforms

These solutions are a type of work experience platform focused specifically on employee development. These solutions incorporate a variety of development resources including tools to help employees identify and track development goals, find and access relevant training, build development relationships through mentors and learning communities, and locate assignments and roles that will help build their capabilities. They may also provide tools so employees can form learning communities to share and discuss development and training content with others.

Learning Content Platforms

These solutions enable training instructors and employees to build, edit, organize, and manage training materials including training assessments and certification tests. They may incorporate a variety of training modalities including video, narrative storylines, virtual reality, interactive exercises, gamification, and integrated curriculums.

Team Management

These solutions help employees coordinate and communicate team activities and projects. They enable employees to set up groups and communities, define goals and share and track information across team members. Some of these solutions are informal in nature, focusing on sharing information across team members in a general way. Others are built to support formally defined team processes and project management methodologies such as Agile, Waterfall, Critical Path, or others.[15] Team management solutions often integrate or incorporate technology solutions focused on supporting electronic communication and collaboration spaces.

Electronic Communication

These solutions include e-mail, chat, instant messaging, calendar scheduling, and other tools that support immediate and asynchronous communication between employees. Many of these solutions support use of visual imagery and audio or visual recordings. Electronic communication is not typically thought of as a tool for workforce management, but the electronic communication solutions available to employees and how companies use them significantly shape employee experience.[16]

Collaboration Spaces

These solutions create shared virtual spaces where employees can meet to discuss issues, explore ideas, and develop solutions. These solutions can be entirely online such as virtual whiteboards or may blend in-person and online technology such as video conference rooms. The availability, design, and use of collaboration technology can be a major factor affecting group cohesiveness and team effectiveness.[17]

Role Clarification/Goal Management

These solutions support communication among employees, managers, and coworkers related to roles, goals, and expectations. They may incorporate goal management methodologies such as goal cascading, OKRs (objectives and key results) and shared team goals.[18] These solutions often include tools for defining and aligning goals, revisiting and revising goals over time, creating shared goals across team members, providing coaching related to both goals and behavioral expectations, and linking employee goals to business operations metrics related to productivity, financial performance, customer satisfaction, or sales.

Self-Management

These solutions provide employees with feedback, information, and insights to help change their behaviors and improve their performance and skills. They may provide employees with nudges[19] to guide and remind employees of things they want to do differently. Many of these solutions collect, analyze, and present data so people are aware of the impact they are having on themselves and others. Examples are solutions that analyze the emotional tone associated with a person's electronic communications, gather survey data showing how a person's behaviors are being interpreted by others, analyze calendar data to provide feedback on how a person is using their time, or track mobile and physiological data to increase awareness of physical activity and health.

General Workforce Technology Applications

These technologies provide functionalities and data that are often integrated into orchestration and collaboration solutions.

Electronic Profiles

These solutions integrate data about employees or candidates to facilitate decisions related to staffing, development, compensation, and performance.

They typically include information such as job title, organizational reporting structure, pay levels, job history and tenure, demographics, past experience and education, and formal qualifications. They may also have information related to past performance, future potential, development goals, career interests, and psychological attributes related to work such as personality and ability traits. Collecting and integrating information about candidates and employees enables companies to make better decisions about them, but it can also create anxiety among employees who, for very valid reasons, may be skeptical about how this data will be used and whether it will be done in their best interest.[20]

Talent Assessments

These solutions are designed to measure employee and candidate attributes, interests, and capabilities. This is typically done through structured questionnaires, tests, simulations, or interviews. Depending on the assessment, this data may be used to guide staffing decisions and/or be used to support employee development.

Experience Measurement

These solutions provide insight into employee and candidate experiences. This is usually done using surveys that ask targeted questions based on an employee's job role, career interests, or after they complete a work activity. Many solutions use embedded analytics to interpret data and provide guidance to managers or other individuals who can act on the results while ensuring data confidentiality and anonymity. Experience measurement solutions may also incorporate data from other sources, such as analyzing patterns of absenteeism to determine if employees are experiencing difficulty managing work and nonwork schedule demands, electronic communication data such as e-mail to provide insight into employee work patterns and attitudes, or data from wearable biometric devices to track employee stress and fatigue. Experience measurement solutions are sometimes referred to as employee listening technology.

Virtual Reality

These solutions create highly realistic, immersive virtual environments to support training, collaboration, or communication. This is one of the faster-growing areas of work technology with some people predicting that it will become so comprehensive and realistic that we increasingly shift much of our work into a massive virtual environment called the *metaverse*.[21]

Robotic Process Automation

These solutions enable companies to automate repetitive online processes and activities. This technology is becoming increasingly robust in terms of the complexity of processes it can support to the point that almost any process that requires people to do the same steps over and over can potentially be automated.

Interoperable Data Management

These solutions enable companies to collect, store, manage, and analyze extremely large datasets containing data from multiple sources in a single system. A key feature of these solutions is their ability to combine workforce data with business operations data found in financial, supply chain, manufacturing, sales, and customer management systems. This is often referred to as "creating a single source of truth" and facilitates the ability to analyze and use data to guide workforce management decisions and actions. A key feature of these solutions is a concept called *interoperability* that enables linking and maintaining data collected from sources that use different data frameworks and structures.

Gamification Platforms

These solutions enable companies to apply the gamification concepts such as storylines, rewards, or contests to encourage engagement and completion of processes, training, and other tasks and activities.

Mobile Enabled

This is more of design feature than a solution. It refers to designing technology solutions so they can be accessed through mobile and smartphone devices. This makes solutions much easier to access particularly for employees who do not work at desks. Most technology solutions can be mobile enabled, but not all are.

Single Sign-On

These solutions simplify security access by creating a unified framework that works across multiple technology systems. Using single sign-on makes different work technology solutions easier to use by employees and, if designed correctly, strengthen system security by reducing the number of access points.

Wearables and Biometrics

These solutions enable collecting data from employees about their physical location and health. These solutions often feed data into solutions used for facilities access, self-improvement, and experience measurement.

Relationship Analysis

These solutions provide data about the nature of employee relationships and how people interact. Many of these solutions use survey data collected using a technique called *organizational network analysis*. Relationship analysis can also be done using data from electronic communication, collaboration space, team management, and facilities access solutions. These solutions are particularly valuable for guiding decisions related to organizational design and workforce productivity. For example, Figure 3.1 shows what an organization looks like based on a traditional leadership organizational chart versus a relationship analysis chart. The figure on the bottom shows how often people interact with each other and identifies Jordan as the person who is central to the organization's operations. This is in contrast to the hierarchical organizational chart on the top that suggest Jordan's role is relatively minor.

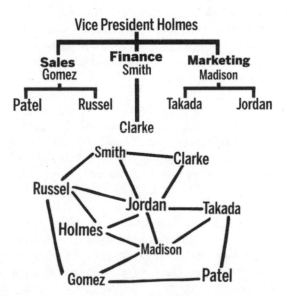

FIGURE 3.1 Hierarchical versus relationship-based organizational charts.

Chatbots

These solutions use artificial intelligence functionality to create user inter-
faces that mimic natural language. Chatbots make it easier to perform certain kinds of administrative tasks such as scheduling interviews or asking
questions about benefits. But they are not always responded to favorably
depending on whether employees expect a chatbot versus a human and
the perceived efficiency of the chatbot for addressing employee needs.[22] It
is somewhat uncertain how they would be viewed if used to perform more
sensitive tasks, such as providing coaching or counseling.[23]

Machine Learning

These solutions use complex iterative mathematical algorithms to identify
patterns and predict future outcomes. These solutions are often used to
guide hiring, staffing, and development recommendations in career matching, scheduling, talent sourcing, talent assessment, and learning experience
solutions. Machine learning can be applied to any solution that generates
large amounts of data used to predict an outcome of interest. For example, it
could be used with experience management solutions to predict employee
turnover or employee profile data to predict likely employee career paths.
However, caution is needed when using machine learning for sensitive talent decisions such as hiring or compensation because most people prefer to
be evaluated by other people, not by machines.[24] This does not necessarily
mean machine learning should not be used for such decisions, but it can
create risks related to perceptions of fairness and equity.

* * *

The list in Table 3.1 covers most of the technology applications that
currently exist to support workforce design and management. New applications are constantly being developed but they can usually be associated
with one or more of the solutions in this list. An experienced HR person
might be surprised there is no mention of common types of HR technology
such as human resource information systems (HRIS) or applicant tracking
systems (ATS). This is intentional because what these systems do can be
thought of as a prepackaged combination of different solutions listed in
Table 3.1. An HRIS is a mixture of electronic profiles, compensation, payroll and benefits management, and facilities and system access. An ATS is
combination of electronic profiles, recruiting management, talent assessments, and job transitions and onboarding. The advantage of thinking of
work technology in this more modular way is it enables companies to mix
or match different solutions to address different needs. Over time I sus-
pect companies will use work technology applications the way we use our

computers and phones: they will have a core work experience platform that they complement with a mix of specialized solutions that frequently change based on their particular needs.

Linking Work Technology to Business Operations Technology

Table 3.1 contains an impressive list of technology solutions that help companies build productive and agile workforces. But none of these solutions actually measure the business value employees provide to an organization. This is because data about things companies hire employees to do, such as drive sales, create customer satisfaction, or build products, are not measured by work technology solutions. It is collected and stored in business operations technology solutions companies use to manage financial data, sales and customer data, and manufacturing and supply chain data. Figure 3.2 illustrates the relationship between these two types of technology. Work technology supports the first three boxes in Figure 3.2. Business operations technology supports the fourth box. To fully leverage technology to create highly agile organizations, companies must break down the wall that often

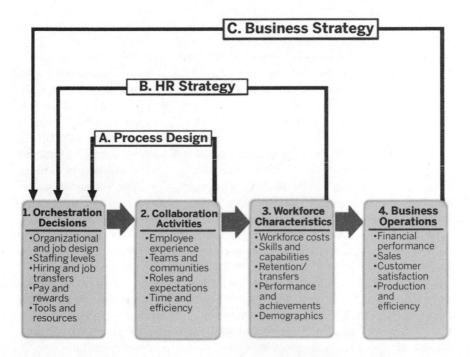

FIGURE 3.2 Linking work technology to business outcomes.

exists between the first three boxes of work technology on the left and the fourth box of business technology on the right. This means creating much tighter connections between workforce data and business operations data.

Figure 3.2 illustrates how different technology solutions support company actions going from workforce decisions to business outcomes. Companies use orchestration solutions to guide and implement decisions related to organizational design, staffing, and talent management. These decisions determine who is in the organization, what roles they have, and the resources available to them. Employees then use collaboration solutions to work together and perform their roles. This in turn influences workforce characteristics such as employee engagement, retention, performance, and skills. These characteristics in turn influence business outcomes. Consider an example of workforce restructuring and job redesign. The process starts when company leaders use orchestration solutions to redesign the company structure and the roles people are expected to perform (Box 1). The company then uses collaboration solutions to communicate the new structure and help employees adapt to their new roles (Box 2). Based on how employees react, the restructuring will change the characteristics of the workforce (Box 3). The changes will create new relationships while weakening others. Some employees will be motivated by the new structure and others may quit entirely. This will change the composition of the workforce and the goals it achieves, which will drive business outcomes such financial performance or productivity (Box 4).

The arrows on the top of Figure 3.2 illustrate how data is used to assess the impact of workforce decisions. At the simplest level, companies measure employee satisfaction with different workforce decisions and processes (arrow A). For example, do employees like a training program? Do they feel they are paid fairly? This data is used for HR process improvement. The next level uses data to see how workforce characteristics are influenced by HR processes (arrow B). For example, are employees who complete a training program more likely to be promoted? Does a new compensation plan influence employee turnover? This data is useful for guiding HR strategy. But companies do not hire people so they can be promoted and not quit. Companies hire people to deliver business results. This is about understanding how a company's workforce management practices affect outcomes such as profitability, growth, customer service, safety, and other critical business metrics (arrow C).

Organizations often have little empirical insight into how workforce decisions affect business outcomes. They know there are relationships between workforce decisions and business performance but lack detail on the strength or nature of these relationships. Companies have a lot of workforce data about staffing levels, how people are paid, what training people complete, and so forth. But they do not know how much these things influence business outcomes such as sales, customers service, or profitability. Historically, very few organizations have actually measured the financial return on investments allocated to salary, benefits, training, and other costs associated with employing people. This was mainly because it was too difficult to access and link the data together. The relatively recent development of interoperable data management technology solutions is changing this. It enables companies to do things such as the following:

- Coordinating retail supply chain solutions with learning platforms so frontline employees automatically receive training on new products before they are shipped to stores, and then seeing how completion of training affects product sales.
- Integrating data on manager skills, employee experience, and sales performance to determine what manager behaviors have the greatest impact on sales team revenue generation.
- Analyzing data on the size, skills, and tenure of customer support teams to determine how team composition affects customer satisfaction.

One of the biggest challenges in HR has been demonstrating the business implications of workforce decisions and practices.[25] HR metrics such as employee engagement and turnover influence business results, but they are not equivalent to business results. By connecting HR data to business operations and financial data, interoperable data management solutions make it possible to calculate the business impact of workforce decisions. For example, determining how changing employee work schedules affects accident rates or determining whether the cost of increasing compensation to reduce turnover is warranted by increased sales resulting from having a more stable, committed workforce. The implications this technology has on the ability of companies to understand the value of people and improve the effectiveness of workforce decisions on business operations are profound.

Adaptability, Technology, and Culture

Technology is central to creating adaptable workforces and agile organizations. How well technology supports this objective depends largely on the culture of the organization. Technology will not make companies more agile if the company's culture reflects the command-and-control leadership styles common in the 20th century that could be characterized as "leaders think, employees do." Organizational agility requires enabling and encouraging employees to question existing practices, explore new possibilities, and take calculated risks to support the mission, values, and strategic objectives of the organization. This comes from leaders and employees using technology to support five key cultural values:

- **Accountability.** Make sure people know what they are expected to achieve, why it matters, and how they will be evaluated. People want to be successful, so clearly communicate how success is measured in their role. Role clarification and talent decision solutions are particularly relevant to supporting this value.
- **Autonomy.** When possible, people should be given freedom to structure work in whatever way makes the most sense to them. Supervisors should avoid micromanaging. As one manager put it, "Work with employees to set clear goals and then get out of their way." Use technology to give employees greater control over deciding when they work, where they work, and how they organize work tasks and schedules.
- **Transparency.** In general, the more transparent the workplace, the better the employee experience. Digitalization enables transparency, transparency drives awareness, and awareness encourages collaboration and accountability. Transparency also promotes equity and fairness. The worst abuses of employees, ranging from unequal pay to abusive supervisory behaviors, tend to occur under the veil of privacy. Whenever possible, use technology solutions to provide the workforce with greater insight into how the company makes decisions and the structures it uses to evaluate and reward employees.
- **Openness to change.** Adaptability is about doing things differently in the future from how they were done in the past. People vary widely in their openness to new experiences.[26] As companies seek to become more adaptable, it is important to manage how employees are reacting to changes. Experience measurement solutions are particularly valuable for monitoring employee anxiety and taking steps to build confidence and enthusiasm, so change is viewed as an opportunity instead of a threat.
- **Psychological safety.** Psychological safety is defined as "the belief that the workplace is safe for interpersonal risk taking."[27] Psychological safety is created when employees feel they will be supported if they take a reasonable risk that does not work out as intended, and when failure is viewed as an opportunity to learn. Employees who experience a sense of psychological safety have higher levels of performance, learning, engagement, information sharing, and commitment. All of these are critical to creating adaptable workforces. Many technology solutions enable actions associated with organizational agility such as information sharing and learning. But without a sense of psychological safety, employees will be reluctant to use it. Experience measurement

solutions can be valuable for diagnosing and address concerns related to psychological safety.

Culture development is an important part of a company's technology strategy. It entails defining the behaviors and actions leaders and managers must take to create an environment where employees feel motivated, supported, and safe using technology solutions to expand, change, and improve how they perform work. It also requires balancing different cultural values. For example, autonomy must be bounded by role clarity and accountability, or the company may fall into chaos. As one customer told me, "We set our employees down clear roads with high curbs and wide lanes. Clear roads and high curbs are about expectations and accountability around what to achieve and how to achieve it. Wide lanes are about giving people autonomy to get there in whatever way works for them, within those guidelines."

Applying These Concepts to the World You Live In

Technology strategies should not start with solutions or processes; they should start by defining the end goal. What is it that you want leaders, managers, or employees to do differently in the future from what they are doing now? How do you want to change the employee experience from what it is now? The objective of technology projects should never be to "implement a new technology solution" or "create a new process." The objective should center on actions such as creating more effective conversations, enabling better decisions, building stronger communities, or optimizing use of people's time and capabilities. There are countless examples of companies deploying innovative and often very expensive technology solutions only to have employees fail to adopt them. Before implementing any technology solution ensure its use will be supported by leaders, managers, and employees. It is always good to ask the following questions about the impact of technology on employee experience:

- Will it make it easier to get things done and save employees' time?
- Will it bring employees closer together and strengthen collaboration?
- Will it make work more meaningful and help employees achieve things they care about?
- Will employees, managers, and/or leaders view it as something that helps them be more successful in their roles?

The answer should be a resounding "yes!" to at least one of these before implementing new technology. If it isn't, then delay the deployment and redesign the technology or develop the culture until it is.

The technology solutions discussed in this chapter will be referred to in the remaining chapters of this book, noting how different solutions help companies address perennial workforce challenges by augmenting or automating decisions and activities. In the 20th century it was possible to find areas of workforce management that did not make extensive use of technology beyond paper forms. Now technology permeates almost every aspect of work. To be fully effective in a highly digitalized world, workforce management must be viewed through a technology-based mindset. This does not require being an expert in the design and use of technology, but it does require making decisions with an understanding of the capabilities and constraints associated with technology solutions. Exploring the following questions can help in thinking about these concepts in the context of the company or companies you work with.

Addressing Barriers That Limit Organizational Adaptability

- What technologies do you use to build a sense of community and collective purpose within your organization? How do you know if it is working?
- How does your company create and maintain a sense of urgency and desire to constantly improve within the workforce? What motivates people to improve their performance? How is this enabled or limited by the use of technology?
- How does your company identify "high-impact" employees? How do you determine which employees are having the greatest impact on the overall success of the company, regardless of their formal role or position? How might technology improve the ability to recognize, reward, and support employee performance?

Using Work Technology to Increase Agility

- Where does your company struggle to make accurate people decisions related to staffing, job assignments, promotions, compensation, or development? How could technology be used to support and improve these decisions?
- What are the barriers to collaboration within the organization? How could technology address these challenges?

- What organizational practices do employees find to be inefficient? What things are often seen as a waste of time? Is it possible to automate or eliminate these activities?
- What are the main security and compliance risks in your organization? How could technology address these?
- Read through the solutions listed in Table 3.1. Which of these is your company using now? Are there solutions that you may not use now that might add considerable value to the organization?

Linking Work Technology to Business Operations Technology

- Could your company calculate the return on investment associated with workforce costs such as compensation, benefits, or employee development?
- What business operations metrics are significantly affected by the skills and performance of employees? How do different workforce characteristics affect these business outcomes?

Creating a Culture of Adaptability

- How well does your organization promote a sense of autonomy, accountability, transparency, openness to change, and psychological safety? Which of these do you struggle with? What can you do to support them more effectively?

CHAPTER 4

Designing Organizations to Provide Positive Employee Experiences

Crafting Jobs to Fit Employees

A manufacturing company realized that a large number of its specialized technicians were scheduled to retire in the near future. These technicians performed complex tasks that took years to fully master, and the company doubted it could develop replacement workers in the time before they left. Then someone asked if it might be possible to change the design of the technicians' jobs in a way that would inspire them to keep working past retirement age. When the technicians were asked about this idea they said perhaps, assuming we get to determine how we do our jobs, and the company provides the resources necessary to allow us to work the way we want to. This led to a collaborative project using a concept called job crafting,[1] where employees and companies work together to define how jobs are designed balancing the interests of both parties.

The goal of job crafting is to create positions that add value to the company but that are done in a way that fits employees' interests and preferences. Common modifications include giving employees greater control over schedules, alleviating them from routine or administrative tasks, providing better physical working conditions, letting them choose their work location, and doing more creative design and instructional work and less repetitive production work. There are two reasons why job crafting makes sense for companies. First, it is usually cheaper and less operationally disruptive to retain skilled talent than to replace it. Second, many skilled employees enjoy the parts of their jobs that challenge them to fully apply their expertise.

Job crafting increases time spent on these tasks and decreases time on routine or administrative activities, which employees find less intrinsically interesting. Performing these highly skilled tasks is also where employees add the most unique value to the company.

If an employee with critical skills says, "I plan to quit my job," do not ask "How can I change your mind so that you stay?" Ask "How can we change your job so that you don't want to go?"

From a company perspective, designing organizations is about figuring out what jobs the company needs in order to achieve its business goals, how the jobs will be paid and supported, where they will be located, how many people are needed in each job, and how the jobs are structured into teams and groups within the organization. It also includes making organizational design decisions related to mergers, acquisitions, and restructuring. From an employee experience perspective, designing organizations is about creating attractive career opportunities, crafting enjoyable jobs, being in effective teams, and working in positive environments. Organizational design has a massive influence on employee experience. As the job crafting story illustrates, company and employee perspectives can be balanced to create mutually beneficial outcomes. But if they are imbalanced, significant conflict and tension between employees and organizations will inevitably occur.

The root issues underlying good or bad employee experiences are often a result of organizational design. Yet employee experience is not always the focus when companies are making organizational design decisions. For companies, a major priority in designing organizations involves controlling workforce costs relative to revenue. Employing people is expensive and companies want to maximize the ROI of money invested in the workforce.[2] Organizational designs that overemphasize cost efficiency can create terrible employee experiences. This was strikingly illustrated when I met with the manager of a scrap metal reclamation plant to discuss their recruiting process. The plant struggled to fill production positions that paid near minimum wage to perform jobs that required working in an aging, poorly lit building wearing uncomfortable protective suits while shoveling scrap metal into hot furnaces for eight-hour shifts. It looked like a scene out of Dante's *Inferno*. I asked the manager who would want to do this job if they had other options and he had no answer. This company's staffing issue could not be solved by improving its hiring practices. The problem was they were trying to hire people for a job virtually no one would want. The solution was either to invest in improving the working conditions or pay people a lot more money to do the work. Solving the staffing problem required rethinking how the organization was designed so the job provided a better employee experience.

Talent tectonic forces associated with the digitalization of work and growing skill shortages are driving significant improvements in organizational design. A highly visible example is the rapid growth in use of technology to support remote working such as electronic communication and online collaboration solutions. This technology makes geographical location less of a factor in the design and staffing of organizations. It improves employee experience by reducing time spent commuting and giving people more freedom to choose where they live. Other examples of technology enabling more effective organizational designs include changing how people are paid, how work is scheduled, and how teams are structured. This chapter discusses these and other innovations by examining five aspects of organizational design from an employee experience perspective.

- **Why do people join organizations?** This section explores the benefits employees get from working for organizations. Money is an obvious one, but it is usually not the primary reason people choose to work for one organization over another.
- **How does job design shape employee experience?** This section explores how job design affects employees' intrinsic and extrinsic motivation toward work. Intrinsic motivation is influenced by the nature of the job such as the work tasks and work environment. Extrinsic motivation is influenced by work outcomes such as compensation, career opportunities, and how the work affects other people or the planet.
- **How does design of groups, teams, and departments affect employee experience?** The people we work with profoundly influence the quality of our work experiences. This section examines how the size, composition, and structure of groups in a company affect employee experience.
- **How do management and leadership structures affect employee experience?** Technology enables use of complex reporting relationships that go beyond traditional hierarchical organizational structures used in the past. This section focuses on ways to rethink the nature of employee-manager structures to better balance workforce productivity and workforce development.
- **Managing restructurings and downsizing with experience in mind.** Organizational structures change over time due to growth, acquisitions, financial constraints, and shifts in business strategy. This section discusses how to carry out restructurings in ways that more positively affect employee experience.

Companies must rethink how they design organizations in response to the growing importance employee experience has for attracting talent and creating agile workforces. This requires viewing organizational design from an employee perspective, moving beyond methods of decision-making that overemphasize cost control at the sacrifice of employee experience, and taking advantage of technological innovations to structure jobs in ways that were not operationally feasible in the past.

Why People Join Organizations

The reasons people join organizations are not the same reasons organizations hire people. Organizations employ people to achieve business outcomes. People join organizations to improve the quality of their lives. Organizations do this by providing people with three things:

- **Roles.** The opportunity to work on meaningful projects and activities that align with their life goals.
- **Resources.** Access to financial, technological, and material assets including compensation.
- **Relationships.** Membership in a community of people they like that values and supports them.

These three things embody the concept of an "organization" in the sense that it is people working together (relationships) using shared assets (resources) to accomplish common goals (roles). People form and join organizations because humans are most successful when we work in groups. Employees are more productive and typically happier when they collaborate in teams and share resources to achieve common or mutually supportive goals. This includes employees who work as independent contractors, who frequently create formal or informal organizations to find work opportunities and share ideas and resources.[3]

From a company perspective, designing organizations is about corporate structures, budgets, job designs, and policies. From an employee experience perspective, designing organizations is about building and joining communities that are meaningful and valuable to them. The design of an organization creates and shapes these communities through its impact on the nature of the roles, relationships, and resources found in the company. Roles define the parts people play in a community. It is about designing jobs in a way that makes people feel their contributions to the community are meaningful, while also showing the community respects their personal goals, needs, and opinions. Relationships are about creating processes and organizational structures that help people form social connections with others in the community based on common interests, goals, and challenges. Resources are about providing community members with information and tools to perform their roles and sharing rewards in a way that makes people feel fairly treated and appropriately valued. In terms of employee experience, the questions to ask when making decisions about organizational design are about how it will strengthen the company as a community. Will the change make the community more successful in achieving the goals of its members? Will it support and attract the kind of members the organization needs to be successful? Or will it make existing members feel less appreciated and connected and make it harder to retain valued members?

There is no such thing as a totally neutral organizational design change. Every change either positively or negatively affects members of the employee communities within the organization. Some changes matter far more than others, but all changes have an influence on employee experience at some level. Changes that seem minor to organizational leaders may significantly affect employee experience. Someone's job title, whether their office has a window, or which department they belong to may seem trivial to some, but these things may not be trivial to employees affected by them. Moreover, if these decisions are trivial, then company leaders should not be making them. A general rule of designing organizations to improve employee experience is that, whenever possible, let employees make organization design decisions themselves. For example, letting employees choose their own job title can provide a stronger sense of autonomy and improved sense of well-being.[4] There are many instances when this level of autonomy does not make sense. But, when possible, it is usually best when the employees responsible for doing the work are allowed to decide how the work should be done.

Companies should not feel like a collection of employees who do similar jobs, share the common work spaces, or have similar e-mail addresses. Companies should feel like a network of communities where employees feel a sense of belonging and connection to their coworkers based on shared interests, values, and goals. The best way to build these communities is to listen to employees, asking them what they want from work and how they think the company can be more successful. This does not mean organizational design decisions always comply with employee desires. Organizations need to achieve business goals or they will cease to exist and not provide any employee experience at all. This often requires employees to accept that, as said in a classic song, "You can't always get what you want." But factoring in the reasons employees join organizations when designing companies makes it far easier to attract, retain and engage the people needed to be successful.

How Job Design Affects the Employee Experience

A study of employee engagement analyzed survey data from millions of employees to determine which questions best predicted employee commitment and retention.[5] The four most important questions asked whether employees knew what is expected of them at work, had resources to effectively do their work, had the opportunity to do good work, and received recognition for the work they did. The answers to all four of these questions are directly influenced by the design of an employee's job, including the purpose of the job, how employees are compensated and rewarded, and the tools, training, and technology provided to employees to fulfill their objectives.

Historically companies approached job design as a somewhat administrative activity focused on defining hiring qualifications, training programs, and compensation structures. It was often shaped by concerns over meeting legal requirements to justify hiring and pay decisions. Many traditional job analysis and design methods break jobs down into specific components and tasks. These traditional methods are valuable for understanding the technical nature of jobs but can fail to surface aspects of a job that determine whether it provides a good or bad experience. This is because they do not look at how the overall design of the job influences employee experience at a broad level.[6] Job design from an employee experience perspective is less about defining exactly what people do and more about understanding the experiences they get from doing it. This includes thinking about the career opportunities it may provide beyond the current work. What makes a job desirable is frequently not only the job itself, but the potential for the job to open doors to other opportunities and experiences.

When designing jobs to maximize employee experience it is useful to look at them from the perspective of intrinsic and extrinsic job motivation. Intrinsic motivation depends on the nature of the work, and extrinsic motivation depends on the outcomes provided by the work such as pay. Both aspects of job design matter but in different ways.[7] Intrinsic job design has a major influence on the quality of people's performance and their ongoing engagement at work. Extrinsic job design significantly influences whether people accept and remain in a job. It can also influence productivity through rewarding performance accomplishments. The following discuss some key questions to think through in each area.

Intrinsic Job Design—Questions That Determine How the Job Itself Affects the Employee Experience

- **What is the purpose of the job?** The most important question to answer when designing a job is why do we need people to do this work at all? This involves identifying the types of objectives people in the job will be expected to achieve, why they matter to the company, and, if possible, how they will be measured. One way to identify the purpose of a job is to ask what happens if the company did not staff the job. What is the impact and cost of not hiring someone to do this work? It is difficult to create a fulfilling employee experience without clear and meaningful objectives. Employees also experience a greater sense of control over their job when they understand the criteria that will be used to define job success. This does not mean defining in detail everything people are expected to achieve. Micromanaged job descriptions tend to be demotivating and ineffectual. But employees should be able to confidently answer the questions, "What do you do, why does it matter, and how can you tell if you are doing it successfully?" Ideally, they should be able to connect their job to broader objectives that give their work meaning beyond just being a source of income. This typically includes things related to helping others, improving the world, or advancing their career. One of my favorite examples of this is from a hospital cafeteria where the job objectives of dishwashers were defined in terms of protecting patient health by ensuring people were not exposed to potential food-born illness. The employees did not think of themselves as dishwashers, but as patient care providers.

- **How many people do you need in this job? Who will they be working with?** The number of people sharing the same job affects the social experience of work. Two people may have jobs with identical objectives, but the experience is a lot different if one works alone and the other works with hundreds of other people doing the same job. When an employee accepts a job, they are joining a community. What is the nature of the community that defines the experience associated with working in this job? It is very different to work independently compared to working as part of a team. For example, a repair maintenance organization struggled to find people who wanted to work all day in remote locations by themselves. This prompted them to hire two people to share a job that could arguably have been done by one person working alone.

- **What skills are needed to perform this job?** Traditional job analysis techniques focus on defining the knowledge, skills, and abilities needed to perform the job. What these techniques do not consider is whether these skills exist in the labor market. The talent tectonic forces of digitalization are changing the nature of skills companies need, and the forces of demographics are changing the supply of people available with these skills. Given these realities, part of job design should include thinking about the developmental nature of job. What skills do employees need on their first day on the job, and what skills must employees learn within a week, month, or even year? Hiring employees based on what they know versus what they can learn has a significant impact on the experience of work. It is the difference between being asked to do something you know how to do versus being asked if you want to learn something new.

- **When and where do people in this job have to work?** Work schedules and job locations have a massive impact on employee experience. Giving employees greater control over when they take breaks and encouraging them to take microbreaks throughout the day is associated with higher levels of performance and decreased work strain.[8] Office space design has a significant influence on how employees work together and can even affect absenteeism.[9] An example from one study found that if employees sit more than 200 feet apart then they almost never interact.[10, (superior)i] Commuting times and work schedules affect the number of people willing to take a job and are common reasons for employee turnover.[11] Another thing to consider is whether to establish expectations on when people will NOT work. Digitalization of work is breaking down the traditional barriers between work and life. A growing problem is people working too much.[12] Employees are suffering from higher levels of burnout caused by the "always connected" nature of work and a sense that there is always more work to do. Job design used to focus exclusively on defining when and where people were expected to work. Now it also needs to include defining when people are expected to disconnect and stop working.

  Giving people control over their work schedule and location is literally giving them control over their lives. Not every employee wants to work remotely or work a flexible schedule, but all employees want the ability to influence decisions about where and when they work. During the agricultural age most work schedules and locations were determined by nature. People got up with the sun and walked to the fields. During the industrial age work schedules and locations were determined by machines. People worked set shifts and commuted to factories. Increasingly, when and where people work will be determined by employees using technology that enables them to balance work demands with life preferences.

- **How long do you expect or want people to stay in this job?** There is no such thing as a permanent job position. Everyone will leave at some point. Communicating expectations about likely job tenure can increase employee commitment and retention. For example, a professional services organization I worked with told newly hired consultants the optimal time to quit the company. The company did not expect

---

[i]Some people say a problem with remote work is it eliminates random "hallway meetings" and "watercooler conversations" that occur in the office, but data suggest these meetings and conversations rarely happen and, when they do, they are almost never about work topics.

or want all its consultants to remain indefinitely as most would never make it to the level of partner. But they also did not want them quitting in under three years before the company had been able to get a return on the investment required to train them. They analyzed the careers former employees had after leaving the company and found the most financially successful people left the firm between five and seven years after they joined. When they started communicating this to new hires their employee retention increased during the first five years.

- **How does the job support employee development?** The developmental value of the job is a major factor influencing employee experience. Does the job give employees a chance to build new skills, acquire new experiences, and develop new relationships? What opportunities can the job provide that might positively influence the course of their career? When designing jobs, it is useful to consider how they help employees create future job opportunities. This may include building activities into the design of the job that are intentionally meant to encourage and promote employee development and career growth. The power this can have on employee experience was illustrated in a conversation I had with a leader who recently left a company known for its extremely high-pressure work environment. He described his former job as being like the surgical rotations medical students complete during their education. It was exhausting and stressful, but he received a lot of developmental growth in a short amount of time. As he put it, the company was not a great place to work, but it was a great place to have worked.

- **Will we employ people directly or as contractors?** Contractors are a critical part of the workforce. From a company perspective, employing contractors provides broader access to skilled talent and greater flexibility to increase or decrease the size of the workforce in response to business demands. Employees performing contract jobs often like the experience of increased autonomy and control over work.[13] There are also risks to employing contactors, including decreased organizational commitment, workforce instability, loss of knowledge when a contract ends, and concerns from noncontract employee that their jobs may eventually be outsourced to contract companies.[14] The decision to use contractors depends on factors ranging from financial costs to availability of qualified candidates. It should also consider the employee experience of contractors and noncontractors. There are legal issues that constrain how companies manage contractors, but at a general level companies should strive to treat contractors as valued members of the larger community of employees. Avoid doing things that make them feel like outsiders or second-class citizens. For example, I once encountered a company that would not allow contractors to participate in company-sponsored birthday celebrations held for employees. Nothing says "you don't belong" more than not being invited to a birthday party. The employee experience of contractors also affects the attitudes of employees who work with them. Employees may view contractors as friends, and we care how other people treat our friends.

Extrinsic Job Design—Questions That Determine How Job Outcomes Affect the Employee Experience

- **How will pay be structured?** Pay influences the employee experience in multiple ways. It affects employees' ability to provide for themselves and their families, communicates how much a company values their skills and contributions, and affects feelings of equity, fairness, and commitment.[15] Salary information is typically the first or second thing people look for when considering a job opportunity.[16] It is important to set pay at a competitive level because candidates and employees will compare pay levels to information on the web to ensure they are paid fairly. Many companies openly share pay ranges on the web to remove any sense of secrecy about pay levels. There is also growing support for legislation that requires companies to post pay levels to ensure pay equity.[17] In addition to pay levels, it is useful to share intrinsic aspects of the job that might make it appealing to candidates, particularly if the pay level could be considered below average market rates. Although pay is an important factor in accepting job offers, it is not the only factor. How pay plans are administered also has a significant impact on employee experience. Plans that reward employees based on their contributions can positively influence workforce productivity and retention. But they can also create tension and resentment if pay differences are perceived as overly large, unfairly allocated, or uncertain to predict.[18] When people receive their pay also affects employee experience. Paying employees weekly or monthly instead of daily can create significant financial hardship for people with limited resources.[19]
- **What resources will employees be given?** One reason employees join organizations is to gain access to things that help advance their career, improve the quality of their work, or enhance their life in general. Think about what the company offers that employees might not get elsewhere. This could be in the form of resources and technology, administrative support, working with skilled or influential colleagues, access to customers or market opportunities, or other things they could not readily obtain outside the company. Employees want jobs where they have the resources needed to be productive and successful.

Conversely, employees may quit in frustration if they are forced to use outdated technology or receive inadequate administrative support.

- **What additional benefits and perks come with the job?** Benefits and perks are financially valuable rewards and resources given to employees beyond standard pay. Benefits convey a sense of appreciation to employees and can differentiate a company's employee experience. Companies may also be legally required to provide certain types of benefits. The most valued benefits tend to be associated with health care, paid time off, and retirement savings,[20] but the list of potential benefits is endless and can include company cars, tuition reimbursement, childcare, free meals, membership to athletic clubs, tickets to entertainment events, or supporting social causes employees care about. Employees may ascribe an emotional value to certain benefits that goes well beyond their financial cost. In my experience, this often happens when providing employees with free or reduced access to company products or services. For example, a coffee company I worked with analyzed how different benefits affected employees' intent to stay. They found that giving employees free coffee beans each week was valued far more than if they had just given them the money to pay for the coffee themselves. The difference was in orders of magnitude; it was along the lines of $10 of free coffee each week having the equivalent impact of increasing pay by $20 dollars per week.[ii]

- **What career advancement opportunities are provided by the job?** One reason people work in some jobs is that they believe it will help them advance to other, more desirable jobs. It can be useful to identify the types of roles people tend to move into after they leave a job. Several retail companies I have worked with use this method to attract and retain high-performing frontline staff. These companies are known for their "promote from within" philosophies and many of their executives started out working in the stores. Employees know that their current job can be a step toward even better jobs.

How jobs are designed shapes employee experience through intrinsic factors such as the purpose of the work and its level of work-life balance, and extrinsic factors such as rewards and career advancement opportunities. If possible, it is ideal to involve employees in the process of designing their own jobs. It is also important to explain why a job is designed the way it is. Employees are more willing to accept aspects of a job they may

---

[ii] I do not recall the exact figures, but it was significant. I have heard of many similar examples such as breweries giving employees a case of beer a month or pork processing companies giving employees free bacon and sausage.

not like if they understand the reasons for the design. There is also value in telling employees if aspects of the job are designed specifically to improve their experience of work.

Job design inevitably involves making compromises between what the company needs, values, or can afford and what employees want or prefer. It is not possible to create a job that everyone will like. Things that one employee might desire may be disliked or deemed unimportant by another. This is particularly noticeable when looking at benefits packages. For example, pet insurance has become a popular work benefit in the United States but how employees feel about pet insurance depends on whether they have pets. Differences in employee preferences can be moderated using technology that lets employees configure things such as benefits or work schedules based on their preferences. However, no job can be all things to all people. A necessary part of job design is identifying what employee experiences matter the most and prioritizing those when designing the position, taking into account the company's business needs and financial constraints.

How the Design of Groups, Teams, and Departments Affects the Employee Experience

Early in my career an executive stood in front of my team and told us we were being moved into a new department. He said this restructuring of our group should not affect the work we did. When a colleague asked why the change was made, he said it was merely rearranging lines on the corporate organization chart. I then asked, if it is just a change to the org chart and does not affect what our team does then why make the change? He gave some noncommittal reply about aligning the organization with the new business operating model and quickly moved on to another topic. This was my first experience with organizational design and restructuring. I soon learned that where my team was placed on the organizational chart did matter. As a result of being moved into a new department, the people we worked with changed, which in turn changed the nature of our work, which ultimately led me to leave the organization. The placement of lines on an org chart matters more than one might think.

How an organization is designed in terms of teams, groups, and reporting structures affects employee experience in two ways. It changes what employees pay attention to as a result of leadership-reporting relationships, reward structures, and department membership. It also changes employee relationships by shaping how often people meet and communicate. Both things should be given considerable attention when designing the size, structure, and reporting relationships of an organization.

Using Organizational Design to Focus Employees on a Common Purpose

One of the challenges in a fast-moving world full of distractions is focusing people's attention on what matters. Organizational design can help address this challenge by putting people into teams, groups, and departments built on a common sense of purpose. For example, if you want people to focus on regional goals and activities then organize them based on regional groups. If you want people to focus on customer service, then make them part of a customer service organization. Then reinforce the strategic focus of these groups and departments when making decisions about their leaders, reward structures, and group names.

This may sound obvious, but make sure groups are led by someone who is interested in what the group actually does. Employees tend to care about the things their leaders care about.[21] Leaders do not need to be experts in the group's work, but they should find the work interesting. It is surprising how often companies put leaders in charge of departments who do not have much intrinsic interest in what the department actually does. This is a common problem in large organizations that use rotational assignments to develop high-potential leaders. Employees can tell when their leaders do not care much about the actual work they do. They can tell when a leader just wants to check the box on an assignment so they can climb up the next rung of the career ladder. This does not mean job rotations are bad—they are not. But when it comes to leadership, if you want employees to care about something, then make sure their leaders care about it as much or more than they do.

The names and reward structures used by groups in organizations should also reflect their core focus. Employee performance should be rewarded based on a mix of individual accomplishments and shared group goals.[22] This increases motivation toward these objectives and creates a sense of collective identity and cooperation among group members. What groups are called also has a significant impact on how employees and customers view their roles within the company.[23] Names should be descriptive of what people are expected to achieve. You know a group has a good name if people outside the group do not have to ask, "What does that team actually do?"

Designing organizations based on shared purpose is valuable for creating focus in a fast-moving world full of distractions, but it can also create silos that reduce collaboration and cooperation across groups. Strong group identities foster information sharing and cooperation within the group, but they can decrease trust and sensitivity toward people outside the group.[24] There are several ways to counter this effect. One is to use cross-functional teams and temporary cross-functional assignments to bring members of different groups together to achieve common goals. Another is to build cross-functional communities that provide opportunities for members of different groups to discuss common areas of interest.[25] For example, one of the benefits of diversity programs and corporate social responsibility initiatives is their ability to unite employees from across different parts of the organization to common causes. A third is to specifically recognize and reward employees who promote knowledge sharing and cooperation among different groups.[26]

Using Organizational Design to Influence Employee Relationships and a Sense of Belonging

Organizational structures do not totally determine how employees work together, but they do heavily influence employee relationships, sense of belonging, and communication styles. People are more likely to communicate with people who belong to the same groups, even if they have never met before.[27] People who remain together in the same team tend to become more comfortable sharing information and constructive feedback with each other.[28] People who feel part of cohesive team show more resilience toward challenging and stressful events.[29] People who work similar schedules, meet regularly, and take breaks together tend to be better at self-managing their performance and solving problems.[30] A sense of connection to team members even decreases the degree to which we find using video conferencing unpleasant and exhausting.[31]

Organization design should be viewed as a way to create, build, and strengthen communities within the company. It should focus on putting people in different groups to foster connections and communication. Here are some aspects to consider when deciding how to group employees into teams, groups, and departments:

- **Task similarity and task interdependence.** Employees form stronger bonds when they perform similar jobs or do jobs that are mutually interdependent.
- **Longevity.** There is value in keeping groups intact over time. Teams with longer tenure tend to have higher levels of performance.[32] This is a result of several factors including greater levels of trust, better knowledge of fellow team members, and more effective task coordination.
- **Background heterogeneity.** Teams composed of members with different cultural backgrounds and work experiences are often associated with higher levels of creativity and performance.[33] The value of team member diversity depends, however, on the degree to which the team has strong collective goals and a supportive and inclusive culture.

- **Size.** The size of a work group changes the nature of employee relationships within the group.[34] How group size affects employee interactions varies based on factors including job design, shared goals, organizational culture, and geographic location. But in general, smaller teams lead to stronger relationships.

Organizational design affects a lot more than cost structures and leadership hierarchies. It focuses employee attention and shapes employee communities. From an employee experience perspective, the primary function of defining organizational structures is to influence how we want employees to perceive the purpose of their work, and how we want employees to work with one another. People define themselves and others largely based on the groups they belong to. Humans are herd animals, and we pay attention to the herds we are in.[35] Whether intentional or incidental, how the lines on an org chart are drawn have real and lasting effects on employee attention, communication, and collaboration.

How Management and Leadership Structures Affect the Employee Experience

One of the most important aspects of organizational design is deciding how teams, groups, and departments will be managed. This includes whether they will be led by a single person at the top of a hierarchical structure, overseen by a collective group of stakeholders, or be self-governed by group members themselves. People have been predicting the downfall of organizational hierarchies and the emergence of leaderless, self-managed teams for over 20 years.[36] Technology is making the use of more complex leadership structures more feasible, but we are not likely to see the end of hierarchical leadership models anytime soon.[37] Collective and self-governed leadership structures can be difficult to implement in a scalable fashion.[38] When they have been successful, it is usually in relatively small companies characterized by highly transparent, cohesive, and collaborative cultures. By contrast, hierarchical leadership structures are very easy to understand and simple to deploy.

Traditional leadership hierarchies are not the best leadership structures,[iii] but they are likely to continue as the dominant management structure in organizations for at least the next several years. The advantage

---

[iii] There is no "best" leadership structure. The effectiveness of leadership structures depends on the purpose of the group or team, the qualities of the leader, and the nature of the group members.

of hierarchical organizational structures is that they are easy to implement. The disadvantage is that they can hurt group performance, particularly in the fast-changing ambiguous environments that characterize the future of work.[39] Hierarchies tend to concentrate decision-making further up the leadership chain and move it away from the frontlines where employees are actually doing the work. This slows the speed of decision-making, frequently hurts the quality of decisions, and undermines employee feelings of empowerment. The challenge is how to retain the simplicity of hierarchical leadership structures and still gain the value associated with collective, group-based decision-making processes. There are a lot of ideas on how this might be achieved.[40] Two more simple methods are distinguishing between leadership approval and leadership decision-making, and separating team managers from talent managers.

Leadership Approval Versus Leadership Decision-Making

Two steps are required before a company acts on a decision. First, the company must decide on the specific course of action. Second, the company must allocate resources, such as people, money, and materials, to execute the course of action. Hierarchical leadership models traditionally put responsibility for both steps in the hands of the senior-most leader in the group. This concentrates decision-making authority in one person and undermines the value of other people's expertise and perspectives. An alternative structure is to task the senior-most leader with responsibility for approving and securing organizational resources to fund actions, and to task a broader group of employees with determining what actions to take. The decision-making group can consist of a predefined leaderless team or be created using an adhocracy where people form temporary teams to address specific issues.[41] Separating leadership approval and leadership decision-making into two roles enables companies to keep the efficiency and control advantages of hierarchies and still gain the benefits of more collective team-based leadership decision-making.

Separating Team Managers from Talent Managers

Most reporting structures define a leadership relationship as being between two people: the employee and their team manager. Some companies are expanding this to include a third person called a *talent manager*. This is a leadership role focused on ensuring the company is building its workforce to achieve longer-term goals. I first encountered talent managers in professional services organizations whose growth depends on having a supply of highly skilled consultants they can assign to new business contracts. I've also seen it used in project-based contract engineering companies to ensure staffing assignments balance short-term operational needs with long-term employee career development.

Figure 4.1 illustrates how the roles of employee, team manager, and talent manager interact. Employees care about successfully performing their current job while progressing toward their long-term career goals. Team managers care about delivering against business targets on time and under budget. Talent managers care about building the capabilities of the workforce to support the company's overall business strategy. The reason this three-way partnership works is because one person cannot achieve their goals without help from the other two. Employees work with their team manager to achieve operational goals, and work with their talent manager to support development goals. The team and talent managers talk about developing the overall capabilities of the workforce to support the company's current and future business objectives.

There are several advantages associated with this three-way structure. First, it helps balance near-term operational goals, long-term company strategy, workforce capabilities, and employee career interests. Managers focused on achieving near-term operational goals will emphasize employee productivity and efficiency. Managers focused on building workforce capabilities to support the company's long-term strategy will

FIGURE 4.1 A three-way performance management partnership.

emphasize employee learning and engagement. This three-way structure helps balance the inherent tension among these things. The structure also addresses the reality that what makes someone a good team manager doesn't necessarily make them a good talent manager. Companies struggle to find managers who can both manage projects and develop talent. Introducing talent managers relieves team managers from having to try to fulfill two roles at the same time. Incorporating talent managers into the leadership structure also provides employees and team managers with a safe environment to discuss development issues. Talent managers focus on overall workforce development but are not involved in day-to-day operational issues. As a result, they can serve as an effective coach for employees to discuss challenges they may be having with their team manager. They can also help team managers address issues they may be having with employees.

Talent managers act as counselors to balance the need to achieve near-term business objectives with the long-term importance of retaining and developing talent. To be effective, talent managers must be respected as someone who has considerable business acumen and company influence. Talent managers must understand the business at an operational level and understand how the organization works at a cultural level. For example, in consulting companies the talent managers are often senior partners. This gives them the credibility and wisdom to effectively work with both employees and team managers.

Managing Restructurings and Downsizings with Experience in Mind

All companies will have times when they must restructure the organization due to acquisitions, workforce cost reductions, changes in business strategy, or even to appease the ego of leaders.[iv] As the pace of change accelerates, organizational restructuring are becoming more common. Restructuring often includes downsizing parts of the workforce. Restructuring decisions and actions, particularly those that involve letting employees go, have a lasting impact on employee attitudes. The following are ways to minimize the negative impact that restructuring can have on employee experience.

[iv] This may not be the ideal reason for restructuring, but it is a reality. Companies sometimes have to change their organizational structure to attract and retain leaders who want more influence over the workforce.

Do Not Downsize Unless It Is Absolutely Necessary

Companies that downsize tend to perform more poorly in the future compared to organizations in the same industry that avoided workforce reductions.[42] These lower performance levels persist for years following layoffs and can create a sense of resentment among employees who remain.[43] Given the risks, layoffs should not be considered until after other cost-cutting methods have been explored. This includes suspending noncritical expenses, eliminating unprofitable projects, and exploring whether employees will take voluntary reductions in pay and benefits to save costs.

Understand the Capabilities You Are Losing by Downsizing

Restructuring decisions often focus on reducing headcount costs without adequately considering employee capabilities. This can lead to catastrophically bad decisions. Consider this example. After a market downturn, a manufacturing company eliminated a department working on a new line of products that they could no longer afford to develop. What they did not consider was the department was staffed with some of the most experienced engineers in the company who had been moved into this department because of their capabilities. It was only after firing them that the company realized they possessed crucial skills the company needed. This led to hiring the employees back as contractors at much higher rates with much lower levels of commitment. Restructuring decisions should not be based solely on employee job titles, cost centers, salaries, and demographics. They should also consider data about employee skills, experience, relationships, and capabilities.

Do Not Restructure the Workforce Without Restructuring the Work

Restructuring should include determining how people's jobs, responsibilities, and work processes are going to change. This is particularly important when reducing headcount. Do not lay off employees and expect the remaining survivors to "do more with less." Such an approach will lead to excessive burnout, poor performance, and turnover among the very employees you most want to keep.

Focus All Reductions into a Single Event

If it is necessary to reduce the size of the workforce, it is better to do one large reduction than several small ones. Multiple recurring rounds of layoffs breeds stress among employees who constantly worry whether they will be the next to be laid off. High performers start to seek job opportunities in other companies that will provide a more stable work environment. Employees who do not have outside opportunities often perform more poorly because of increased anxiety over their job security. It is better to make one difficult but significant workforce reduction rather than making a series of shallow layoffs over time that give the feeling of the company slowly dying.

Treat People with Respect

There are many examples of companies using downsizing processes that treated hard-working, loyal employees almost as though they were criminals. I once worked with a company that brought people into a meeting room, told them they had been let go, and then sent them out another door directly into the parking lot. Another company escorted employees to their desks to clear out their belongings under the watch of security guards in front of the shocked faces of their former coworkers. There are also instances of companies sending termination notices to employees via mass e-mail. There are two major problems with insensitive downsizing processes. First, assuming the organization survives and begins to grow again, you may want to rehire these employees. They are more likely to return if they were treated fairly and respectfully when they were let go. Second, treating downsized employees poorly undermines the morale and trust of employees who remain. Employees will resent the company if they feel it treated their former coworkers like excess baggage to be thrown away when things got bad. They will also wonder, "Is that how they will treat me if I'm let go?" When planning layoffs, costs associated with severance packages and outplacement services should not be viewed as money spent on laid-off workers but as investments to ensure the loyalty and commitment of the employees who remain.

Actively Communicate

Two-way communication during restructuring helps create a sense of fairness and confidence among employees. Discuss reasons why the company restructured and what it means for the long-term growth of the organization. Let people know what is being done to ensure proper and fair treatment of employees who may lose their jobs. Build employee confidence by explaining the company's strategy to emerge from the current change and the opportunities it will provide to those who remain on board. Give employees a sense of control by providing information about the challenges and constraints the organization is facing, enlisting their support in overcoming these challenges and listening and acting on their suggestions.

There are many examples of companies that intentionally hid information about planned restructurings, suddenly surprising employees with announcements of workforce reductions. This secrecy can permanently undermine the trust of any employees who remain. By contrast, one restructuring I witnessed started with the company telling employees it would be reducing the size of the workforce in six months, explaining why it was necessary, and outlining support employees would receive if they were affected. One can imagine why a company might not want to share this information widely, but leaders felt it was important for employees to know since it might affect major life decisions such as whether to buy a house or explore other job options. This kind of honesty and transparency is what it means to believe in the value of employee experience.

Restructurings, particularly those involving workforce reductions, are difficult, risky, and emotionally exhausting events. Avoiding the mistakes outlined here cannot guarantee a rapid return to full productivity, but actively considering the role of employee experience in restructurings does reduce the risk of creating long-term or permanent loss of company value.

How Work Technology Is Influencing the Design of Organizations

Technology is influencing the design of organizations in several ways. It is providing new data and insights to guide decisions about the design and size of the workforce, creating tools to change the nature of jobs and how they are performed and managed, and enabling companies to more effectively reallocate employees based on shifting business needs and organizational structures. The following is a look at some specific technology solutions that are particularly relevant to the topic of organizational design.

Solutions That Help with Designing the Organization

Technological innovations are providing leaders with much greater insight into the nature of the current workforce and the relationship between future business needs and future workforce capabilities. Workforce design solutions enable companies to forecast future staffing needs based on existing internal and external talent supplies, considering business growth and employee development and turnover. Interoperable data management solutions are providing the ability to understand how the skills, capabilities, size, and structure of the workforce affect business outcomes such as sales revenue, customer service, and manufacturing productivity. Relationship analysis tools enable companies to understand how the nature of employee relationships and communication patterns are affecting business performance. Taken together, all three solutions enable companies to much more clearly understand how the current organizational structure needs to change to support future business goals.

Solutions That Help with Defining Jobs

Compensation, payroll, and benefits management solutions enable companies to create more tailored and effective pay structures for different jobs. Work scheduling solutions provide companies with flexibility to enable employees to have greater control over their time. Contractor management solutions make it far easier to employ contractors in a way that makes them feel like a valued part of the workforce, and not as "temporary help." And experience measurement enables companies to actively involve employees in the process of shaping, evaluating, and improving the design of their jobs.

Solutions That Help with Creating Teams and Groups

Work experience platforms and team management solutions enable companies to create and support different communities within the organization. This includes creating cross-functional teams and communities that bring different groups together and reduce the risk of silos. Relationship analysis tools enable companies to understand how the design of the organization shapes employee interactions and diagnose and solve barriers that are hindering communication.

Solutions That Help with Managing Restructurings

Electronic profiles and talent management solutions can provide detailed data to understand the skills, capabilities, and performance of the current workforce. This data can be fed into workforce design and interoperable data management solutions to guide restructuring decisions including decisions about workforce reductions. Opportunity matching and job transition solutions can help with moving and reallocating headcount from one organizational structure to another, or supporting offboarding if necessary. Experience management solutions provide a way to assess and address employee experience concerns during the restructuring process.

Applying These Concepts to the World You Live In

The design of the organization plays a critical role in a company's ability to attract, engage, develop, and retain talent. Companies often fail to fully appreciate the impact organizational design has on employee experience or take advantage of the technology available to improve the design and restructuring of organizations. The most important thing is to simply recognize and accept that the way organizational design was done in the past is not how it should be done in the future. Exploring the following questions can help with thinking about these concepts in the context of the company or companies you work with.

Designing the Organization

- List your company's business strategies and objectives two to three years in the future. What will the workforce need to look like to achieve these goals? How will it require changing the current workforce in terms of types of jobs and number of people?
- Why is your current organization designed the way it is? Does the design make sense to employees? Is it easy to determine what different groups do and how they work together? What changes might employees make to the organization if they were given the authority?

Defining Jobs

- What aspects do people most like and dislike about their jobs? Are there ways to change jobs so people get to do more of what they enjoy and less of what they dislike?
- What makes jobs in your organization unique and special? Compare jobs in your organization to similar jobs in other companies. Why would someone want to do these jobs in your organization versus another? What might lead them to accept an offer in another company instead of yours?

Creating Teams and Groups

- What impact is the design of your organization having on how people interact across groups and departments? Are the right people talking with each other? Are there parts of the organization that tend to be isolated from other areas?

■ How do you promote a sense of community within different teams and groups in your company? How are you using technology to shape and understand the communities and networks in the organization?

Creating Leadership Structures

■ What methods or processes are used to ensure leadership decisions are made by the right people? If you have leadership hierarchies, how do you ensure leaders at the top are not making decisions without adequate input from employees farther down the hierarchy?

■ How do you ensure a balance between managing people for near-term operational productivity versus managing them for long-term development? What elements of organizational or job design help ensure support for employee development?

Managing Restructurings

■ What processes do you have in place to guide restructuring? What data are available and used by leaders when making restructuring decisions?

■ Do you have a philosophy or set of guidelines to follow in the case of workforce reductions or layoffs? How do you ensure that the employees who survive a layoff are not negatively affected by the experience of seeing their colleagues let go?

CHAPTER 5

Filling Positions and the Experience of Moving into New Roles

A Wealth of Opportunity Without Any Potential

A group of leaders in an aerospace engineering company had received funding to develop a new generation of products and needed to quickly ramp up their project teams. They worked with a recruiter in HR to define the job requirements, posted the positions on their career site, and got ready to interview candidates. But then no one applied. The pay for the roles was competitive and the project involved the kind of innovative, boundary-breaking work many engineers dream about doing. Why was no one interested?

The recruiter began contacting people who were qualified for the role but had not applied. What they learned was few of these potential candidates knew about the company. The company had been around for decades, but its products involved highly specialized components that did not have a broad market. Plus, it was located in a part of the country not known as a hotspot of engineering innovation. The candidates were interested in the kind of work the company was doing, but they did not know the company did this work. Many did not even know the company existed at all.

This prompted the company to begin a recruiting campaign that was run more by their marketing department than HR. The program used web marketing technology to build awareness in the engineering community about who the company was, what they did, and why they were a great place to work. Targeted outreach campaigns were built focusing on people with the unique skills the company needed to develop its products. The messages explained the mission of the organization, the people who worked there, and the unique culture found in the company given its more rural location. The company eventually found itself in the enviable position of having more high-potential candidates than it could hire, but it took a lot of effort to get there.

The lesson learned is that there is little value in having great career opportunities unless they can be matched to candidates with the potential and desire to pursue them.

The most important decision a company makes about an employee is the decision to hire them.[1] Every other decision is a consequence of the initial action of bringing them into the company. Historically, most hiring discussions stressed the importance of selecting the right candidates. The focus was on improving how companies made hiring decisions. This is changing as talent tectonic shifts associated with digitalization increase demand for specialized skills and demographics shrink the relative size of the labor pool. This creates more competition among companies to find and hire qualified candidates. As a result, the most important staffing decision is often not which candidates the company decides to hire. It is which company the candidates decide to work for. The story of the engineering company[i] in this chapter's opening captures this new reality. The employees hired for a job are entirely determined by which candidates choose to apply in the first place. Candidates do not apply to jobs to fill positions. They apply to jobs to fulfill career goals and obtain resources that support their needs outside of work. Selecting good candidates still matters, but increasingly the main challenge is finding qualified candidates and getting them to apply. This includes viewing existing employees and contractors as potential sources of talent and staffing positions using short-term assignments and ad hoc teams. From an employee experience perspective, the challenge of filling positions is not about hiring decisions; it's about life decisions. The jobs people perform affect their near-term goals and long-term career opportunities. The decision to accept a job is a decision about how to spend a large portion of our waking hours.

Most candidates have multiple job opportunities, although some opportunities may not be very appealing. Typing the words "Open job positions near me" in a search engine will usually return hundreds if not thousands of opportunities. This is generally true even in recessions, although it may

---

[i] The story is based on a company a colleague worked with. It is modified for brevity and illustration.

not be true in all locations. The question most candidates must answer is not "Can I get a job?" but "Can I get a job that takes my life in the direction I want to go?" Filling roles from an experience mindset requires rethinking staffing from this perspective. It is not about evaluating candidates to see if they can do the job; it is about aligning what the company needs with what candidates want and are able to do. It is also useful to think of every position as a temporary assignment that lasts only until the work changes or the people move on to something else.[2] It is unrealistic to expect someone to do the same job for their entire life, although they may stay in the same company and do different jobs.

This chapter examines finding, matching, and transitioning people into new roles from an employee experience perspective by looking at the following topics:

- **How job characteristics affect staffing.** The challenge to filling positions can change depending on the nature of the job, the number and types of positions being filled, the availability of qualified candidates, and whether the position is for a relatively short or fixed amount of time.
- **Finding candidates and creating career paths.** The process of recruiting or "sourcing" candidates can start years before an employee is actually hired. This section looks at the candidate and employee experiences that lead to a person ultimately expressing interest in a position.
- **Selecting candidates and getting the right fit.** Hiring someone into a job they are ill-suited to perform is bad for employees and companies. But most people do not like being evaluated and screened. This section discusses assessing candidates in a way that makes them feel engaged, respected, and fairly treated.
- **Transitioning, welcoming, and departing.** The experience of starting a new role creates a lasting impression and shapes subsequent employee decisions and actions. This section discusses ways to welcome candidates and create smooth transitions when employees leave one role to start another.
- **Dynamic and temporary staffing.** Positions are increasingly being filled through use of temporary internal assignments or short-term contractors. These methods can be highly effective but create their own challenges in terms of employee experience.

The chapter concludes with a discussion of the role technology solutions are playing in reimagining how companies address the challenge of filling positions.

How Job Characteristics Affects Staffing

The biggest variable that affects filling a position is the structure of the job itself. The nature of job roles determines which people can or will perform them. Chapter 3 discussed several elements of job design that affect staffing through their influence on employee experience. The following are four additional job design–related questions to consider when filling positions:

- How many people does the company need to hire?
- How many qualified candidates exist in the labor market?
- How long are people expected to stay in the role?
- What can candidates change about the job?

How Many People Does the Company Need to Hire?

The experience of filling positions is different based on whether it involves high volume hiring in which a company is placing hundreds of people into identical or highly similar positions versus low volume hiring in which a company is hiring just one or two people for specific roles. High-volume hiring is common in the retail, hospitality, and manufacturing industries where workforces include thousands of people all performing the same basic kind of job. The biggest challenge to high-volume hiring is efficiently sourcing and processing thousands of candidates in a way that each candidate still feels they were treated with care and respect. Use of technology has a massive impact on candidate experience in high-volume hiring processes. Used poorly, it can make candidates feel ignored, unfairly eliminated, and treated as "just another number."[ii] Used effectively it can create an engaging and highly interactive experience. Examples include providing websites where candidates can listen to current employees talk about what it is like to work at the company, allowing candidates to apply using their mobile phones, using chatbots to guide candidates through the hiring process and answer questions about the status of their application, and creating interactive simulations that enable candidates to experience what the job is like and determine if it is the right fit for them.

The challenge of low volume hiring is about creating human interactions with the right people at the right time. Low volume hiring jobs tend to involve positions that require candidates to possess specialized knowledge

---

[ii] This is a significant challenge for retail and hospitality companies where candidates are frequently customers.

and skills. The first challenge to low volume hiring is getting qualified candidates to apply. Candidate search technology is making it easier to find people with specialized skills, and company careers sites can be designed to show different career options based on a candidate's background similar to how online shopping sites show different products based on customer preferences. The most effective recruiting methods for low volume hiring also make extensive use of personal relationships and connections.[3] This may involve technology solutions that encourage employees to recommend jobs to people they know or solutions that alert recruiters to reach out to qualified candidates as soon as they show interest in a role. When hiring for specialized roles with relatively few candidates, it is important to ensure qualified candidates are connected with the right people in the organization to keep them engaged. In the past, companies used recruiting technology as a barrier to reduce the time recruiters and hiring managers had to spend talking with candidates. This is a poor strategy in a world where qualified candidates have multiple opportunities. Methods for low volume hiring should emphasize connecting recruiters and hiring managers to high-potential candidates as early in the hiring process as possible. People often change their careers based on a conversation, but few people rethink their life direction based on an online application form.

How Many Qualified Candidates Exist in the Labor Market?

Most staffing techniques assume that somewhere in the labor market people exist with the qualifications to do the job. Recruiting is about finding these people and convincing them to join the company. But what happens if the assumption that qualified candidates exist is not true? This is a real possibility when filling positions that require new or highly specialized skills. In this case, traditional recruiting methods will not work. A key question to ask when filling positions is whether there are any qualified candidates who would accept the pay the company is offering to do the jobs the company wants them to do. One way to answer this is to use workforce analytics technology to generate statistics about available labor. This question can also be answered in a more qualitative way by asking existing employees, "How many people do you know who are qualified to do this job and might realistically accept our job offer?" If employees struggle to come up with many names relative to the number of positions you want to fill, then you will likely struggle to find qualified candidates. When this happens, it may make sense to shift the goal from hiring someone who has the skills to do the work to hiring someone who can learn the skills to do the work. In other words, you may need to fill positions based on future potential instead of past qualifications.

Focusing on hiring for future potential is advantageous for multiple reasons. First, there will always be more people who can learn to perform a job than there are people who can already do the job. Second, many candidates view the opportunity to learn new skills as an important factor when deciding to apply for a job.[4] Third, companies that hire candidates based on their ability to learn skills instead of whether they already have these skills are less affected by economic shifts that may increase demand for people with these skills. This does not mean any candidate is qualified to learn any job. Hiring for potential requires using talent assessment solutions to measure attributes and motives that predict how quickly candidates can acquire new skills and effectively apply them at work.[5] The strategy of hiring for potential also affects job design and financial staffing models. Jobs need to be structured to provide an effective learning environment and more resources are needed to support employee training and development. The company must also manage its business operations knowing that newly hired employees may not reach full productivity until weeks, months, or even years after they start. There are costs associated with hiring for potential, but these are often balanced out by reduced compensation levels compared to those needed to hire "ready now" candidates, access to a more stable flow of talent, and increased engagement and retention caused by supporting employees' career growth.[6]

How Long Are People Expected to Stay in the Role?

In the past, companies tended to fill positions with an implicit assumption that roles are relatively stable. This worked when the world moved at a slower pace, but as the pace of change accelerates, companies often find themselves filling positions that are expected to last a year or even less. These positions may be more effectively filled through a short-term assignment instead of a permanent hire. The benefit of hiring for short-term assignments is it enables greater use of contractors or temporary internal transfers of existing employees. The downside is it can undermine organizational stability and knowledge retention because people leave after a relatively short amount of time. This will be discussed more later in this chapter when we explore dynamic and temporary staffing.

What Can Candidates Change About the Job?

One of the best ways to attract candidates is to let them structure the job to fit their needs and interests.[7] This includes influencing work objectives, job tasks, work schedules, and work location. It may also include letting employees set different pay structures or benefits arrangements, although this can create risks related to internal equity. It may sound odd to let candidates define their roles, but it is not new. Companies filling senior leadership positions often work with candidates to jointly define the nature of the role and its compensation structure. In the past, it was not feasible to expand this more broadly because there was no effective way to track and manage different work arrangements across large numbers of employees. This is changing with advances in work technology that support employees defining job expectations, setting work schedules, and defining more personalized compensation structures. As this technology evolves, the biggest barrier to job flexibility may be willingness of leaders to let employees control decisions about how to do their work.

Finding Candidates and Creating Career Paths

Figure 5.1 describes the experiential stages candidates go through that lead to joining a company. It includes creating interest in exploring careers in an industry, attracting candidates based on a company's employment brand, focusing candidates' attention on specific roles they are qualified to perform, and enticing candidates to complete an application. Some of these things involve experiences that can happen years before the candidate applies for the current role.

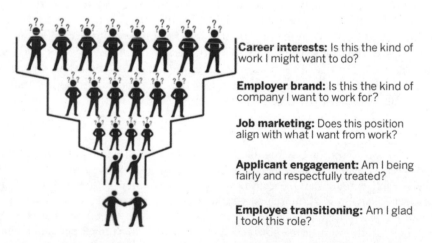

Career interests: Is this the kind of work I might want to do?

Employer brand: Is this the kind of company I want to work for?

Job marketing: Does this position align with what I want from work?

Applicant engagement: Am I being fairly and respectfully treated?

Employee transitioning: Am I glad I took this role?

FIGURE 5.1 The candidate experiences associated with filling positions

Career Interest: Is This Work Something People Would Consider Doing?

There is a concept in psychology called *possible selves* that describes mental images people have about the type of person they could imagine becoming over time.[8] If you ask a child "What do you want to do when you grow up" and they say, "Become a nurse," what they are sharing is one of their possible selves. We all have multiple images of possible selves even though they may not be fully defined. They are influenced by the people we know, what we see around us, and whom we view as role models.[iii] Possible selves influence our life choices at a conscious and unconscious level, including the kinds of work we consider.

A challenge facing companies trying to fill positions in many industries is that few people may consider working in that industry as a possible self. This is a significant problem for industries that are staffing new types of jobs. For example, in 2012 virtually no high school students were thinking "I want to be a solar photovoltaic installer when I graduate," but 10 years later in 2022 it was one of the fastest growing jobs in the United States.[9] It is also a challenge for industries that are rarely portrayed in the popular media. A leader of a wholesale distribution company once told me people rely on packages showing up at their homes with little understanding of the nature of the distribution industry that made it happen. He lamented that people do not realize it is possible to have a very meaningful and fulfilling career focused entirely on the distribution of materials to individuals who need them. Wholesale distribution is a critical and technologically advanced industry, but it is not well known compared to industries such as health care, manufacturing, retail, or information technology. This is one reason they struggle to get people to consider the industry as a career.

Building an industry career brand is a long-term investment, particularly in the case of jobs that require specialized skills acquired through advanced education. It starts with making people aware of the positive qualities associated with the industry, the kind of work people do in the industry, and the likely future growth of the industry. Examples of career branding websites can be found by searching online using terms such as "career opportunities in retail" or "career paths in manufacturing."[10] Other methods use activities

---

[iii] This is one reason diverse role models are critical for increasing diversity of the workforce. Children tend to identify with people who look like them in terms of demographics and social characteristics. This was powerfully illustrated by a medical student I knew in graduate school who told me he first thought about going into medicine when he was 14 and met a black doctor. As he shared, "All the doctors in my life had been white, so before I met this man, I didn't think people like me became doctors."

that give people exposure to the kind of work done in the industry. This is often done while people are still in school.[11] My favorite example is First Lego League, a program where children from 6 to 16 years old work in teams to build robots using Lego toys linked to computers. My kids participated in this program, and I was not surprised to learn it was sponsored by several engineering and technology companies interested in building future pools of qualified engineering job candidates.

Company Brand: Do People Want to Work for Your Company?

A person's decision to apply for a position is influenced by the job and the company. In many cases, the company has a larger impact than the job. Companies can develop a strong reputation or "employment brand" as being a good or bad place to work.[12] One factor influencing employment brand are online reviews by current and former employees on public web sites sharing their employee experiences at the company.[13] Another factor is the company's consumer reputation and public image. People like to work for companies that are considered to be innovative and socially responsible.[14]

How a company markets its employment brand also influences the diversity of job applicants. As the number of people in the labor market relative to the number of jobs available declines, companies need to get better at finding qualified candidates from demographic groups that have been affected by a history of discrimination. This includes women, people from different ethnic and racial groups, and people with physical and neurological disabilities. The likelihood of a person with a diverse background applying for job at a company is influenced by how the company presents itself as an employer.[15] In particular, does the company seem like the kind of community where the person will feel welcomed and supported? Employment brand marketing materials and career sites should incorporate pictures and information so candidates will feel that "people like me work at this company."[16] This includes guidance for people who have questions about the level of support given to people with their interests and concerns. Also avoid language that might appear offensive or alienate some groups. For example, I once saw a company refer to its salespeople as "aggressive ninja warriors." This term was both factually incorrect and implied a stereotypically masculine, confrontational sales culture that many candidates might find unappealing.

Marketing Jobs: Are People Looking at Your Positions?

There are three basic ways to generate applicants for a position: posting jobs, searching for candidates, and utilizing references. Job postings should be written using search engine optimization techniques so they appear prominently in internet search engines. Postings should clearly communicate why a candidate might be interested in the job and what makes it appealing from an employee experience perspective. Leave information about job qualifications further down the description and ensure they are specific enough so candidates can quickly determine if they meet the criteria. This ideally includes salary ranges so candidates can determine if the compensation matches their expectations and requirements.[17] Simply posting a job on a company career site may not be very successful unless the company has a strong employment brand. Recruiting marketing technology addresses this by posting jobs across a range of job boards, online communities, and other sites likely to be frequented by candidates. This should include sites used by internal employees who may be looking for the next step in their career. Internal transfers are often more successful than external hires.[18]

Job posting is a passive way to find candidates. By contrast, searching for candidates involves actively looking for qualified people using data found on the web and through privately managed candidate databases or "talent pools." Talent sourcing technology solutions are transforming the ability of companies to find potential candidates through use of highly advanced machine learning algorithms. But these solutions are only as valuable as the candidate databases they are searching, which is why many companies create and maintain electronic profiles of past job applicants, current employees, and former employees (aka, "alumni") that they can draw on as potential sources of candidates. Paying for access to online candidate databases is another way to get more value from talent sourcing solutions. It may also make sense to employ professional recruiters whose careers are focused on finding and placing candidates in different types of jobs.

The third way to market jobs to applicants is through employee referrals. Referrals can be a particularly effective way to find qualified candidates when hiring for specialized roles. As a recruiter told me, the best candidates are usually two degrees of separation from the hiring manager. The hiring manager may not know them, but they know someone who knows them. Candidates hired through employee referral also tend to be more successful particularly if the person who referred them is a high-performing employee. The performance and commitment of existing employees can also increase when people they referred are hired.[19] People like it when their company hires their friends. The downside of employee referrals is they can limit diversity of applicants. This is because the people we know tend to come from similar socioeconomic backgrounds as we do.[20] This is why some recruiting management solutions include specialized applications that extend referral networks to incorporate a more diverse range of candidates.

Engaging Candidates: Are People Completing the Application Process?

The difference between a candidate looking at a position and completing an application is the difference between a customer going into a store and a customer buying something. The job application process should be easy and engaging. This includes allowing people to apply using mobile technology and automating tasks associated with data entry. An entire sub-specialty of recruiting analytics has arisen focused on understanding applicant drop-off rates.[21] As a general rule, shorter applications fare better because most drop-outs occur within the first 20 minutes of the application process. However, if candidates are interested in a job, then they are often willing to spend an hour or more in the application process, provided they understand the reason for completing different forms and exercises.[22]

Companies should not assume qualified candidates will show up when they want them. People only pursue positions that match their conception of a possible career self, and they prefer companies that are known as a desirable place to work. It can take years to build candidate interest in a job, but only moments to lose candidates due to a bad experience during the application process. The ability to cultivate and recruit candidates will increasingly be the difference between companies that are able to staff positions and those forced to rethink business strategies due to a lack of qualified people.

Selecting Candidates and Getting the Right Fit

Hiring someone who cannot or does not want to do the job is more than just a waste of money and time. When a new hire struggles to perform or quickly leaves the organization it creates a bad experience for other employees. It may even cause turnover of existing employees, which creates additional staffing challenges. It also means the company did not hire a different and more qualified candidate who, in all likelihood, has since accepted an offer elsewhere. There are many highly sophisticated talent assessment technology solutions that can be used to guide hiring decisions.[23] These assessments are designed to predict job performance, developmental potential, and retention. They do this by collecting and analyzing data about candidates' interests, skills, abilities, experiences, and qualifications to assess fit with the job and/or company culture.

One problem with assessments is not all of them work as advertised. Before using an assessment, it is important to review how it was developed and ensure it predicts job performance fairly and accurately. There are significant operational and legal risks to using poorly built talent assessments.[24] Another problem with assessments is candidates may not like them.

Although no one wants to be hired into a job they will not enjoy, most people dislike taking tests. Candidates are evaluating the company at the same time the company is evaluating the candidates. If candidates dislike a company's hiring process, then they are less likely to accept an employment offer.[25] Avoid creating experiences where candidates are being asked a lot of questions while receiving little information in return. Instead, create a two-way exchange between the company and the candidates using personal touch points, work previews, company insights, job crafting, and providing feedback.

Personal touch points are events built into the process that give candidates a chance to talk with an actual person about the job, the company, and the hiring process.[iv] These can involve conversations with hiring managers, recruiters, current job incumbents, or other people who can build a human connection with the candidate. This helps change the staffing process from a "cold formal evaluation" to a "friendly conversation about career options."

Work previews provide candidates with a sense of the tasks involved in the job, the work environment, and the company culture.[26] This can be done using simulation exercises, articles, videos, employee informational interviews, and real or virtual tours of the work environment. Some simulation-based talent assessment solutions provide work previews while simultaneously gathering selection data by having candidates perform tasks similar to what they would do on the job.

Company insights provide candidates with information about the benefits of working for the company, the company's mission, history, and culture; and potential longer-term career opportunities; for example, structuring interviews to include a portion of time for candidates to ask questions about what it is like to work for the company and training interviewers on how to answer these questions to put the company in the best possible light.

Job crafting involves putting steps in the hiring process where the candidate and company discuss possible modifications to the job to better fit the candidate's skills or interests, or to accommodate disabilities or nonwork commitments such as childcare. Job crafting can improve employee commitment and support greater levels of workforce diversity,[27] but it must be done in a way that ensures equity of treatment across candidates.

Providing feedback to candidates about their status in the hiring process is fundamental to creating a positive experience. One of the main complaints by candidates about hiring processes is the absence of feedback on job applications. It is important to let candidates know when they will hear back about next steps, including telling them if their application has been rejected.

[iv]A chatbot is not a person, no matter how realistic it may seem!

Some countries have laws that require telling candidates the reason they were eliminated. Regardless of legal requirements, it is a good idea to offer candidates information about why they were not chosen if they ask.

Candidates understand the need to evaluate applicants. What they dislike is being asked to provide information without understanding how it will be interpreted and why it matters. Candidates do not want to pass hiring tests. What they want is to explore their fit with the job. The selection process should be designed as an ongoing information exchange between the candidate and company until a final hiring decision is reached. This includes providing information to candidates explaining why they may be asked to complete different assessments, what these assessments measure, and how the data will be used.

Transitioning, Welcoming, and Departing

When people start a new job, they tend to be highly sensitive to their own employee experiences and how they are being perceived by others.[28] It is both folk wisdom and psychological truth that first impressions are lasting impressions. How employees experience their first weeks or months on a job has a lasting impact on their long-term job performance, development, and retention.[29] The term often used to describe transitioning employees into the company is *onboarding*. But newly hired employees do not want to be onboarded! That sounds like a form of torture. They want to be welcomed, supported, and set up for success. This involves attending to all three categories of employee experience that determine how people feel about work: fulfillment experience, task experience, and social experience.

Fulfillment Experience: I Know Why I'm Here

Employees ideally start the first day of work with a clear sense of their job objectives. If someone were to ask "Why were you hired?" they should be able to confidently answer by explaining how they will contribute to the company's success. Unfortunately, it is surprisingly common for employees to start a new role and not even meet their manager for several days to discuss their job objectives. Most employees will not complain about this lest they come across as lacking confidence or whining. But think about what this experience is like from an employee perspective. The employee made a decision that will affect their life in profound ways and define how they spend most of their waking hours over the coming months or years. At the very least, their manager should find time to welcome them and establish a bit more clarity about why they are here.

Task Experience: I Have the Tools I Need to Be Successful

The first few weeks at work can feel very awkward for new employees. They want to add value but may not have the resources needed to be effective. This can include simple issues such as getting security access allowing them into the building, a computer set up so they can begin communicating with colleagues, or knowledge of how to use machines or computer programs fundamental to their jobs. This lack of resources can make people feel like an incompetent outsider instead of a valued employee. It puts them in the position where they feel stuck between either bothering others for help or simply remaining ineffective. This is why companies should strive to ensure employees are fully equipped with everything they need to be successful on their first day at work. Companies should also seek to reduce or automate administrative tasks associated with joining the organization. Filling out forms is a lousy way to start your first day on the job.

Social Experience: I Feel Connected to the Right People in the Company

A critical part of starting a new job is establishing relationships with coworkers. New employees need support getting to know their colleagues. In addition to meeting the people they will work with directly it can also be beneficial to connect with fellow employees who share common backgrounds or interests. The goal is to create relationships that give employees a sense of belonging and connectedness with their teams and the larger organizational community. This may include training employees on how to welcome new hires into the company.

* * *

The previous discussion of transitions is focused on engaging new employees. But another important and often overlooked aspect of job transitions is managing employee departures. Every employee is going to eventually leave, but few companies proactively plan how to manage turnover. The following are a few ways to lessen the impact when people leave.

- **Embrace rehiring employees.** Many company cultures treat employees almost like traitors if they decide to leave. This does not make sense given that rehired employees are often more productive and tend to stay in the job longer.[30] Assuming the person is leaving under positive circumstances, let them know they are welcome to reapply for future opportunities that might interest them.
- **Have a socially networked offboarding process.** Identify what people, departments, or projects will be affected by the employee's

departure. Then create a method for departing employees to share resources with key stakeholders to lessen the impact of their departure.

- **Educate managers to talk with employees about turnover before it happens.** The best time to talk about turnover is before people decide to leave. Encourage managers and employees to discuss potential turnover concerns far enough in advance to explore alternative opportunities in the company that might inspire them to stay.
- **Manage deprovisioning.** There are many stories of companies forgetting to collect computers, turn off security access, or otherwise failing to deprovision former employees and contractors. One company discovered employees were eating free lunches in the company cafeteria months after they had stopped working. Make it easy for people to return their equipment and put processes that automatically turn off their system and facilities access.

Job transitions can create considerable stress for employees and managers. But if done right, they lay a foundation for lasting and strong relationships. Job transition technology can help employees start new jobs with a positive experience by guiding employees and managers through exercises to establish role expectations, automating procurement and training processes to ensure employees start with the tools and resources needed to be effective, and coordinating meetings and conversations with new coworkers. This technology can also support internal job transfers and employee departures. Job transitions are inevitable, making job transitions smooth is a choice.

Dynamic and Temporary Staffing

Many positions can be filled through employing contractors or creating dynamic teams that move employees into short-term roles to address specific project or operational needs. These dynamic, temporary staffing methods are becoming more common as companies adapt to an increasing pace of change. Although they may not be thought of as staffing in the traditional sense, they should be treated as an aspect of a company's strategy for addressing the challenge of filling positions.

Filling Roles with Contractors

Contractors are people who perform work for the organization but are not on the company's payroll system. They are paid based on fulfilling a specific work contract typically with a defined start and end date.

Rules and regulations governing contractors vary across countries, but the core concept is the sense of working for an organization without being a formal part of the organization. There are two main reasons why companies use contractors. First, they enable quickly increasing or decreasing the size of their workforce based on business demands. Second, they can provide access to skilled talent the company might not be able to hire as a regular employee. From an employee perspective, the advantage of contract work is greater control of their work and work schedule, greater variety of work, and in many cases the opportunity for higher levels of pay. It is also common for contractors to work for multiple organizations at one time. The disadvantage of contract work is greater levels of job uncertainty, frequent job change, and inability to access company benefits provided to full-time, permanent employees.

Companies should have a defined strategy for when to hire contractors and how to manage them. There are complex legal rules that govern the use of contractors in many countries. These rules are intended to protect contractors from being exploited as "second-class" labor and are a result of companies creating poor employee experiences for people in contractor roles. I have worked with companies that manage contractors through their procurement departments in a way that feels more like they are line-item costs than members of the workforce. Managers and employees should be accountable for giving the same level of respect to contractors as they do to full-time employees. This includes having processes for welcoming and transitioning contract employees into the organization. When contractors feel valued and appreciated, they are more motivated to do the best job possible.[31] They are also more likely to accept future contract assignments.

Filling Roles Using Dynamic Teams

Many companies are shifting from fixed organizational structures to more dynamic team models where positions are filled by moving people into new roles and groups to solve specific problems.[32] These dynamic teams have three characteristics:

- **Temporary.** They are created to achieve a specific objective and typically disband after the objective is achieved.
- **Multifunctional.** Team members are chosen based on having relevant skills and capabilities needed to achieve the objective and often come from different departments in the organization.
- **Informal leadership structure.** Teams may or may not have a designated team leader. Team leaders usually do not have formal management authority over other team members.

Dynamic teams can be used to avoid the costs of hiring new employees or contractors. They can also increase employee engagement and development by giving people new experiences. But they pose unique challenges. This starts with getting the right people on the team. Companies need to find employees with the right skills and interests who also have the flexibility to leave their current roles. This can get very complex in large organizations. Issues may arise if an employee funded by one part of the company is asked to join a team in another area without provisions for backfilling their current role. This can create resentment among employees if they are prevented from joining a team and frustration for managers if they lose current staff to another part of the company. Another challenge is transitioning people into and out of team roles. This includes situations in which teams disband without finding new roles for their members. Such situations can create anxiety among employees concerned about employment stability and career growth.

In the past, companies tended to think of contractors and dynamic teams as being separate from other recruiting and workforce planning activities associated with filling positions. This creates confusion over the true nature of the company's workforce and what they are doing. As one HR leader shared, "Our company has a lot of contractors in the workforce, but we know almost nothing about them, their level of engagement, and what would happen if they left." Companies should seek to manage contractors and agile teams alongside the other methods they use to staff the organization, viewing them as a way to fill positions that do not require hiring new employees.

How Work Technology Is Changing the Ways Organizations Fill Positions

The challenge of filling positions underwent a massive technology transformation when the process of finding and applying to jobs migrated to the internet in the early 21st century. Since then, this has become one of the most technologically advanced areas of HR. At a general level, the technology falls into three areas: marketing career opportunities, matching candidates to positions, and managing job transitions.

Marketing Career Opportunities

Technological innovations in this area include talent sourcing solutions that enable companies to create tailored job sites designed for different candidate communities, place targeted job advertisements across hundreds of websites and job boards, and track data showing which recruiting market-ing methods are generating the most qualified candidates and hires. Some work experience solutions help cultivate candidates by supporting alumni communities where employees, potential candidates, students, and former employees can share information related to the company and/or the indus-try it belongs to. These solutions may incorporate technology supporting use of employee referrals to discover candidates. Learning platforms can also provide free training to potential candidates to generate interest in the skills the company needs.

Matching Candidates to Positions

Opportunity matching and talent assessments solutions use mathemati-cal algorithms, machine learning functions, and psychometric formulas to assess the probability of candidates being interested, qualified, and success-ful in different roles. These solutions, when designed correctly,[v] are valu-able for identifying candidates with specialized skills, selecting the highest potential candidates among hundreds or thousands of applicants, and pre-dicting whether candidates will succeed in a job or company if hired. The effectiveness of opportunity matching and talent assessments depends on having access to data needed to match people to jobs. This includes data on people's work skills, interests, abilities, personality traits, education, and certifications. It can also include data about extrinsic work topics such as pay expectations, schedule requirements, and willingness to relocate. Elec-tronic profile solutions that collect and store this data have a central role in the evolution of technology to match candidates to opportunities. How these solutions will evolve is uncertain given concerns about data privacy and potential misuse. Although these concerns are well founded, there is a tendency to think of talent assessment and opportunity matching in terms of people who were not selected for jobs. But this overlooks people who are given job opportunities as a result of these solutions. This includes situ-ations in which use of mathematical matching algorithms helped people find employment in entirely new industries based on measuring their future potential in addition to their past experiences.[33] For example, opportunity matching and talent assessment technology was used during the 2020 pan-demic to help employees who were laid off in the hospitality and services industry find new job positions in the grocery and medical fields.

---

[v] The talent assessments market is known for two things: complex, evidence-based selection tools that predict candidate job success and complex, well-marketed selec-tion tools that do not predict anything. It can be hard to tell one from the other with-out guidance from an expert who understands the concept of empirical validation.

Managing Job Transitions

Recruiting management solutions provide tools to handle the complexity of keeping track of different job candidates, communicating with applicants and hiring managers, extending job offers, and welcoming new employees to the company. These solutions can be integrated with job transition, contractor management, work experience, and team management solutions, which enable companies to fill positions in a holistic fashion incorporating external hiring, internal transfers, contractors, and dynamic teams. Combining this with interoperable data management solutions enables companies to get an accurate picture of the entire workforce, identify their current roles, and determine which cost centers are paying them.

* * *

Historically, technology solutions developed to fill positions placed more emphasis on supporting company needs than creating positive employee experiences. This is reflected in the names used to describe these solutions such as applicant tracking, candidate screening, staffing section, and employee onboarding. Staffing technology was sometimes described as a form of supply chain technology implying candidates are like a bulk resource that needs to be tracked, screened, sorted, and selected. Is it any wonder candidates disliked the experience of using this technology?[34] The impact of staffing technology on candidate experience has significantly improved but there are still concerns.

Candidates want three basic things from the experience of filling job positions: opportunity, visibility, and transparency. Opportunity is about making people aware of industries, companies, jobs, and positions that align with their career interests, capabilities, and life goals. Visibility involves providing insight into the realities, good and bad, that are associated with work in various jobs and companies. Transparency concerns clarity about how companies determine who is hired into different jobs. Modern staffing technology is giving candidates more opportunity and visibility by providing greater access to information about careers and employers. But the growing use of complex assessments to evaluate and match employees to job opportunities is often decreasing transparency in selection decisions. People can accept that not everyone will get hired, but they want to know the processes to evaluate them are fair, job relevant, and unbiased. The complex mathematical and machine learning algorithms increasingly used for staffing are sometimes called *black box* technology because people do not understand how they work. Helping people understand how this technology works is critical to improving candidate experience related to their use. A friend who builds machine learning staffing systems calls this "turning black boxes into glass boxes."[35]

Applying These Concepts to the World You Live In

Filling positions should feel more like a series of conversations and communications about careers than a process focused on evaluating people. This dialogue should start well before the company needs to fill a specific position, focusing on topics that generate interest in what the company does. Bad experiences happen when people are placed in roles that they are ill-suited to perform, but great experiences happen when people are given opportunities that match their interests, capabilities, and potential. One way to move in this direction is to use experience measurement solutions to ask current and potential candidates how they feel about company's employment brand and hiring practices. Pay attention to the views expressed by people whose capabilities would add value to the organization but who have for one reason or another decided to work elsewhere. It is also important to have processes for managing the transition when employees leave a role. Exploring the following questions can help with thinking about these concepts in the context of the company or companies you work with.

Generating Candidates

- How does your company find job candidates? Where does your target audience search for employment opportunities?
- What inspires people to apply for jobs in your company? How can you improve your employment brand to attract more and better qualified candidates?
- What is the overall supply of potential candidates in the job markets your company hires from? Are enough people pursuing careers in your industry to ensure your company has access to enough skilled candidates in the future?
- Who are people in the workforce that your company would like to hire either now or in the future? Why would these people decide to work somewhere else instead of working for your company? If you made them a job offer now, would they be likely to accept? If not, why not?

Engaging Applicants

- How easy is it for people to apply for jobs in your company? How long does it take? Are there any steps that are particularly cumbersome or difficult?

- What does your company do to ensure high-potential candidates get connected with actual people early in the application process? How do you use human interaction to drive applicant engagement?
- What methods do you use to evaluate candidates for job fit? How are these methods presented and explained to candidates? How do candidates feel about these methods?
- What methods do you use to ensure candidates can get information and feedback about their application? How do you communicate to candidates when their application is denied?

Transitioning Employees into New Positions

- What happens to an employee on their first day? What about their first week or month? How do you ensure they start work with a clear sense of their objectives and the resources they need to be effective? What methods are used to help employees build relationships with their new coworkers?
- How does your company manage employee turnover? What happens when an employee gives notice that they are leaving? What things are or could be done to ensure turnover does not negatively affect coworkers?

Filling Positions Using Contractors and Dynamic Teams

- How many contractors does your company currently employ? How can you tell what they are doing, where they are working, and how much they cost?
- What guidance is given to managers and employees regarding the treatment of contractors? How do you ensure contractors feel like valued and respected parts of the workforce?
- How many of your employees are currently working as part of a dynamic team? What factors limit your company's ability to use dynamic teams to address staffing needs?

CHAPTER 6

Developing Capabilities and the Employee Experience of Learning

How Do You Prepare Truck Drivers for a World of Self-Driving Trucks?

A 50+-year-old courier company employing thousands of truck drivers and warehouse workers had to address this and similar questions to prepare its workforce for a changing future. Their industry is being transformed by technological innovations. Online retail shopping has expanded its customers from shipping clerks working in offices to individual consumers living in homes and apartments. Package delivery times that used to be measured in days or weeks are now measured in hours. Robotic automation and Internet of Things (IoT) tracking technology are altering how packages are sorted, stored, and retrieved. And the predicted development of self-driving trucks and drones is poised to totally change how packages are delivered.

Given labor market skill shortages, it is unrealistic for the company to transform its workforce just by hiring people with new technical skills. More important, the company values its employees and wants to avoid layoffs. So how could they get their workforce of long-tenured truck drivers and warehouse employees to view technological change as an opportunity instead of a threat? The answer lay in its frontline managers.

The first person many employees approach when confronted with change is their immediate supervisor. Frontline managers are the human face of the company to its employees. Frontline managers in this company were historically hired for operational, technical, and project management skills. The company sought to turn these frontline managers into change agents and coaches who could help employees and the company navigate digitalization and its impact on the workforce. They did not downplay the effort this would take. Executive leadership, including the CEO, is directly involved in the program. Frontline managers participate in extensive development programs that combine leadership training with on-the job learning projects. The company also works with the frontline manager's immediate supervisors to ensure learning and development is treated as a core part of their job expectations.

As frontline managers build their coaching capabilities and start embracing the role of change agent, they have become a major source of ideas and guidance within the company. In two years, the program generated sales revenue and operational costs savings equal to more than 12 times the initial investment. Customer satisfaction increased, and union grievances and accidents decreased. Employees feel like an active part of the company's digital transformation as their mindsets shift from "surviving change" to "shaping change." The company knew its survival hinged on the ability and willingness of its workforce to embrace and guide change. The actions of company leaders demonstrated confidence and support for their employees' ability to adapt, and although their jobs will change due to technology, their value as people will endure.

This chapter focuses on maximizing an organization's most valuable resource for dealing with change: their employees' ability to learn. Adaptation is the competitive niche of humans. We are the only species on earth that has the capability to alter our behavior to live in highly unfamiliar environments.[i] We are amazingly good at change. Nevertheless, people often view job change as a threat instead of an opportunity, which hinders our ability to adapt.[1] Adapting to change involves learning. Learning takes energy and people are neurologically predisposed to conserve mental and physical resources (or put another way, we are hardwired to

---

[i] One could argue single-celled life forms like bacteria also have this ability, but they do it by evolving over multiple generations and not through learning during a single generation.

be lazy).[2] An analogy might be drawn between employee development and maintaining a healthy diet. People know it is important and they want to do it, but they struggle to do it consistently. People are good at learning, but only under the right conditions. Those conditions are when they feel the effort to change will benefit their lives, feel supported by those around them, and believe they will be successful. The challenge organizations face is creating an employee experience that provides these conditions.

This chapter examines how to create adaptable workforces by shaping the work environment to support employee development. It focuses on four elements of employee experiences that play a critical role in promoting learning and growth:

- **Context.** Designing jobs that encourage and enable development by giving employees the time, opportunity, and motivation to build new capabilities.
- **Capabilities.** Helping employees identify what knowledge, skills, and experiences to develop to achieve their goals and prepare for the next chapter in their careers.
- **Content.** Providing employees with access to the development resources they need to build new capabilities.
- **Culture.** Creating an organizational environment that supports employee development, with particular focus on the role managers play in supporting employee development efforts.

All four areas must be addressed to create an employee experience that encourages and supports ongoing learning and development.

Context: Designing Jobs That Motivate and Enable People to Develop

An old joke asks, "How many psychologists does it take to change a light bulb?" The answer, "Just one, but the light bulb must want to change." This joke may not be funny, but it contains a valuable insight about employee development. People are unlikely to develop if they do not feel motivated to learn. For employees, this usually means tying development to job goals. The best way to do this is to make development part of the job itself, including accepting the implications this has on productivity.

Designing Jobs for Development

When people think about supporting employee development, they often focus on helping employees create development plans, setting time aside for learning, or giving employees access to training courses. These actions are useful but are often not very effective. In my experience, career development planning solutions are among the most widely deployed but least used features in talent management technology platforms. Learning professionals constantly struggle with getting employees to complete training courses.[3] And company efforts to give employees dedicated time for learning and innovation have mixed results.[4]

Employees say they value development, so why is it so difficult to get them to use development resources such as career planning, training, and dedicated learning time? The answer is because these things take people out of the flow of work. They create a feeling among employees and managers that development is separate and may even compete with time spent doing actual work. The goal of designing jobs for development is not to create dedicated time and activities for learning. It is to build learning into work itself, defining job tasks and objectives in a way that optimizes the balance between employee productivity and employee development. This requires managers and employees working together to set job goals that balance organizational value and developmental value.

- **Organizational value** reflects how important a goal is to the company. Goals high in organizational value are usually the most important part of an employee's job. They are the reason why the job exists. Goals low in organizational value are still valuable but are not as critical.
- **Developmental value** reflects how much a goal exposes the employee to unfamiliar work environments, problems, or business situations that require building new skills or applying existing skills in new ways. Goals with low developmental value are typically things an employee has done before.

The greatest levels of development happen when employees are given goals high in both organizational and developmental value. These goals create learning through on-the-job experiences.[5] For example, the best way to help an employee develop project management skills is to give them an important project to manage and then support them with learning the skills they need to be successful. But if employees are given too many goals that require extensive learning, they will become overwhelmed. The challenge is defining people's jobs in a way that maximizes their developmental value without overwhelming them. Figure 6.1 places work goals into four categories based on their organizational value and developmental value:

- **Business-driven development goals** are high in organizational value and high in developmental value. These are activities employees must do for work that require them to gain new experiences and develop

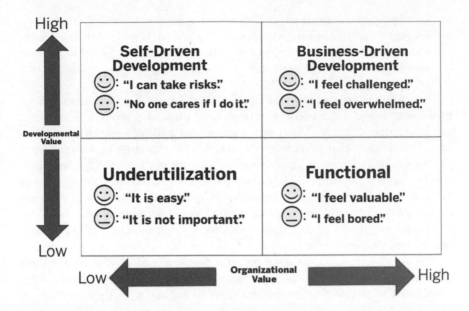

High

Developmental Value

Low

Self-Driven Development
☺: "I can take risks."
☹: "No one cares if I do it."

Business-Driven Development
☺: "I feel challenged."
☹: "I feel overwhelmed."

Underutilization
☺: "It is easy."
☹: "It is not important."

Functional
☺: "I feel valuable."
☹: "I feel bored."

Low ← Organizational Value → High

FIGURE 6.1 Mapping job goals for development.

new skills. The downside of these goals is they tend to be mentally demanding. They require learning how to do the work while getting the work done at the same time. People with too many business-driven development goals risk becoming overwhelmed.

- **Functional goals** are high in organizational value but low in developmental value. They are not necessarily easy, but the employee knows how to achieve them. Functional goals enable employees to contribute to the organization by focusing on important but familiar tasks. They give employees a sense of confidence and value. The disadvantage is they do not push employees to develop new capabilities. People with too many functional goals may feel they are stuck in a rut doing the same things over and over.
- **Self-driven development goals** are low in organizational value but high in developmental value. These goals enable employees to take developmental risks because failure will not have a major impact on the business. Their disadvantage is employees may never get around to these goals because they are not important to the organization. I refer to this quadrant as the "books I want to read" or "classes I keep hoping to take" section of a job.
- **Underutilization goals** are low in organizational value and developmental value. These goals may have once had more value but became less important or less challenging over time. It sometimes makes sense

to reassign these goals to other employees who will gain more developmental value from performing them. What may be a low development value goal for one employee might be a challenging goal for another employee with less experience.

Based on my experience, the optimal mix of goals is approximately 45% business-driven development, 45% functional, 10% self-driven development, and 0% underutilization. Using this approach to goal setting enables organizations to build future workforce capabilities by changing how employees perform their current jobs. It also makes jobs more meaningful to employees because it supports their career aspirations, avoiding problems that occur when employees feel overwhelmed by too many development goals or feel stuck in a dead-end job due to too many functional goals.

Developmental job design creates a work environment where employees constantly learn new things. An old saying in the training world is "Employees are responsible for their own development." If that is true, then companies are responsible for creating an employee experience that enables employees to develop. If companies want to future-proof their workforce, they need to structure current jobs with the future in mind. This also reduces the likelihood of employees losing their jobs due to digitalization because it discourages doing the same things over and over. As a general rule, once a person can learn to master a task then a machine can learn to copy them. A health care technician once asked me what they could do to avoid losing their job to a robot. My answer was, "Structure your role so you are always being challenged to learn new things. Things that take effort to learn are rarely simple, routine tasks. These, are the things least likely to be automated."

Development Versus Productivity

Designing jobs to support employee development puts employees in a constant state of growth, which creates more adaptable workforces and agile organizations. It also helps companies find and retain talent. The opportunity to develop new skills and capabilities is a key factor in attracting candidates and engaging employees.[6] The downside of designing jobs for development is it reduces short-term productivity. People are most productive when they are doing things they already know how to do. Designing jobs for development intentionally asks people to do things they do not know how to do.

Devoting time and resources to employee development is a long-term investment that requires accepting short-term costs. It is easy to build a theoretical case for investing in long-term learning, but it is difficult to build data-based financial models given the difficulty of measuring the value of a skilled workforce.[7] This was illustrated in a story a colleague shared about telling an executive how many salespeople had completed a training program. His response was, "All you've told me is how many hours these people have been sitting in training courses instead of selling to customers." Showing the financial value of development is getting easier as technology improves the ability to link employee data to business operations data, for example, creating links between knowledge of sales techniques and salesperson performance[8] or showing how emotional resilience training leads to improved customer service performance.[9] But it will always be difficult, particularly for jobs that do not have clearly defined financial performance metrics.

The most critical factor for designing jobs for development is having executives who put a priority on employee growth and innovation.[10] Leaders differ in their belief that employees can develop new capabilities. In psychology, this is referred to as the difference between a fixed and growth mindset.[11] Leaders with strong growth mindsets believe employees can significantly improve their capabilities through effort. By contrast, leaders with fixed mindsets doubt people can change their abilities much over time. It is hard to convince a leader with a fixed mindset that restructuring jobs for development is worth the potential loss of short-term productivity it may create. In such cases, companies may be limited to making incremental improvements until the leader is replaced by a more growth-oriented executive.

Managers also play a pivotal role in designing jobs for development.[12] They must be encouraged to use job assignments as a way to develop employees in addition to getting work done. They should be guided on how to use goals to balance the company's short-term operational needs with employees' longer-term career development objectives. Managers should be supported when, instead of giving a challenging assignment to an experienced employee because they know they can do it, they give the assignment to a less experienced employees so they can learn how to do it even though it may take longer to achieve. Organizations must also reward managers for helping to build employee capabilities.

It is surprising how many companies say they value development but do not reward managers for developing employees. To illustrate this, I often pose the following scenario to leaders: "Managers who are good at development encourage employees to move into new roles in the company when they have outgrown their current jobs. These employees are usually top performers. How does your company reward managers who develop and promote top performers out of their teams?" The typical response to this question is "We don't do anything for them." Many companies inadvertently punish these managers by not backfilling the positions left vacant as a result of promotions. If companies truly value employee development, they should reward managers who enable and support development of employees even when this means sacrificing short-term operational productivity to build long-term workforce capability.

Capabilities: Helping Employees Define Development Goals

Employee development starts with structuring jobs to create a work context that encourages and allows employees to build new capabilities. The next step is helping employees figure out what capabilities to build so they can find the right development resources. The actions associated with doing this differ based on why the employee is learning. Employees undertake learning for three basic reasons:

- **To fulfill a requirement.** Certain jobs require completing training courses and demonstrating specific knowledge and skills (e.g., safety training). Employees must complete these development activities to be allowed to work.
- **To perform their job.** Employees may need to learn something new to carry out a work task or improve effectiveness in their current role.
- **To advance their careers.** Employees may want to engage in a development activity to create future career opportunities and achieve longer-term life goals.

These three things can be thought of as the difference between *having* to learn to meet job qualifications, *needing* to learn to perform their job, or *wanting* to learn to advance their career.

Developing Capabilities to Meet Job Requirements

In this situation, development goals are defined by the company instead of the employee. The company informs employees what they need to know to be allowed to work and then helps employees complete relevant development activities to ensure they know it. The development activities associated with this particular situation are often related to ensuring safe and secure work environments. There may be significant operational and regulatory risks if employees fail to meet training requirements. The challenges in this situation are primarily related to determining what employees need to learn, making it easy to learn, and ensuring they learn it. The employee experience of development is different when it is about completing training to meet job requirements. People's attitudes toward activities change when they are told they must do them. That applies even when what they are being asked to do is in their best interest. In this situation, focus on making development easy, efficient, and effective.

Technology often plays a critical role for managing learning activities focused on meeting job requirements. Large companies may have thousands of people moving between different work assignments at hundreds of locations on any given day. The development requirements for a specific employee can change based on their current work location, job tasks, and how long since they last completed a training or certification activity. Learning experience technology solutions are extremely valuable for ensuring employees have completed required training and development activities associated with their jobs. These solutions can be integrated with work scheduling, job transition, and facilities access management solutions to reduce the risk of employees doing job activities they are not qualified to perform. For example, when an employee receives a job assignment, their qualifications are automatically checked, and they are informed via text messaging if they need to complete a required training course through their mobile phone. If they do not complete the course, then their security badge may be turned off denying them access to the work site. In some cases, employees may be able to complete the required training at the work site using mobile technology rather than having to go sit in a classroom.

Employees sometime view required development activities as a waste of time, which decreases the attention they put into mastering the material.[13] There is a difference between completing a required learning course and learning the course content. It is important to communicate to employees why the development matters beyond simply telling them "It is a requirement." It is useful to share stories that illustrate what is gained by completing the training. If possible, have leaders role model completion of required development activities and talk about what they learned with their employees.

Another reason employees have a negative view toward required development activities is that the training may not be very effective.[14] It is beyond the scope of this book to talk about effective training design, but one area worth calling out because of its impact on employee experience is use of virtual reality (VR) technology to create immersive learning programs. Immersive learning gives people the experience of being physically present in a specific environment. It is valuable for learning things that require being aware of physical surroundings or managing emotions under stress. This is relevant to safety and security training courses required for many jobs. Consider the following examples:

- **Physical awareness.** Loading trucks involves organizing parcels to maximize the use of space while considering issues related to weight, load balancing, and the order things will be unloaded. Employees must also pay attention to subtle cues that indicate potentially dangerous situations. VR training enables companies to train employees on hundreds of loading scenarios and create the time pressure and intensity of a loading dock in an efficient and safe manner.
- **Emotional control.** It is critical to remain calm when faced with a life-threatening event. VR training enables companies to create the

emotional intensity associated with situations such as facing an armed robber or escaping from a damaged building in danger of collapse. These simulations help people learn how to respond to situations they will hopefully never face in real life.

VR does not have to be totally realistic to be effective. What is important is the simulation re-creates specific mental states or physical images that are central to the person's development.[15] VR can also make training more memorable and enjoyable. As one training professional shared, "It was the only time employees have ever asked to stay after work to take a safety training course for a second time." VR is not relevant for every type of required training. But if part of learning something requires people to experience the actual situation, then VR training may be an ideal solution.

Developing Capabilities to Improve Job Performance

In this situation the challenge is helping employees identify capabilities that will help them be more effective in their current roles. This challenge is fairly easy to solve when dealing with simple actions related to performing routine tasks. In these cases, it can usually be addressed by providing mobile or online tools so employees can quickly find the information they need, for example, having chatbots answer questions or using videos to walk through process steps. The challenge becomes more difficult when the goal is not to instruct employees simply on how to do something but on how to do it well. The former is about giving employees access to knowledge to do specific things. The latter is about making employee aware of what they need to know to be more successful when they do it.

In the past, companies often rolled out learning programs to large groups of employees as though they were all the same, regardless of each person's unique interests or existing capabilities. Any distinction between employees was based on broad categories tied to job titles and departments. This approach ignores the fact that development activities that will help one employee improve their job performance might be a waste of time for another more experienced employee. This practice of treating every learner like they were identical was so widespread it was given a derogatory name: sheep dip training.[16] This compares corporate learning programs to the process by which herds of sheep are pushed through pools of disinfectant solution to kill bugs and bacteria regardless of whether they need it or not. It should be no surprise employees often view sheep dip training programs as a waste of time. It is also a waste of company resources to give training to people who do not need it.

Advances in technology are helping companies match development resources to the unique needs of each employee. This starts with providing employees with search engine tools so they can find training that meets their interests. The challenge is employees may not know what development activities to search for. "Unskilled and Unaware of It" is the name of an influential research article that examined the relationship between a person's current performance and their ability to determine what to change to increase their performance.[17] It found that people who would benefit from development are often unaware of what they need to develop. Or as the saying goes, you don't know what you don't know. Companies are addressing this issue using a variety of methods:

- **Learning communities** are online workspaces where employees share ideas, pose questions, and recommend resources related to development. Employees identify new capabilities to learn by drawing on the experiences and knowledge of other people performing similar roles.
- **Opportunity matching** are analytic solutions that recommend development activities to employees based on matching skills, interests, experiences, job types and other data to learning and development resources available in the company.
- **Talent assessments** are measures that help employees identify what skills or behaviors to develop to improve their effectiveness.

Most employees want to get better at their jobs but may not know which development resources will help them improve. And engaging in development activities that do not provide value is a waste of time. It is not enough to provide employees with access to development resources. Companies must help employees identify what capabilities to develop so they maximize the value of time spent on development activities.

Developing Capabilities to Advance Careers

The manager of my first job after graduate school gave me this advice: "Having a successful career comes down to figuring out what you want to do and finding someone who will pay you to do it. The first is often harder than the second." This describes a challenge many employees face when developing capabilities to advance their careers. They do not know what to develop because they do not know what they want to do in the future. In a world where the nature of jobs and organizations is constantly shifting, it is possible the capabilities most valuable for an employee to develop may have little do with their current work. For example, I know a person who went from working in sales to a career in data analytics. This shift was enabled by learning data analytic skills that were totally unrelated to the sales jobs he had earlier in his career. Career development used to assume people would follow relatively well-defined career paths where one job leads into another job in a somewhat linear fashion. Companies talked about employees being ready for a promotion or new role in one year, three years, and so forth. Linear, time-based development methods no longer work in many industries due to the pace of organizational restructuring and rapid emergence of new job types. As one leader told me, "If I do not even know what a job will look like in three years, how can I tell when someone will be ready for it?" In response to this new reality, companies are using technology to help employees build careers in a world without defined career paths by enabling the following activities.

- **Skill projections** use workforce analytics solutions to predict what skills the company is likely to need three to five years in the future. This information is shared with employees along with guidance on ways to build these skills while in their current roles.
- **Work communities** use work experience platforms to bring together people who share an interest in different industries or professions. People share ideas about how the nature of work in these industries and professions is changing, what capabilities it will require, and how to get them.
- **Development relationships** use opportunity matching solutions to create partnerships to guide employee development, such as finding mentors, sponsors, coaches, or in some cases simply putting two people together who have common interests but different perspectives based on their level of experience, location in the organization, or background.[18]
- **Job recommendations** use opportunity matching solutions to recommend career directions employees may not have considered. Some solutions use machine learning methods to uncover opportunities that may not be readily apparent based on a person's existing skills.
- **Temporary assignments** use opportunity matching solutions to help employees to join dynamic teams or complete short-term fellowships that expose them to different kinds of work, experience different environments, and develop new capabilities that could open up career opportunities in the future.

Developing careers in a highly digitalized world is like shooting at fast-moving targets. By the time you get to where you were aiming, the goal may have moved or disappeared entirely. Detailed, long-term career plans do not work when possible career paths are constantly changing. Instead, employees need a general career direction based on the capabilities they have, the capabilities they could develop, and the sort of work they want to do in the future. This requires giving employees a sense of what they could become in the future given their current skills and previous job roles. There is a tendency to assume that if employees know how to do something now, then they will be interested in doing it in the future. In reality, it is often the opposite. For example, I know a highly experienced, highly paid project manager who has little interest in working as a project manager. What she wants is to leverage the skills gained as a project manager to do something very different from what she did before. The ultimate goal is to help employees build capabilities throughout their careers so they are constantly in positions where they are getting paid to do something they want to do.

Content: Giving Employees Access to Resources to Build New Capabilities

Once employees figure out the capabilities they want to develop, the logical next step is to engage in development activities to start building them. This includes providing access to training resources such as classes, books, simulations, and other resources to develop specific knowledge and skills. Structured training is often criticized as not being an effective form of development, and it is true that training does not work as well as on-the-job learning. However, training delivered in the right manner at the right time is a very effective development tool. Furthermore, it is far easier to provide employees with training than it is to give employees tailored, on-the-job learning experiences. Training may not be the most powerful form of development, but it is highly scalable. The challenge companies face is making training resources easy to find, simple to access, and enjoyable to complete. In many ways, this is similar to some of the challenges faced by media companies, and corporate training programs are increasingly incorporating characteristics that were originally developed by online media platforms such as YouTube and Netflix. This includes recommending training content based on specific employee interests, enabling employees to create and share their own content, and providing communities where employees can discuss and share training materials. The following are ways technology is helping companies address these challenges:

- **Learning communities** use learning experience platforms to make training a social activity where employees interact with others who are having the same training experiences. This can be likened to creating an online version of the kind of social environment experienced by people at college when they form study groups and support relationships with fellow students.
- **Learning curriculums** use learning experience platforms to link together training programs into a coherent framework that supports broad development objectives tied to specific goals or outcomes, for

example, providing a series of training programs that cover the skills someone needs to start a career in a new profession.

- **Guided recommendations** use analytics to recommend training courses based on an employee's existing skills, interests, job history, or reactions to previous training. These solutions are somewhat similar to streaming music platforms that recommend songs based on analyzing a person's stated music preferences and previous listening history.
- **Employee-generated content** use learning content platforms that enable employees to create and share training materials. These are similar to the way people use public platforms such as YouTube to create and share instructional videos. It is important to monitor employee-generated content to ensure it is accurate and appropriate. But when used correctly, this is an extremely powerful form of training, as illustrated by the following example. A few years ago, there was a short fad in the United States for a baked good called *cronuts*.[ii] A grocery chain was getting customer requests for cronuts, but the stores did not carry them. A baker in one store figured out how to make cronuts, recorded an instructional video, and put it on an online learning community accessible to employees in other stores. Because the same kitchen equipment in the video was used in all the stores, the training was highly effective and soon all the stores were making cronuts. This was done faster and at a fraction of the expense of a formal training program. In fact, the cronut fad would have passed by the time the company could have rolled out a formal training program. Plus, employees were excited to see a colleague show up in the training video.
- **Micro-learning** provides employees with access to training courses consisting of stand-alone segments typically lasting less than three minutes each. These are often delivered using mobile technology so employees can access them at any time. Employees can quickly scan these courses and take ones that seem relevant, with one course often leading them to another.
- **Gamification** delivers learning activities in the form of stories, puzzles, or competitions. Employees complete the game though engaging in different development activities. Putting learning activities in the context of a larger narrative or competition can increase employees' interest and engagement when completing them.

Although training plays a critical role in development, it is not the most effective method for building new capabilities. The best development comes

---

[ii] Cronuts are a deep-fried combination of a croissant and a donut. They are not a healthy food, but they are good.

from job assignments. Staffing and job design should be incorporated into development programs in coordination with training. This may include using technology that helps employees find short-term assignments, fellowships, mentorships, and other work experiences that support their development goals. Training is valuable, but the best development comes from engaging with people and doing work, not just attending training courses.

Culture: Creating an Organizational Environment That Supports Development

The process of learning involves doing something we either do not know how to do at all or learning how to do something in a more effective manner. Any significant effort to learn something new almost always involves making mistakes of one kind or another. Effective learning environments use training and other resources to reduce the number and impact of the mistakes people make during the learning process. But any major learning experience will at some point involve discovering something we did not know, changing our minds about something we thought we knew, and understanding how to fix something we did incorrectly. Demonstrating incompetence is an inevitable step on the path toward developing competence, but people do not want to participate in development programs if they might be punished for mistakes made due to a lack of experience. Nor will employees ask for feedback or advice if they feel it might be interpreted as a sign of weakness or naivete. The degree to which employees engage in active learning and take on challenging developmental assignments is heavily influenced by two aspects of organizational culture: psychological safety and belonging.[19]

- **Psychological safety** is defined as "the belief that the workplace is safe for interpersonal risk taking."[20] It depends on employees experiencing work as a place where people are not negatively evaluated for sharing their concerns or asking for help and where people do not fear they may be unfairly judged or punished for making honest mistakes. Leadership trust and authenticity are critical for creating psychologically safe environments.[21] It is built by leaders being clear in their expectations and support for development, consistent and transparent in the processes they use to evaluate and make decisions about people, and open in sharing information with employees about things that could affect them, whether good or bad. A work environment becomes psychologically safe when employees know they will not be unfairly judged for engaging in development activities that require them to take risks, make and learn from mistakes, and seek guidance and feedback.

- **Belonging** is defined as "the feeling of being accepted and approved by a group or by society as a whole."[22] When employees worry about whether they belong, they often adopt a survival mindset instead of growth mindset. Instead of focusing on developing and making more of an impact, they focus on showing they are important and "needed" to protect their jobs. They are less likely to take risks for fear that they will be viewed as incompetent. Companies create a sense of belonging by showing they care about employees, are considerate toward employees' needs, and are compassionate in their treatment of employees. The first of these is about ensuring employees understand the value they provide to the company. Every employee at one point or another wonders, "Am I doing a good job?" It is hard for employees to understand their value if the organization does not have some process to measure and recognize their contributions. The second is about listening to employee concerns and demonstrating sensitivity and inclusivity in the company's response. This includes recognizing that people from different backgrounds may have very different experiences of work. The third is about employee's sense of employment stability. Employees' fear of job loss can create behaviors that undermine organizational adaptability and can ultimately lead to actual job loss. Organizations seeking to create a culture that encourages development must ensure employees feel they belong in the company—that they are wanted, not merely needed.

Employees feel a sense of safety and belonging when they believe their leaders care about them and can be trusted to share things with them that might affect their lives. This requires leaders to openly engage with employees about occasionally difficult topics. Leaders are often reluctant to do this out of concern they may appear incompetent or ineffectual.[23] We often forget that leaders are employees, too. They also shy away from development activities for fear that it might make them look bad. When leaders role model interpersonal risk taking and share stories about learning from mistakes, it sends a message to employees that it's okay not to be perfect as long you learn from the experience.

Technology can also help create cultures that support learning. Experience measurement solutions enable companies to understand and take actions to increase people's sense of belonging and safety, talent management solutions can increase transparency in how the company evaluates people, and work platforms can create forums for leaders and employees to openly share information. But what ultimately matters most are the behaviors of leaders.

Applying These Concepts to the World You Live In

Accelerating changes in business markets, technology, and socioeconomic conditions are forcing employees to learn to do things that are much different from what they did in the past. This has led to a massive increase in the development of learning technology. This technology plays a critical role in creating adaptable and agile workforces, but the technology will not work if it is not implemented in the right way and supported by the right culture. Just as people "learn how to learn," so must companies learn how to use learning technology effectively to build strong development cultures. Exploring the following questions can help in thinking about these concepts in the context of the company or companies you work with.

Context

- What methods does your company use to ensure development activities and experiences are incorporated into an employee's job?
- How are managers rewarded for developing employees? What barriers do managers and employees face in terms of supporting and encouraging development?

Capabilities

- How many jobs do you have where people are required to complete training in order to work? What is the employee experience like in terms of completing this training? How could it be improved?
- What methods are available to help employees define their development goals? How does the company help employees identify the capabilities they should develop to be better at their jobs and/or more successful in their careers?

Content

- How do you connect employees to relevant training materials? What methods can employees use to find training? What methods are used to proactively suggest training to employees?
- What technology does your company use to make training materials more accessible, engaging, and effective? Does your company use gamification, micro-learning, learning communities, or VR applications?
- Does your company have methods to support user/employee-generated training content?

Culture

- How do you measure employees' sense of psychological safety and belongingness? What processes are in place to ensure the company culture supports learning and development?
- What actions and methods are used to ensure leaders display the behaviors that drive employees' sense of psychological safety and belongingness? Do you train or assess leaders on behaviors that create a feeling of trust, authenticity, caring, concern, and compassion?

Creating Engagement and Employee Experiences That Inspire Successful Performance

Engineering Employee Engagement

From about 2014 to 2016 there was a trend for companies to elimi-nate employee performance ratings.[1] This was based on a belief that evaluating performance created anxiety in employees that dam-aged engagement and development. These claims were not exactly true,[i] but the message resonated with many leaders who found the process of rating performance to be stressful, time-consuming, and ineffective. Several companies I worked with at the time embraced this idea, only to discover it did not work as intended.

When one particular engineering company stopped formal evalu-ations its employees and managers initially welcomed the change because it meant they did not have to write performance reviews or have difficult conversations about performance ratings. But over time employees started to wonder how the company made decisions about pay and promotions. Some expressed concern over the fair-ness of these decisions. Things reached a critical point when sev-eral high-performing engineers left the company. These engineers felt their contributions were not properly recognized and expressed

---

[i]The actual problem was not the use of performance ratings. The problem was many companies were using poorly designed and ineffective performance rating processes.

*frustration at working with colleagues who did not share their com-
mitment to doing the best job possible. This led the company to adopt
a new performance rating process that incorporated techniques that
previous consultants had told them hurt employee engagement, most
noticeably comparing employees against one another. There were
two significant differences between the new performance rating process and the prior one the company had used. First, managers rated
performance using group discussions with other managers and leaders. Managers did not make ratings by themselves. Second, company
leaders were actively involved in the process and used the results to
guide decisions related to staffing, compensation, and development.
Employees were told exactly how they were evaluated, who was evaluating them, and why the evaluations were being done.*

*After the new process was deployed, employee engagement went up
along with greater retention of high-performing talent. They also saw
a small increase in turnover among employees who were considered
to be skilled and valuable, but not particularly effective. When the
company shared these results with me, I was reminded of what other
customers had said about eliminating performance rating processes.
Companies can eliminate formal ratings, but they cannot eliminate
people judging each other. Employees know they will be evaluated
in some manner. They want to know how it is done and what data
are used. Employees want transparency in how the company makes
compensation and staffing decisions that affect their careers and
their lives. Being evaluated can be stressful, but knowing you are
being evaluated and not knowing how it is done is even worse.*

This chapter is about how to engage employees to execute the company's
business strategy, in other words, how to maximize employee performance.
Employee performance is one of the biggest sources of variability in business operations. Employees are capable of amazing performance with the
right motivation, engagement, and support. They can also be incredibly
unproductive if they receive poor guidance, recognition, or coaching. Their
productivity immediately goes to zero if they quit based on how they are
being treated. And they can switch between these states based on a single
employee experience.

Fully engaging employees is one of the most difficult challenges faced
by large and growing organizations. The engagement and performance of
employees tends to decrease as the workforce expands.[2] This is due to
multiple factors, including complexity of coordination among members,
lack of individual recognition, decreased feelings of accountability, and less
urgency for organizational survival. Companies must work to ensure the
experience employees have at work inspires everyone to do their best.

This means dealing with the reality that not everyone has the same level of performance. The challenge is how to manage differences in performance while maintaining a psychologically safe environment where people feel a sense of belonging regardless of their performance level. This chapter looks at five topics relevant to creating engaging work environments that foster high levels of employee performance.

- **The performance management dilemma.** Creating an environment where every employee feels valued even though some employees provide more business value than others.
- **Aligning performance expectations.** Ensuring employees understand what they are expected to achieve, know why it matters, and are committed to doing it.
- **Increasing awareness of performance.** Providing employees with feedback and guidance about what they can do to be more successful without making them feel overly criticized or evaluated.
- **Managing differences in performance.** Managing the reality that not everyone performs at the same level and that the performance of employees influences the performance of their coworkers.
- **Compensation and performance.** Using pay and other tangible rewards to motivate performance and engage and retain talent.

Managing performance requires balancing multiple activities, is easy to get it wrong, and there is no one best way to do it. Nevertheless, it has to be done. The question is not whether a company manages performance but rather how effectively it does it.

The Performance Management Dilemma

Engaged employees feel a sense of commitment, focus, and energy toward supporting the goals of the company. Engagement is directly influenced by the formal and informal performance management methods used in a company to communicate job expectations to employees, support them in meeting those expectations, and recognize them for their contributions and achievements.[3] Companies often rename performance management processes to make them sound more employee focused (e.g., success paths, career conversations), but regardless of what they are called, companies have to practice performance management in some form. The alternative might be called "hire, pay, and pray," when employees are encouraged to do their best without specific expectations or accountability for results. This approach has been studied and it does not work. Simply put, "When people are asked to do their best, they do not do so."[4]

At its core, performance management requires balancing two types of activities (see Figure 7.1). One involves coaching individuals by providing guidance, feedback, and recognition to support the performance, development, and retention of individual employees. The other involves making decisions about how to use pay, promotions, job assignments, and development resources to create high-performing teams. Both require assessing employee performance but not for the same reason. Building teams involves assessing employee's past performance because it predicts future behavior. This is critical for making decisions about how to structure roles and invest pay and other limited resources based on the strengths and contributions of each team member. These decisions often require comparing employees against each other. By contrast, coaching individuals is based on the belief that people can change, and past behavior does not totally define future behavior. Coaching individuals involves assessing employee's past performance to provide feedback and advice to improve their future performance. It often avoids comparing people against one another because this can trigger defensive responses that limit learning.[5] These two activities conflict in the sense that past behavior does predict future behavior, but it does

Maximizing performance, development, and retention of individual team members
- Focuses on coaching and avoids comparing people against one another
- Assumes past performance behavior does not limit future performance

Putting the right people in the right positions with the right tools
- Requires comparing people to assign roles and allocate resources
- Assumes past performance behavior predicts future performance outcomes

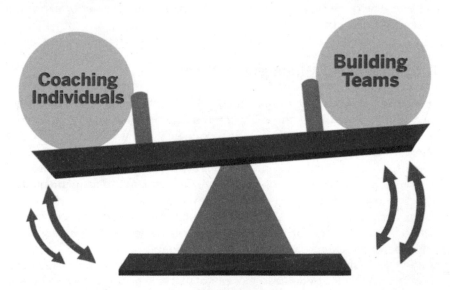

FIGURE 7.1 The performance management dilemma.

not completely determine future behavior. Comparing employees based on their past performance is necessary to guide decisions when not everyone gets the same outcome, but it can increase employee anxiety, which can hurt individual performance.[ii] Balancing these two things is something I refer to as the *performance management dilemma.*

Solving the performance management dilemma starts by recognizing that performance management is not one process. It is several processes that must be linked together without becoming overly intertwined. Figure 7.2 illustrates the three main parts of performance management: setting expectations, discussing progress, and assessing contributions. Each involves a different set of activities and affects performance through different sets of psychological pathways, but how one part is conducted also influences the effectiveness of the other two parts.

- **Aligning job goals and expectations.** This is about ensuring employees understand what they must accomplish, why it is important for the success of the organization, and how it affects achievement of their own career goals. This includes updating goals and job expectations to reflect changes in the company strategy. Psychologically, this is about focusing employee attention, energy, and motivation.
- **Ongoing coaching and development.** This is about employees understanding their level of performance and helping them change their behaviors to be more successful. It involves giving employees ongoing performance feedback about their progress toward meeting

FIGURE 7.2 The three parts of performance management.

[ii] People vary widely when it comes to having their performance compared against others. Some people find it threatening or distasteful, and others enjoy competing against their peers.

their job expectations and achieving their career goals. Psychologically, this is about increasing employee self-awareness and self-management.

- **Staffing and investment decisions.** This is about evaluating employee performance and using this to guide decisions about how to manage, reward, and develop people. This includes ensuring pay and staffing decisions are made and communicated to employees in a way that increases their sense of equity and motivation. Psychologically, this is about making effective and fair decisions about employees that recognize the contributions they are making to the organization.

These three parts might be described as "tell me what you want me to do," "help me do it," and "recognize me for what I did." Although they are related, it is important to treat them as separate activities. For example, in the past companies tended to use goals primarily to guide future compensation decisions. When this happens, employees set expectations based more on what they want to get paid and less on what they can accomplish to support the organization. Companies also encounter problems when there is no clear link between the different parts. For example, it is impossible to give people effective feedback if they do not have clear job expectations. If people do not know what they are supposed to be doing how can they know how to do it more effectively?

It is important to be transparent about how actions in one part influence actions or decisions in another but also to be cautious not to link them too closely. For example, there should be a connection between goal achievement and promotion decisions, but employees should not feel the best way to advance their careers is to set goals that are easy to achieve. They must have confidence that career success will come from setting difficult goals and actively working with their manager throughout the year to achieve them. Additionally, an employee's previous performance should influence their future goals and job assignments. For example, if an employee's past performance suggests they have leadership potential, then they might be given job goals that allow them to develop and demonstrate their leadership skills. Conversely, if an employee struggled to meet certain goals the previous year, they might be given a different set of goals that better play to their strengths.

Solving the performance management dilemma requires doing each step in Figure 7.2 while also linking them together in an effective manner. Employees often wonder, "What does the company expect me to achieve?" or "How can I tell if I am meeting expectations?" or "How will my current actions influence future decisions about my pay and career opportunities in this organization?" Employees who cannot answer these questions are likely to feel confused about their roles and uncertain about their futures. Employees who can answer these questions are likely to feel engaged and in control of their careers. The remainder of this chapter is about how to make this happen.

Aligning Performance Expectations

I once had lunch with a person who had analyzed engagement survey data collected from millions of employees across thousands of organizations. When I asked if any single survey question was most strongly associated with engagement, his answer was the question, "Do you know what you are expected to do at work?" It is hard to make work engaging if employees do not know what they are supposed to do, why it matters, or whether they are doing it effectively. Providing employees with meaningful, challenging yet achievable goals is fundamental to creating high-performing organization.[6] Clear goals give employees a sense of purpose, clarity, and strategic direction. If employees do not have clear goals, then managers and employees will struggle to have effective coaching conversations because it will be unclear what to talk about. And the organization will struggle to make effective talent management decisions because it will be difficult to assess what employees have accomplished. The problem facing companies is how to provide employees with effective goals in a world of shifting priorities and changing business needs. It is even more challenging to do it in a way that employees feel like they are participating in a conversation and not simply being told what to do.

In the past, companies tended to treat goal plans as a kind of contract between employees and the company to guide future compensation decisions. Goal setting was a quarterly or annual event, and once goal plans were set, they rarely changed. Goal plans were often created through a method referred to as *goal cascading* (see the left side of Figure 7.3). In this approach, company executives set an overall company goal plan that defined key business outcomes. Senior leaders then broke the plan into smaller components and objectives that they communicated to their directors and managers. Directors and managers then assigned even more specific tactical goals to their employees. Goal cascading works if things remain relatively stable over time and leaders have the best insight into what goals to set. This is often no longer true. Shifting priorities are a part of life in most organizations, and there is little chance that goals will remain unchanged throughout the year. And the best tactical goals for achieving company strategies often come from people further down the leadership hierarchy who are dealing directly with operational challenges.

Organizational agility depends on the ability to rapidly realign employees on shifting business strategies. This is better done by establishing goals through ongoing dialogue (see the right side of Figure 7.3). In this method,

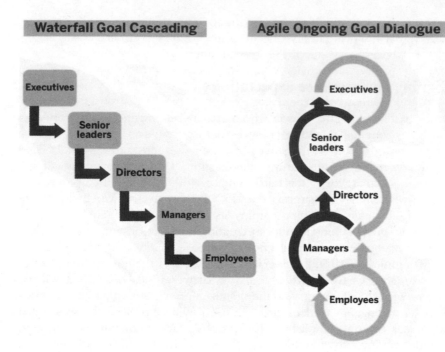

FIGURE 7.3 Goal cascading versus goal dialogue.

goals are discussed, clarified, and modified through frequent conversations. Leaders, managers, and employees regularly meet to discuss what is happening, what needs to happen, why it is important, and what is required to be successful. Role clarification and goal management technology help employees and managers to coordinate these conversations, update expectations, identify challenges, and track progress. These solutions also enable employees to see the goals of colleagues and leaders across the company, which promotes alignment and collaboration across the organization.

Three employee experience problems related to goals often can occur in a world of constant change: being fixated, distracted, and disconnected. **Fixated** happens when leaders make a change in the company strategy, but employees are not informed and continue doing what they were always doing. For example, one company inadvertently rewarded salespeople for selling a product line for several months after it had been discontinued. **Distracted** happens when employees react to changes in a way that detracts from what matters to the company. For example, I have seen employees devote time to studying market trends that were related to their profession but unrelated to what their company did. Just because employees feel something is relevant to their job does not mean it is that important to achieving the organization's objectives. **Disconnected** happens when senior leaders fail to recognize challenges in the business market that limit the ability of employees to achieve their goals. Leaders may not become aware of these challenges until the company starts to miss key strategic objectives. When this happens, leaders may blame poor employee performance when the real issue was that the strategy was based on flawed assumptions about the market or capabilities of the company. Ongoing goal dialogue reduces the risk of people being fixated, distracted, or disconnected by emphasizing two-way information flow up and down the leadership chain.

The best methods for setting goals depends on the type of job and culture of the company. But the following tends to make goals more engaging and meaningful to employees.

- **Goals should be defined through dialogue.** People want to know what they are supposed to do at work, but few people like to be told what to do. Goal setting should be approached as a two-way conversation between the manager and employee to align what the company needs to accomplish, what employees want to achieve in their careers, and what employees are able to do. Giving employees influence over the nature and definition of their goals increases their sense of ownership and commitment to achieving their job expectations.
- **Goals should be tangible.** Goals should define specific accomplishments or outcomes that demonstrate the contributions the employee is making to the organization. Even if someone never saw an employee perform their job, it should be possible to determine their contributions by looking at the goals they have accomplished.
- **Goals should be public.** There should be no secret to what people are trying to accomplish at work. Employees cannot effectively collaborate without knowing each other's goals. In addition, the more public people are about their goals the more accountability they will feel about achieving them.
- **Goals should be expected to change.** There are few jobs in which an employee's goals will stay exactly the same over 12 months. Although there may be financial targets and operational commitments that cannot be changed, the tactical goals employees pursue to fulfill these commitments are likely to change over time. Managers and employees should set goals with the expectation that they will be refined and modified based on shifting business demands and strategies.

If a company can do only one thing to improve employee engagement, it should be ensuring employees have concrete, inspirational, and business-relevant goals. At a minimum, companies should ensure that managers and employees regularly discuss and update goals, because simply talking about goals increases employee's motivation toward achieving them.[7]

Increasing Awareness of Performance

Goals create employee engagement by giving work a sense of meaning and purpose. Performance feedback amplifies engagement by providing employees with encouragement, support, and insight to achieve their goals. When feedback is effectively delivered it is simultaneously a form of education and recognition. Knowing how to receive feedback is a critical skill for employees. Not all employees will be expected to coach others, but all employees will have to react to feedback from others. How they respond will have a significant influence on their long-term career success. My father called this to my attention when I was in middle school and delivered a presentation to my class. He asked if I received questions or comments from my classmates. When I told him no, he half-jokingly said, "You know what it means when people don't give you feedback? It means either your work is so good that they can't think of any way to make it better or it is so bad or boring they don't want to put energy into helping you improve it. Guess which is more likely." His point was that people should want feedback because it shows others care about their work. The problem is that feedback is not always delivered in an effective or supportive manner.[8] When this happens, feedback feels more like an attack on our competence than coaching to help us improve our work.

There are many ways employees can receive feedback. The easiest is to give them goals that can be measured using well-defined metrics. These metrics become a form of feedback. Sales jobs are a good example. Salespeople do not need to ask for feedback to know whether they are on track to have a successful quarter. They just look at their performance relative to their sales targets. The challenge is many jobs cannot be linked to clear metrics such as sales quotas. In addition, performance is not just about what goals people achieve. *How* they achieve goals is also important. This is about how people interact with others, the things they do that go beyond formal job expectations, and the quality and efficiency of their work. It can be difficult to measure these things using objective metrics. This sort of qualitative feedback is best delivered through conversations with managers, coworkers, or customers.

Manager-Based Feedback

The quality of manager feedback has a significant impact on employee engagement, but coaching does not come naturally to people in managerial roles for multiple reasons.

- **Managers are not expected to coach.** Few companies promote people to manager based primarily on their coaching skills, and many companies put little emphasis on coaching when they evaluate manager performance. Managers may also report to leaders who do not role model effective coaching. Managers tend to manage employees based in part on how they are managed themselves.[9] If a company wants its managers to spend more time coaching employees, then senior leaders in the company should spend more time coaching the managers who report to them.

- **Managers do not understand the nature of coaching conversations.** Managers tend to divide employee meetings into two general categories: check-in conversations, in which they discuss near-term tactical issues related to job activities, and development planning conversations, which are focused on the long-term career direction of the employees. Check-ins are often held daily or weekly. Planning conversations are held only a few times a year. The main questions asked in check-in conversations are "What did you get done recently and what are you doing next?" The main question in planning conversations is "Where do you want to go with your career?" Many managers do not understand that a coaching conversation is a third type of meeting somewhere between a check-in and a planning conversation. The focus is not on day-to-day tasks, nor is it on long-term career planning. The focus is on revisiting and clarifying expectations and performance in the employee's current role. In coaching conversations, the main question is "How is your current role going and what would help you be more successful?" A coaching conversation might start by reviewing the employee's job goals to see if they need to be revised based on changes in the broader business or company strategy. It could also focus on discussing challenges the employee is facing in their role. The key to effective coaching conversations lies in having them often enough to proactively identify and address concerns before they become problems. Or as I like to put it, it's a relaxed discussion of issues before they become issues.
- **Managers do not know how to coach.** It is important to train managers on how to have effective coaching conversations. This starts with having a clear agenda about what these conversations are designed to cover. It is also important managers be trained on how to effectively deliver, receive, and discuss performance feedback. Many managers are anxious about coaching because they think it requires addressing sensitive topics related to employee feelings and performance issues. Coaching can involve these topics, but most coaching is more about role clarification than employee behavior or attitude. Coaching conversations often start with questions such as "Let's talk about the five or so major things you are working on. What is going well? What could be going better? What might we do differently?"
- **Employees do not expect or know how to receive feedback.** Employees should be encouraged to request coaching conversations

with their managers and be trained on how to respond to feedback, including feedback they may not agree with. Some companies include training on how to request and receive feedback in new hire development programs. Others periodically hold team-building sessions centered on giving and receiving feedback. These sessions often extend feedback beyond employee-manager relationships by encouraging employees to provide feedback to each other.

- **Managers forget to provide coaching.** Managers may forget to hold coaching conversations simply as a result of having hectic schedules. Goal management technology solutions can be used to remind managers and employees to meet on a regular basis, suggest topics to address during coaching sessions, and keep track of what was discussed so it can be revisited in future conversations.
- **Managers are not rewarded for being good coaches.** As mentioned in Chapter 6, for years, I have asked companies the following question: "How do you reward managers who encourage high-potential employees to leave their teams to take other roles in the company?" This is what good coaches do. Rather than horde talent, they develop and share it. But many companies do not reward managers who share talent, and some even punish them by not backfilling the role.

Most managers know they are supposed to provide coaching, but coaching is not something that people will do just because they know it is the right thing to do. Furthermore, managers who try to coach but lack the right skills can damage employee engagement. Managers need to be trained on how to coach, reminded to hold coaching sessions, be held accountable for the quality of their coaching, and be rewarded for doing it well.

Coworker and Customer-Based Feedback

Coworkers and customers are a valuable source of feedback given their unique perspectives on employee performance. The challenge is creating an environment in which providing this feedback is viewed as easy and appropriate. Experience measurement technology is making it easier for employees to collect feedback from customers and coworkers, for example, by texting someone two or three simple questions after a presentation or meeting. The willingness of coworkers and customers to provide this feedback is influenced by their understanding of how it will be used. This is particularly important for feedback from coworkers. Information should be provided so people providing feedback know who will see it and, if relevant, what steps are taken to protect the confidentiality of the person providing it.

There is also an increasing trend toward using self-management technology solutions to provide coaching and feedback. Self-management technology is designed to make people aware of their current behaviors and provide guidance on what to start, stop, or continue doing to be more successful in achieving their goals. It often makes use of data collected directly or indirectly from coworkers or customers. These solutions are based on two psychological concepts: self-regulation and nudges. Self-regulation involves making people aware of how their current actions and behaviors are helping or hindering their success.[10] For example, smart watches can make us aware of how much sleep we are getting or how often we are walking instead of sitting. Nudges are visual cues or simple reminders that encourage short-term actions that help us achieve long-term goals.[11] My physician spouse refers to these as "healthy choices." An example is keeping healthy snack foods like fruit on the counter and putting less nutritious choices like cookies in the closet. Simply making fruit more visible influences our choice about what to eat when we are hungry. The following lists some common types of self-management solutions. This technology field is advancing rapidly with more solutions available every year.

- **360 surveys.** These solutions ask an employee's coworkers to provide employees with feedback to guide their development efforts.[12] 360 surveys have been around for decades, but their complexity and effectiveness has greatly increased with the development of experience measurement technology. Automation has made them far easier to use and embedded analytics enables faster interpretation of the results while still keeping survey responses anonymous.
- **Electronic communication analytics.** These solutions analyze patterns in the frequency and content of e-mail, text messages, calendars, and other electronic communication to provide people with feedback on how they are interacting with others. They can, for example, make managers aware of how much time they spend with some team members compared to others, how responsive they are to different individuals' questions and requests, or how the tone of their language may influence people's perceptions (e.g., using too many critical words or rarely providing complements).
- **Event and project feedback.** These solutions are used to collect feedback during or after some activity. This is usually done by sending a short set of questions to participants during or after an event, meeting, or project. Another method is to use data that show if people are actively participating in the project or event based on how frequently they attend meetings, contribute ideas, or actively pay attention to a presentation.[iii]

[iii] This technology can create concerns about privacy. For example, it is valuable for someone doing a web presentation to know if people in the audience are paying attention. This could be done using eye tracking technology on computer cameras, but people may not be comfortable being measured in this manner.

- **Triggered nudges.** These provide employees with targeted suggestions triggered by occurrences in the employee's environment. For example, an employee could set their calendar to send them a nudge to take a micro-learning course on "how to make a good first impression" shortly before an important customer meeting. These nudges can be thought of as proactive feedback in preparation for an upcoming action or decision.

Self-management solutions have the advantage of being automated and may feel more objective than feedback from managers or coworkers. They should not, however, be viewed as a replacement to talking to others. Effective performance depends on effective relationships, and the strength of relationships is driven by having quality conversations.

Managing Differences in Performance

All employees provide value to the business, but some employees generate more value than others. This statement is true in any large organization[13] but calling it out makes some people feel uncomfortable. It can trigger feelings of evaluation, favoritism, and exclusion and may seem antithetical to the concept of belongingness as a key cultural value. Yet, it is a reality, and how companies deal with it has major consequences for employee experience and organizational adaptability. Failing to manage differences in performance creates bad experiences for employees. High-performing employees want to be recognized for their contributions, and a company cannot recognize outstanding accomplishments without categorizing employees based on performance.[14, iv] Tolerating poor performance may be even worse. Most people have experienced the frustration of having to rely on coworkers who are unresponsive, are not committed to delivering quality work, or are rude or disrespectful toward others.[15] Overlooking differences in performance even creates bad experience for low-performing employees, who may know they are struggling but do not know how to change their situations. Employees who were fired for low performance sometimes look back on the event as a positive step in their career growth because it got them out of being stuck in a role where they could not succeed.[v, 16] Failing to manage differences in performance also hurts company performance.[17] And the best employee experiences come from working for successful companies.

[iv] This concept was explored in the popular animated movie *The Incredibles*, in which the plot centered on the observation that "if everyone is super then no one is."
[v] I am not advocating firing employees. To the contrary, companies that are good at hiring employees and managing differences in performance rarely fire people because they prevent issues from reaching this point.

I have worked with more than 1,000 companies exploring ways to manage performance differences and read countless articles on the topic. Based on this collective experience, there are three major aspects companies often overlook when managing differences in performance:

- It involves subjective judgment as much or more than objective measurement.
- It requires comparing employees but does not require ranking them.
- It is about knowing the capabilities of the workforce to guide future decisions.

Keeping these things in mind is key to creating positive employee experiences while dealing with the reality that not everyone performs at the same level.

Managing Performance Involves Subjective Judgment More Than Objective Measurement

The first step to managing differences in performance is understanding what these differences are. This requires placing employees into categories based on job performance, in other words, rating them.[vi] Rating performance is one of the most difficult things to do well when it comes to managing employee experience. Many rating processes fail to accurately assess performance or do it in a way that makes people feel unfairly judged. The worst methods use strict forced ranking methods that compare employees in a zero-sum manner so that if one employee is rated higher, then another employee must be rated lower. These competitive methods often create traumatic stress for managers and employees. Some companies I work with no longer use words such as *calibration* or *rating* because they trigger strong emotional reactions in employees as a result of previous use of forced ranking methods.

The underlying problem with many performance rating processes lies in how they are conceptualized. People often approach performance rating as a process of measurement. They create checklists and formulas designed to objectively determine employee performance levels. These methods

---

[vi] Rating requires placing people into categories but does not require assigning people numeric ratings or ranking employees. The most effective rating processes use descriptive labels such as "exceptional," "solid," or "valuable but needs improvement." Labels should also describe the performance and not the person. This emphasizes that performance is a temporary state based on what we do; it is not about who we are. There is a big difference between calling someone's performance "below average" and calling them a "below-average person."

almost never work because the main purpose of performance rating is not about objective measurement. Performance rating is a process for making social judgments. Ratings should be influenced by objective metrics, but ultimately the rating assigned to an employee is a judgment about how much the organization values having the person as a member. When people argue with me on this point, I ask if it would be possible to create a computer formula that could accurately measure the value of their performance without any human involvement. No one has done it. Even if it could be done, people dislike having their value assessed by machines.[18] And using machines to evaluate performance would still be a result of someone's subjective decision about how performance should be measured.

Objective metrics play an important role in evaluating performance, but the weight given to metrics depends on subjective values of the company. For example, is a salesperson who consistently exceeds their quota but treats colleagues disrespectfully a high-performing salesperson? Some leaders would say yes, and others would say no. Many things companies value about employees are difficult to measure objectively. This includes being collaborative, creative, caring, committed, resilient, and agile. Metrics should influence how companies evaluate employee performance, but how people judge performance will always be based on impressions and observations in addition to mathematical measures. It's a bit like evaluating friendships. There are objective metrics one could use to evaluate friendships such as how quickly friends return your calls or how often they ask you for money. But the actual evaluation relies on subjective beliefs about what makes a good friendship. The same concept applies to rating the performance of employees.

What the most effective rating processes do is create consistency and clarity in how subjective performance evaluations are made. These processes emphasize using talent review conversations instead of complicated scales or formulas to ensure performance ratings are fair, consistent, and job relevant. The talent reviews start with defining observable behaviors, specific goals, and other tangible metrics that should be considered when evaluating performance. They also encourage managers to consider input from multiple sources when evaluating employees (e.g., coworkers, peers, customers, direct reports). And most important of all, they require managers to discuss, explain, and justify their decisions to peers to ensure that how an employee is rated reflects what the employee has actually done and not the idiosyncratic beliefs and perceptions of the person rating them.

Managing Performance Requires Comparing Employees but Does Not Require Ranking Them

A few years ago, I had the opportunity to work with someone who had studied leaders of famous music schools, sports training academies, and other organizations that consistently produced people who achieved "world record" performance in their fields.[vii] The leaders were asked how their organizations consistently produced people who achieved amazing results. Their answers emphasized two key principles. First, they put a tremendous focus on selecting people with the right skills and aptitude. Second, they stressed that managing low performers was as important as time spent on high performers. For example, the head of a music conservatory said the best musicians possess an inner talent that cannot be taught. What these musicians need is to be in an orchestra that pushes them to realize their full potential. An orchestra is only as good as its weakest member, and it was critical every player perform at their best even if they will never be the best. The success of these organizations lay in knowing how to get the highest performance possible out of lower-performing members.

The performance of people is influenced by the performance of those around them. What we believe is impressive, possible, or simply expected at work is defined in part based on what our peers are accomplishing. To use an analogy, imagine you go out for a stroll with a group of people and start walking at your normal pace. Whether you will think your pace is too fast or slow will depend on the pace of the people walking with you. Even if you do not feel competitive pressure to keep up with the fastest person in the group, you are likely to feel some pressure not to fall too far behind the slowest person. People draw energy and ideas from people they work with, and they lose energy and inspiration if they have to work with people that do not share their dedication to doing the best job possible. Creating highly engaging work environments requires managing employees based on their level of performance relative to the group.

Comparing employees against each other can be ego threatening particularly for low-performing employees. When done wrong it can create problems related to unhealthy competition and inequity. But some form of comparison is a fact of life in a world where "not everyone gets a trophy." The solution lies in using methods that manage differences in employee performance without making people feel unfairly judged or ostracized. First, it is critical to distinguish between low performance and counterproductivity. A person with low performance still adds value to an organization. As one manager put it, "Most employees with poor performance are good, just not good enough." A counterproductive person hurts the value of the company. The methods for dealing with counterproductive employees should be very different from those used to manage low-performing employees. Second,

---

[vii] The graduates of many of these programs went on to achieve actual world records in athletic competitions or the artistic equivalent in terms of global achievement awards.

it is important to stress that employee performance levels change over time. In other words, just because an employee didn't "get a trophy" this year does not mean they will not get one next year, and vice versa. It is also important to emphasize rating performance is not about getting rid of or punishing low-performing employees. Most poor performance is not intentional. It is usually a consequence of people not being aware of their level of performance or not understanding how their actions affect others. It can even be a result of being overlooked while all the attention is given to their higher-performing colleagues. Last, even if they wanted to, few companies have the capability or desire to fire lower-performing employees and replace them with better external candidates. These so-called rank and yank performance management techniques are financially ineffective and culturally toxic. The goal of rating performance is not to identify low-performing employees. The goal is to improve the adaptability and success of the organization by improving the performance of employees at all levels.

Rating employee performance can be stressful for employees and managers alike. Nevertheless, it is part of improving employee experience. How a company manages employees at different levels of performance affects the engagement of employees at all levels of performance. This does not mean some employees are better than others. Performance is something we display. It does not define who we are. But differences in performance have meaningful consequences for how people should be managed. It is not fair, effective, or accurate to pretend everyone performs at the same level. Effectively managing differences in employee performance is one of the most difficult aspects of leadership. In recognition of this challenge, a model is provided in the Appendix that can help leaders understand and manage differences in employee performance in a manner that protects people's sense of belonging and psychological safety.

Managing Performance Is About Knowing the Capabilities of the Workforce to Guide Decisions

A company cannot effectively respond to change if its leaders do not know what its employees are capable of doing. The better company leaders understand the existing workforce, the more intelligent their response to change. The best way to learn about employees' capabilities is to talk with them and others who work with them. This should be seen as the primary reason for conducting talent review sessions.[19] Talent review sessions bring leaders, managers, and other stakeholders together to discuss the performance contributions of different employees within a team, department, or group. Talent reviews are far more effective for assessing performance than having managers fill out performance rating forms. Managers often lack insight into how employees affect people outside of their team and may have idiosyncratic biases and assumptions that influence how they rate people. Having managers discuss and justify ratings increases the accuracy of performance evaluations, ensures people are using the same definitions of performance across the company, reduces bias, and provides greater knowledge and sharing of talent across teams and departments. Leaders learn about the impact employees are having on the company, their skills and contributions, their performance compared to their peers, and their potential to move into other roles. The main value of these sessions does not come from rating employees but from talking about how employees are being rated and discussing the implications this has for future employee management and development.

The primary reason for conducting talent reviews is to help managers and leaders build teams that maximize the performance of the organization. An outcome of talent reviews is providing recognition and opportunities to people based on their contributions to the organization. This may be in the form of job assignments, developmental activities, or compensation. Because talent reviews affect employees' careers, employees should be informed when talent reviews are conducted and what information is used to evaluate their performance. This transparency gives employees a sense of fairness and greater control over their careers. Most people can accept not getting the highest performance ratings provided they believe the rating process is fair, that it is based on appropriate criteria; conducted in a consistent, unbiased manner; and communicated in a sensitive and appropriate manner.[20] It is also important that managers communicate the results of talent reviews in a way that encourages employees to ask questions and seek clarification if necessary. When it comes to employee experience, there are few moments that matter more than discussions about employee performance.

A big part of talent reviews involves identifying, rewarding, and supporting high-performing employees. It is equally critical to address concerns of low performance. How a company treats low-performing employees has a major impact on employee experience.[21] Failing to address issues of low performance sends a message that performance does not matter. But addressing low performance in a way that is uncaring, unsupportive, or disrespectful sends a message that people do not matter. Managers should be supported, guided, and held accountable for addressing performance differences. Terrible managers blame the performance of their team on the performance of their direct reports. Lousy managers lose high performers and tolerate low performers. Good managers attract and retain high performers. Great managers turn low performers into high performers and promote high performers to even more impactful roles outside of their group.

There are many ways to conduct talent reviews,[22] but one crucial element is incorporating data about employee goals, interests, accomplishments, and skills. Advances in employee profile and talent management technology have significantly reduced the time needed to prepare and conduct talent reviews. For example, one company that used to spend over 60 hours gathering employee information for talent reviews now completes the task in less than one hour. As a result, they changed from having day-long talent reviews once a year to having much shorter sessions each quarter. They also expanded the use of talent reviews further down into the organization. This more frequent and wider use of talent reviews gives their leaders much greater awareness of the capabilities of people in the workforce.

Compensation and Performance

Money is not the only reason why people work, but it is a major reason why most people work. If you do not believe me, try not paying employees for a month. Furthermore, most employees will worry at some point in their career if they should be getting paid more. The reason people become anxious about pay is not necessarily because they are being paid unfairly, but because they do not understand how their pay is determined.[23] It is very easy to demotivate people through inequitable pay. Companies can avoid many of these negative motivational problems by monitoring pay equity and ensuring employees are not grossly under- or overpaid relative to their peers doing similar work. This is becoming more important as a growing number of public websites provide information to help employees determine if they are getting paid as much as their peers. Social demands for pay equity are also creating pressure on companies to be more transparent about compensation levels.

Pay equity does not mean paying everyone the same amount; it means paying people fairly based on their contributions and skills relative to their peers. Paying people differently is critical to the creation of high-performance company cultures. However, as was succinctly summed up in review of research on compensation practices, "Pay for performance seems capable of producing spectacularly good results. It can likewise produce spectacularly bad results."[24] Given that companies often approach compensation more as a financial activity focused on managing budgets than a motivational activity focused on increasing employee experience, it is not surprising pay methods often fail to motivate employees in a positive manner.[25] Financial constraints limit pay levels, but small variations in pay strategies can significantly improve employee experience at little to no extra cost. Keeping the following four things in mind help with building compensation practices that positively impact employee engagement:

- Pay is a tool to direct employee attention and motivation, including not quitting the organization.
- Employees have a strong reaction when they learn they are paid more or less than their peers.
- The motivational value of pay depends on employees understanding how pay decisions are made, being confident they can influence these decisions, and being comfortable discussing pay decisions they may not agree with.
- It is rare for companies to lower pay levels, but in some situations, this is the best way to optimize employee experience.

Pay Is an Investment, Not Just a Reward

A customer once told me, "We don't pay people for what they have done in the past; we pay them based on what we want them to do in the future." Compensation can motivate employees to do more of certain things and less of others, including not quitting the organization. It does this through two mechanisms. First, it rewards people for past contributions that increases their sense of equity and commitment to the company. Second, it focuses attention on future goals. But these mechanisms only work if employees know how their pay is determined and believe the pay structure is fair, appropriate, and equitable. To maximize the motivational value of pay, it is critical to link pay decisions to strategic objectives employees are expected to support. One method for doing this is to create commission-based pay plans that link financial incentives to the accomplishment of specific actions or goals. This method works well for jobs in which employees are assigned clearly defined sales, service delivery, or manufacturing targets. The problem with commission-based pay plans is they do not work well for jobs in which it is hard to link individual employee performance to specific and easily measurable outcomes.

In many jobs, pay is not used to reward single isolated acts or accomplishments but to demonstrate appreciation for contributions resulting from months or years of work. For these jobs, the easiest method to link pay decisions to strategic objectives is through use of performance evaluations. This is commonly done by giving managers a recommended range for compensation increases based on different performance categories. For example, outstanding performers might be eligible for a 3% to 6% increase and contributing performers are eligible for a 2% to 4% increase. This creates a link between performance and pay but allows leeway for pay to also be influenced by other factors unrelated to performance such as retention risk. Creating a link between pay decisions and employee performance creates a stronger sense of equity because the company is investing more resources in employees who are creating the greatest value for the organization.[viii] It also increases employees' sense of engagement because they understand how compensation decisions are made and how they can influence them.

Some companies have taken the concept of "pay as an investment" even further by approaching compensation more like funding projects than rewarding people. In these companies, managers do not make pay decisions. Pay decisions are made by leadership teams that look at recommendations made by managers along with other factors related to the company's business strategy and internal and external pay equity. Two interesting things happen when leadership teams make compensation decisions instead of individual managers. First, pay decisions reflect a more holistic view of the workforce and the company's long-term strategy. Second, it changes how manager and employees discuss compensation. Managers still have to explain compensation decisions, but it is more like the conversations managers and employees have about obtaining budgets to fund work projects. The manager and employee work together to provide information to the company to justify their request, but neither the manager nor employee makes the decision. As a result, discussions about compensation are less likely to devolve into tense arguments over money between employees and managers.

Pay Differences Often Matter More Than Pay Levels

If you want an employee's attention, tell them you are increasing how much they are paid. If you really want their attention, tell them their coworkers are getting a bigger pay raise than them. Employees have strong reactions to even small differences in pay levels, especially if they do not meet their expectations.[26] There is no such thing as a trivial difference in pay. Any difference will be seen as either motivating and equitable or insulting and unfair.

The term *pay dispersion* describes differences in compensation across employees working in the same job or organization.[27] Zero pay dispersion, which means paying everyone the same, tends to be demotivating. It is particularly demotivating for high-performing employees who are sensitive to being recognized for their contributions to the organization.[28] As pay dispersion increases, assuming pay differences are allocated based on performance, motivation tends to increase. But at some point, this starts to reverse.

[viii] A common misperception is the belief that paying people to do something decreases their enjoyment of the activity. This applies only when paying people to do things that they did not expect to be paid for, for example, paying people to play a game that they had been playing just for fun. People expect to be paid for work.

"Getting a bigger bowl"

Fixed pay
What it is: salary or hourly rates,
merit increases, base pay adjustments,
benefits, stock units
What it says: We value who you are;
we believe you will make positive
contributions in the future.

"Getting treats"

Variable pay
What it is: commissions, bonuses,
spot awards
What it says: We value what you did;
we want you to do these things in the
future.

FIGURE 7.4 Compensation from an employee experience perspective.

If pay dispersion becomes too great it creates feelings of anxiety that hurt performance. It can also create unhealthy competition that undermines people's sense of teamwork and collective commitment. In sum, paying high-performing employees more than low-performing employees is motivating, but not if the differences become too large. The challenge is figuring out the right level of pay dispersion for different types of compensation.

From an employee experience perspective, pay differences can be divided into two basic categories: fixed pay and variable pay. Figure 7.4 illustrates these using an analogy from a dog-loving colleague who is also a compensation expert. Fixed pay involves rewards such as salary or stock awards that are paid out over time. Employees receive this pay as long as they remain with the company regardless of their future performance levels. One-time pay involves commissions, bonuses, and other financial awards that employees receive once based on some sort of triggering event, such as achieving a sales quota or being recognized for a work accomplishment. These two types of pay create different employee experiences. Fixed pay sends a message about how much the company values having the employee in the organization. Variable pay tells employees how much the company appreciates specific things they did in the past or might do in the future. The difference between variable pay and fixed pay can be thought of as the difference between saying "I value what you did" versus "I value who you are." In general, people will accept higher levels of pay dispersion tied to variable pay than fixed pay. This is because variable pay is based on achieving objective targets that someone did or did not achieve. It is easy to link differences in variable pay to specific accomplishments. By contrast, fixed pay is based on a person's perceived value as an employee, which is far more subjective and sensitive.

Using pay to increase engagement requires figuring out how to use fixed and variable pay to motivate employee performance and retention. If pay differences are too large, then employees may become anxious about their future compensation. If differences are too small, then they may feel underappreciated and unmotivated. The first will result in employees quitting due to concerns about income stability, but the second will result in employees quitting due to concerns about income inequity. To make things even more confusing, people differ widely in their tolerance for changes in compensation. Some people like working in high-risk, high-reward environments where pay levels may swing widely from one year to the next based on individual and company performance. Others prefer stable, predictable pay structures where compensation changes very little from one year to the next regardless of individual or company performance. When building pay strategies, it is critical to ask employees what pay structures would be most meaningful to them. One company did this and discovered that employees wanted higher levels of variable pay in exchange for lower levels of fixed pay, which allowed high-performing employees to make more money but actually lowered the total overall cost of compensation.

Even the most optimally designed pay strategy will fail if employees do not understand how their pay is determined. For example, imagine a high-performing employee is given a 2% pay increase. The employee might initially view this change as insulting thinking "that doesn't seem like very much!" However, if the employee is told they received a 2% merit increase when most of their peers received 1.5% and that this difference is based on the relative strength of their contributions, then that .5% difference is likely to have a significant impact on their motivation. The key is that employees must be told that they are receiving a different level of rewards than their peers and be told what they did to earn it. This is a sensitive conversation, and training managers on how to explain compensation significantly increases the motivational value of pay.[29] This includes how to share information comparing an employee's compensation to average pay levels in the company. It does not mean sharing information about the pay levels of specific individuals. Although this is done in some companies, it can create problems related to confidentiality and resentment if not carefully handled.

Pay Processes Should Give Employees a Sense of Appreciation and Empowerment

The motivational value of pay is a result of employees feeling appreciated for past accomplishments and feeling empowered to influence future compensation decisions. This depends on employees seeing a connection between compensation decisions and performance levels.[30] It requires providing employees with a clear explanation of the details about how the company makes pay decisions, including who makes these decisions, when the decisions are made, the data used to guide the decisions, and what checks and balances are in place to ensure the decisions are fair and accurate. Simply understanding how pay levels are determined by itself can increase employee performance.[31]

No matter how well a company designs and communicates its pay processes, employees will inevitably have questions about their compensation. This is particularly likely if they feel they are not being paid appropriately. Part of showing a sense of appreciation to employees is showing sensitivity to these concerns. Employees, at least the kinds of employees you want, do not want to create tension by raising an issue that could be interpreted as being greedy or accusing their company of treating them unfairly. It is easy to do things that will cause employees to shut up rather than share their concerns about pay. Something as simple as a joke by a manager about "everyone wanting more money" could prompt employees to bottle up pay anxiety rather than discuss it. Managers should be trained on how to have conversations about compensation and welcome questions from employees about their pay levels. The alternative is to stay quiet until they find a job somewhere else that pays better. Conversations about pay should also be used to explore concerns that may not be strictly about compensation, for example, feeling undervalued in general. Raising pay may temporarily alleviate the pain of feeling stuck in the wrong job, but it will not fix the issue. And although you do not want people quitting over pay, you probably do not want money to be the only reason they stick around.

Sometimes It Makes Sense to Lower Compensation

In most jobs, compensation is something that stays flat or goes up, but it almost never goes down. However, changes in the business and labor market can create situations when it may make sense to lower pay levels. Employees will naturally be wary of decreases in compensation, but research suggest that employees will accept lower pay levels as fair if they believe the decision is based on valid criteria and is consistently implemented and appropriately communicated.[32] Money is an important part of work but is not the sole reason why people work. People frequently accept lower salaries to move into jobs that better fit their career interests or life prefer-ences. The financial value of an employee's skill sets can also change over time based on job demands. When a company lets someone go as part of a downsizing, they are implying the person's contributions do not justify their cost. But it seems unlikely the person has no value. An alternative is to adjust compensation down, so their contributions justify their pay.

Compensation is one of the largest operational costs in companies and significantly influences employee engagement and retention. But many companies approach compensation more in terms of managing financial costs as opposed to creating better employee experiences, which results in getting a fraction of the ROI pay can generate in terms of higher perfor-mance levels. If you want to gauge the effectiveness of your compensation methods, try asking your employees the following questions:

- Do you understand how the company makes decisions that affect your compensation?
- Do past pay decisions adequately recognize the contributions you make to the company?
- Are you confident you can influence future pay decisions that will affect your life and career?

Of these three questions, the third is the most important. We don't pay people merely to recognize the things they have done in the past. We pay people to positively influence future actions.

Applying These Concepts to the World You Live In

Creating employee engagement would be much easier if everyone per-formed at the same level, if no one felt threatened by performance evaluations, and it made sense to manage high-performing and low-performing people the same way. But none of these things is true. Engaging employees starts by creating cultures that promote feelings of belongingness and psychological safety. This is necessary to sup-port employee development and learning. However, to fully engage employees it is also critical to ensure they feel valued, appreciated, and recognized for their contributions. This requires creating a culture of transparency on how the company defines people's roles, evaluates their contributions, and makes decisions related to pay and staffing. The reason many companies lack transparency is that they do not use clear, consistent, fair, and equitable processes to evaluate employees and make pay and promotion decisions.

One way to improve engagement is to create transparency in how talent management decisions are made. Similarly, one way to ensure pay inequity is to publish and share employee pay levels.[33] Employees appreciate knowing that their career success does not depend on hidden backroom decisions but on honest and constructive discussions about what they have contributed and how they could add more value to the organization. People working for companies that use transparent methods for making performance related decisions do not wonder, "What do I have to do to be successful?" They know when and how they will be evaluated, how to influence these evaluations, and how these evaluations will affect their career. This does not mean creating highly critical or competitive environments in which people are pitted against one another. It just means being honest and open about how the company makes decisions about people.

Terrible employee experiences happen when companies use unfair or insensitive methods to deal with differences in employee performance. Frustrating employee experiences happen when companies pretend that everyone performs at the same level, even when they do not. Engaging employee experiences happen when companies constructively deal with the reality that some employees perform at higher levels than others and then use methods that value the contributions of everyone regardless of performance level. It can take a lot of work to create effective methods for managing performance, but just because something is hard does not mean we can or should avoid doing it. Exploring the following questions can help you think about these concepts in the context of the company or companies you work with.

The Performance Management Dilemma

- What methods does your company use to set job expectations, provide ongoing coaching, and evaluate contributions? How do these methods support one another?
- Imagine a high-potential job candidate asked you this question: "How does the company ensure decisions about pay are equitably based on employee contributions and aren't influenced by arbitrary opinions or political maneuvering?" How would you answer?

Aligning Performance Expectations

- How are goals established in your organization? What methods are used to ensure employees' goals are kept current and reflect changes in the company's strategy or tactics over time?

- Imagine your CEO asked employees across the company the following question: "What are the top three goals in your job, and how do they support my top three goals?" Would employees be able to confidently answer this question? If not, why not?

Increasing Awareness of Performance

- What sort of expectations and training do employees and managers have when it comes to giving and receiving feedback? What is working well currently? What would make things better?
- What tools and resources do employees have available to them to help monitor and develop their performance? How can employees tell if they are meeting expectations in their role?

Managing Differences in Performance

- How does your company identify critical, high-performing employees? What actions are used to ensure high-performing employees feel recognized and appreciated for their contributions?
- What methods are used to manage differences in performance within the organization? How does the company help managers improve the performance of employees who may not be meeting expectations?

Compensation and Performance

- How do you ensure employees in your company understand how pay decisions are made? Are they confident in their ability to influence future pay decisions that affect their careers? If not, what would increase their sense of confidence?
- What steps are taken to create a link between pay decisions and employee contributions? How do you ensure employees feel they are being fairly and appropriately paid?

CHAPTER 8

Increasing Efficiency, Ensuring Compliance and Security, and Building Culture

A Great Place to Work Even When You Aren't Working

The 2020 COVID pandemic devastated the hospitality industry. At one point 75% of hotel rooms were empty and annual revenues dropped by almost 50%.[1] Hotel companies had to radically reduce operating costs to stay solvent, and an obvious way to save money was reducing hotel staff. Most hotel companies furloughed or laid off employees, but one hotel chain focused efforts on protecting the well-being of its employees. The company continued providing health care benefits to employees even though they were not working and created a program to help employees find jobs in the grocery and distribution industries that were growing due to the pandemic. At a time when the company had clear reasons to cut employee programs to save costs, it invested in creating programs to support employees. The company kept its reputation as a great place to work even when its employees were not working, which made it far easier for the hotel to ramp back up when people started traveling again.

Money is sometimes called the lifeblood of organizations. If a for-profit company does not make money, then at some point it will go under or be acquired. Government and nonprofit organizations have to control costs relative to the services they provide, or they may be defunded or restructured. Given the role money has on company survival, every company considers the financial implications of workforce decisions and practices by looking for ways to increase revenue or decrease costs. But as the story at the beginning of the chapter illustrates, money is not the only thing that matters from an employee experience perspective. It is one thing for a company to say it values things beyond money, but another to demonstrate this through action. The hotel company in this story demonstrated that it valued employee well-being by making significant changes to its policies and operations to help employees through the crisis, even though it meant spending money at a time when money was in short supply. One might argue these changes were financially intelligent because it might help the company rehire staff after the crisis subsided. But the company leaders did not know if that would happen. In fact, many employees found and permanently switched to higher-paying jobs in other industries. The main reason the company invested in providing employees with benefits and job transition support was because they believed it was the right thing to do. It was not about reducing costs or increasing revenue. It was about placing a value on employee well-being.

The previous chapters discussed four perennial workforce challenges organizations must address simply to employ people (designing organizations, filling roles, developing capabilities, engaging performance). These actions define *what* a company must do to build and manage its workforce. This chapter discusses three perennial workforce challenges that reflect *how* the company does these things. From a company perspective, these challenges are about increasing efficiency, managing risk, and creating effective cultures. From an employee experience perspective, they are about valuing employees' time, rights and security, well-being, and social communities. Companies do not value these things just by talking about them. Companies value these things by thinking about them in much the same way companies think about money. They influence how decisions are made at every level of the organization. They are important simply because they are valuable, and they are valuable because they are important. There are strong financial benefits associated with saving employees' time, protecting their safety and security, and supporting their communities. Increasing employee efficiency improves workforce productivity; decreasing security breaches or contract violations can save companies millions of dollars; and having more diverse, healthy, and socially responsible cultures is associated with higher levels of company performance.[2] But companies that strongly value these things do not do them solely for monetary reasons. They do them out of a belief it is the right thing to do.

What It Means for an Organization to Value Something

Values reflect the "relative worth, utility, or importance" placed on actions and outcomes.[3] The values of an organization are expressed in three ways: what it says, what it does, and what it rewards. Of these three, the first is the most visible but frequently the least impactful. Truly demonstrating support for values requires tangibly changing what a company does and how it rewards employees. For example, most companies say they value workforce diversity and inclusion. Making a visible commitment to supporting demographically[i] diverse workforces does affect how an organization is perceived by employees and applicants.[4] But saying a company values diversity does not mean its workforce practices support hiring and retention of diverse employees. The challenges of workforce diversity and inclusion are a result of social biases and economic situations that create inequality in the distribution of career opportunities and the judgment of people's value and potential.[5] The only way to create inclusive workforces is to eliminate biases that affect how career opportunities are distributed and how talent decisions are made. Many corporate diversity efforts focus on sharing statistics that highlight the lack of corporate diversity and stress the importance of inclusion but do little to actually change how jobs are designed and staffed or modify how employees are developed, managed, and rewarded. If companies want to create inclusive organizations, they must do more than talk about diversity. They must change the processes that influence job design, staffing and pay decisions, management behavior, and employee development.

Organizations that truly show value for diversity and social responsibility do not treat these things like programs or marketing campaigns. They incorporate these values into ongoing decisions and business operations. In a sense, these values are treated similarly to how companies demonstrate the value they place on money. The role of the chief financial officer in a company is not just to talk about the importance of being financially solvent and track profit and loss. It is also to influence how the company makes business decisions so it achieves its financial targets. All companies value money, but not all companies value it in the same way. Companies differ in how much they emphasize controlling costs and their willingness to invest in ventures to drive future revenue. These financial values influence how

---

[i]The term *demographics* refers to non-job-relevant employee characteristics that are associated with bias and discrimination at work. This includes race, ethnicity, gender and gender identity, age, sexual orientation, health, and disability status.

jobs and organizations are designed and how the workforce is managed and rewarded. The same approach is necessary if companies wish to truly value other nonmonetary outcomes that influence employee experience.

It is unlikely a company would design a compensation process or staff a new business function without input from finance. But many do it without input from people in the company focused on topics related to diversity and corporate social responsibility. This was illustrated in a conversation I had with a chief diversity officer about gender pay equity. When I asked what her company was doing to address the issue, she shared that executives were given a report showing disparity in pay between men and women in different parts of the company. When I asked if the company was making changes to the processes used to set pay levels and award salary increases, she told me that compensation was managed by a different group. The company expressed a commitment to gender pay equity but was not changing the one thing that directly creates pay inequity: the processes that determine pay levels. By contrast, consider this story about a technology company's efforts to increase the neurodiversity of its workforce. Autism spectrum disorder affects about 2% of the adult population.[6] Many people with autism have valuable job skills, but they often struggle with social interactions involved in the hiring processes and onboarding methods used by most companies.[7] A global technology company wanted to tap into this vastly underutilized talent pool. As a person involved in the program told me, the goal was not to employ people because they have autism but to find a way to identify and employ autistic people who possess job skills the company needs. The company created a process for selecting and developing employees that was not biased against people with autism. It replaced job interviews with work simulation exercises and made new employee training compatible with how people with autism prefer to interact with others. The company demonstrated its commitment to diversity by investing in changing its hiring and training programs to remove bias against people with autism. Companies demonstrate their true values based on what they do, not what they talk about.

Increasing Efficiency: Valuing Employees' Time

Many conversations I have with companies focus on topics of user adoption related to getting employees to use systems, complete processes, or take training programs. In one instance a company was getting resistance toward a self-service system that enabled managers to create new job requisitions. Having managers do this task enabled the company to save money by eliminating support staff. The process struck me as cumbersome and nonintuitive, and my initial thought was "Why would anyone want to do this if they didn't have to?" I asked if the company's senior executives used the system. The response was, "No, their time is too important to spend on this sort of administrative task." I then asked in the most respectful way possible, "At what level down the org chart does people's time cease to be important?"

The most precious resource employees give to an organization is their time. How we choose to use our time is literally how we choose to use our lives. At the risk of sounding overly dramatic, when companies do not value employees' time, in a sense they are not valuing employees' lives. Psychologists use the term *illegitimate tasks* to describe work activities that employees view as an unreasonable or improper use of their time given the purpose of their job.[8] This includes performing administrative or routine work that employees feel should not be part of their role or requiring employees to use tools and methods that are overly cumbersome, inefficient, and time-consuming. These tasks create significant stress and frustration for employees because they prevent them from focusing on the core purpose of their work. They also send a message to employees that their time is of less value than other people in the company who do not have to do these tasks. This can create a sense of organizational class hierarchy that negatively affects employee engagement, commitment, and innovation.[9]

Organizations frequently make decisions that save the company money at the cost of employees' time. For example, a hospital decided to save money on facilities staff by limiting waste collection to patient rooms. Doctors and nurses were told they had to remove trash from their workspaces themselves. This decision may have made sense looking at a financial spreadsheet somewhere, but it did not make sense to the highly trained health care professionals who were now expected to spend part of their workday throwing out garbage instead of caring for patients. Issues related to wasting employees' time are common when it comes to use of self-service technology solutions that enable employees to complete administrative tasks instead of having them completed by support professionals. This includes activities such as procuring job materials, completing regulatory paperwork, filing expense reports, posting job openings, and other actions associated with the bureaucratic side of work. Self-service solutions enable companies to save workforce costs by eliminating support services roles. They also provide employees with the ability to perform tasks independently, which can create a greater sense of efficiency and autonomy. However, these advantages are predicated on the assumption that self-service solutions are effective. Sadly, many of these systems are nonintuitive, difficult to access, and time-consuming to use.[10] Forcing employees to use bad self-service solutions is stupid, ineffective, and cruel.

- **Stupid.** The pay rate of line employees is often higher than the pay rate of administrative support staff. Line employees are not employed to do administrative work, nor are they hired based on their administrative skills. Many self-service systems require higher paid line employees to complete non-value-adding tasks that could be done by lower-paid, skilled administrative staff in much less time.

- **Ineffective.** When self-service systems are poorly designed, employees will try to minimize time spent in the solution. This includes leaving out or changing information to make the process faster. For example, a manager might reclassify an employee turnover reason from involuntary to voluntary to avoid going through additional required steps if they instead provided the real reason why an employee left the company. The result is a solution that systematically creates bad data.

- **Cruel.** Self-service solutions often support tasks that employees must complete to move forward with their work (e.g., get a new computer, hire a staff member, complete expenses). Forcing employees to use poorly designed self-service solutions to perform these tasks can create considerable stress and anxiety. Many employees openly admit to having lost their tempers due to bad experiences with self-service technology. Companies are requiring employees to use systems that literally raise their blood pressure.

Technology solutions that employees are required to use should be simple, intuitive, and efficient. The best examples of this kind of technology are found in online consumer platforms where sales depend on creating effective customer experiences. These solutions use mobile access, chatbots, artificially intelligent search engines, and robotic process automation to make it easy for customers to find, purchase, and track the delivery of products. The best solutions also make it easy for end users to talk to a person if the technology is not providing them with the experience they want. A user design expert once told me that technology should not prevent system users from contacting an actual person if they feel they need it. What technology should do is connect them to the right person and maximize the value of the interaction. It is insensitive to design technology solutions that make it hard for employees to get help so a company can save costs on administrative support staff. Access to support staff also affects employee resilience and productivity, particularly in hybrid/remote work environments.[11]

Decisions that affect how employees spend their time should be reviewed as being appropriate and relevant to their role. It is financially inefficient and culturally disrespectful to ask people hired for their specialized skills to spend time on tasks that are unrelated to the purpose of their job. For example, some retail companies have deployment teams assigned to protect the time of store managers and frontline staff. Any corporate action that will affect store employees is reviewed by this team. Actions that are overly distracting or time-consuming are sent back to be further refined and simplified. As a member of one of these teams explained, they wanted store employees focused on selling and delivering products and services to their customers, and so the company was extremely sensitive to any requests that might reduce the time they spent on this core activity. Another way to ensure a company truly appreciates the value of their employees' time is to require executives to use the same self-service solutions they expect other employees to use and make sure they do it using the same level of administrative support other employees receive. I have only encountered two global companies that actually do this. Before a technology solution is rolled out to employees, senior executives have to use it themselves. If the technology is deemed by the executives to be too cumbersome, nonintuitive, or time-consuming then it is sent back to be reworked before it is deployed.

Companies cannot protect employees from the accelerating pace of change they face at work. Nor can they protect employees from the increasing levels of distractions and stress caused by a hyper-digitalized world. But companies can protect employees' time so they can focus on what matters most in their jobs. The more engaged employees are by the purpose of their work, the more frustrated they become when forced to devote time to administrative tasks or use inefficient systems.[12] Burnout is not simply a result of spending too much time working; it also is a result of spending too much time on tasks that are not seen as important to what really matters at work.[13]

Managing Risks: Valuing Employees' Security, Legal Rights, and Safety

People are experiencing increasing anxiety as a result of many things associated with digitalization including economic uncertainty, social unrest, and the modern "always on/always connected" nature of work and life.[14] People do not perform well when they are anxious, and an important element for creating an effective, adaptable company is ensuring employees feel safe and secure in the workplace.[15] This includes trusting that the company is acting in good faith in terms of fulfilling contractual obligations and engaging in legal business practices.[16] This requires managing employee experiences related to security, privacy, compliance, organizational safety climate, and corporate ethics.

The Employee Experience and Security

Employee concerns about security can be divided into physical protection and data protection. Physical security can be a major issue in jobs where robbery and other forms of assault may occur (e.g., retail store employees).

Employees who witness or experience physical threats often suffer from anxiety for years afterwards.[17] Advances in security technology are providing companies with a number of tools to protect the physical security of employees. This includes solutions that enable real-time control over people's access to facilities, active workplace monitoring, and remote intervention in the case of security incidents. These solutions can significantly improve physical security. At the same time, how and why they are being used should be clearly communicated to employees; otherwise, they may be perceived as a way for the company to monitor employees as opposed to protecting them.[18]

Data protection has become a major concern in all jobs due to growing incidents of identity theft and ransomware attacks.[19] Most data security breaches are unintentional results of employees clicking on phishing e-mails or doing online activities that expose company data to outside attacks.[20] Employees are the greatest source of vulnerability when it comes to protecting workplace data.[21] Creating data security is largely about protecting employees from themselves by influencing three aspects of the work environment: ability, awareness, and attitude.

- **Ability** involves making it easy to be secure or, more specifically making it hard to create security risks. This involves what are called *frictionless* security measures that automatically address security vulnerabilities, for example, integrating staffing systems and security systems to ensure employees are automatically given appropriate access to data when they start new job roles and automatically shutting off security clearances when employees transition out of positions.
- **Awareness** is about ensuring employees understand how to avoid security risks. This can be addressed through training and creating a culture that encourages and values secure behavior,[22] for example, employees asking others for appropriate identification before giving them access to secure locations.
- **Attitudes** is about employees feeling a commitment to keeping the organization secure. It involves employees feeling a sense of engagement and ownership toward protecting the welfare of the company, its employees, and its customers. This is achieved by managing employees in a manner that makes them feel respected, cared for, and valued.

One of the consequences digitalization has on employee experience is increased security risk. The same tools that enable worldwide communication and data sharing also facilitate global data theft and misuse. A single security breach, intentional or otherwise, can do lasting damage to thousands of employees and customers. As security becomes even more critical over the coming years, a key part of creating positive employee experiences will be ensuring employees feel secure from harm.

The Employee Experience and Privacy

Privacy has become a major social topic both inside and outside of companies. Many countries have stringent laws that protect and limit the collection and use of employee data.[23] This is creating a unique challenge for companies given the inherent conflict between security and privacy. Security is about controlling access to information and physical spaces through surveillance and prevention. Companies monitor physical and electronic information to ensure the right people have access while keeping the wrong people out. Surveillance and prevention also trigger employee concerns about privacy and freedom. Employees do not like to be constantly monitored and many view privacy as a human right. Employees also do not want their access to data and physical locations to be highly constrained. Access to information is necessary to create agile, collaborative, and innovative organizations, and nothing hurts a person's sense of belongingness quite like a locked door that implies they are not welcome here. Employees want the freedom to access secure systems, data, and locations to get their work done without feeling like they are being constantly monitored. This requires balancing security access, personnel surveillance, and perceptions of privacy.

Companies find themselves in a difficult situation of needing to restrict and track access to data to protect security but not wanting to give employees an experience of feeling unfairly constrained and monitored. Achieving this balance requires giving employees insight into what data are being collected and why this collection is relevant to their work.[24] Employee attitudes toward privacy are influenced by the level of transparency and control they have over how data are being tracked and used.[25] Employees are more accepting of data monitoring when they know what data are being collected, understand why it is relevant to their jobs, and have some ability to access and control how the data are used over time.[26] People do not like the feeling that someone is secretly watching them. Companies can lessen employee concerns over data privacy through explaining how the organization uses data and, if relevant, providing employees with feedback based on the data (e.g., sharing data that provides insight into work patterns or other behaviors that might increase their self-awareness).[27]

The book *The Second Machine Age* noted that "when information was mostly analog the laws of physics created an automatic zone of privacy. In a digital world, privacy requires explicitly designed institutions, incentives laws, technologies, and norms."[28] As security threats increase, the conflict between protecting employee privacy and employee safety will only become more challenging. Addressing this challenge will require actively listening and collaborating with employees to create employee experiences that effectively balance surveillance, security, privacy, and freedom of access.

The Employee Experience and Compliance

The concept of employment is at its core a legal contract between an individual and a company that defines the terms of the work relationship and conveys certain regulatory protections. Compliance is typically thought of as an administrative activity to keep track of details related to actions such as payroll accuracy, job training certifications, and use of equipment. But how a company manages compliance can have a significant influence on employee experience. Even small contract breaches or violations of work rules, whether intentional or not, can significantly undermine employee trust in the organization.[29] It can also create significant financial costs and tarnish a company's employment brand.

The primary technology solutions used to ensure compliance are compensation, payroll and benefits management, contractor management, certification management, and facilities and systems access. The obvious benefits of these solutions are about efficiency. Automating compliance activities reduces paperwork and saves people from having to manually sign up for new systems, enroll in new processes, and request new resources. It also supports data security by ensuring people's data permissions match their roles. Compliance solutions also affect organizational agility and employee engagement. A company's ability to create new organizational structures, add new employees, manage acquisitions, or change pay practices is constrained by compliance solutions. For example, payroll solutions limit the ability of companies to add employees in new countries or regions with different compensation practices and regulations. Compliance solutions also damage employee engagement if they do not work properly, for example, failing to give employees access to the resources needed to do their role or messing up someone's paycheck.

A powerful example demonstrating the strategic value of compliance solutions for shaping employee experience occurred in a consumer products company in spring 2020. This company employed hundreds of salespeople whose pay was based on selling almost a thousand different products. Their monthly income was tied to achieving sales targets using a complex formula of commissions incentivizing different product sales in different regions. COVID's impact on consumer behavior made it impossible for salespeople to realistically achieve these targets, which meant they were going to lose most of their monthly income. The company was also facing significant financial losses, and its survival depended on finding ways to achieve some level of sales revenue. Fortunately, the company was using a compensation management technology solution that made it possible to quickly redesign and implement a new commission plan that reflected the changed economic environment. This provided employees with a way to preserve much of their income by selling against revised and achievable targets. Company leaders commented that without this technology it would have been impossible for the company to adapt its sales compensation structure so quickly, and they would have lost a lot of valuable sales employees when they most needed them.

If you asked someone to list technology solutions based on their impact on employee experience, it might seem unlikely that they would include compliance solutions such as payroll and compensation management. But if that person was an HR leader who has managed a complex global work-force or supported a company going through significant organizational change, then compliance solutions such as payroll and compensation management might be near the top of the list.

The Employee Experience and Organizational Safety Climate

Safety climate describes the shared perceptions employees have toward how safety is managed within the organization.[30] Fostering a strong safety climate can have a major influence on employee experience, particularly in jobs and organizations where there are considerable safety risks. A company's safety climate influences how jobs are designed and how employees are trained and managed. It is also visible in how people act such as employees being mindful to wear safety glasses in certain work areas or reminding each other to hold handrails while on a stairway. Safety climate affects the frequency of accidents and injuries that occur in an organization and influences employee attitudes toward the organization as a whole.[31]

There are right and wrong ways to build a safety climate. The wrong way is to reward employees for not having accidents or injuries, because this can lead to people intentionally hiding safety incidents.[ii] The right way is to focus on designing jobs and work schedules in a way that reduces risk of injury, ensuring employees have proper safety training and equipment, and recognizing and role modeling behaviors that reduce the likelihood of accidents and injuries.[32] This may include using learning and certification management technology to ensure people have the right training and skills to safely perform different jobs, using wearable and biometric technology to monitor employee health statistics, and using experience measurement technology to track employee safety perceptions.

[ii]A safety expert told me an employee once continued to work with a broken leg rather than report it and lose the bonus the company was offering for no accidents on the work-site.

The Employee Experience and Corporate Ethics

An organization's commitment to ethical behavior influences the attitudes of employees and potential job applicants.[33] People, at least ethical ones, want to work for companies that share their commitment to integrity, honesty, and legally and socially appropriate actions. A company's ethical integrity is influenced by a range of factors. It starts with setting clear expectations with employees when they are initially hired. It then requires holding leaders and employees accountable for ethically appropriate behavior. How people act should be as important as what they achieve. The company should also have methods and safeguards so employees can report ethical concerns without fear of retribution.[iii] A common characteristic of ethical companies is the willingness of employees and leaders to openly discuss topics associated with ethical issues.[34] Experience measurement technology can help promote ethical behavior by providing a forum for employees to safely raise ethical concerns and questions. Talent management technology can also be used to ensure ethical behavior is considered when evaluating the performance of employees, particularly those in leadership roles.

Maintaining corporate ethics becomes increasingly difficult as companies grow. The CEO of a large global company told me his biggest concern was that in a company their size someone somewhere was inevitably doing something they should not be doing. He said it was both impossible and improper to try to monitor every employee's behavior around the world, which was why the company placed a lot of emphasis on managing employees in a way that would make unethical behaviors easier to spot.

Building Socially Responsible Cultures: Valuing the Well-being of Employees and Their Communities

The concept of corporate social responsibility refers to organizations supporting the needs and welfare of the communities where they operate.[35] Examples include actions to improve social equity, health and well-being, economic development, and environmental sustainability. People want to work for companies that support their communities and social beliefs. Building socially responsible cultures is associated with higher levels of employee commitment and greater applicant attraction.[36] Socially responsible cultures

---

[iii] I experienced this at a previous company in my career. People had misrepresented the effectiveness of a solution being sold to customers. After privately sharing my concerns with our corporate counsel, I was abruptly moved from a leadership role into a minor position. I soon left the company, which was subsequently sued based on topics related to the concerns I had raised. The company no longer exists.

take a variety of forms. Companies may focus on issues associated with products and services they sell or the customer communities they support. Examples include supporting local businesses, promoting children's sports, or improving parks in local communities. There are also broad socially responsible objectives that are frequently emphasized by companies given their global importance. Four of the most important are creating inclusive and diverse workforces, supporting remote work models, improving employee health and well-being, and building environmentally sustainable work practices. Remote work is not usually viewed as a socially responsible practice but is included because of its impact on employment opportunities, employee well-being, and environmental sustainability.

Creating Inclusive and Diverse Workforces

Companies have been working to create more diverse and inclusive cultures for decades. This work has taught us several things. First, there is financial value in creating fair, equitable, and inclusive organizations.[37] Second, there is no simple fix to create diverse workforces and build inclusive cultures. Despite years of effort, companies still struggle to achieve demographic equity, diversity, and inclusion. Diversity programs are frequently successful but rarely successful enough.[38] Third, two aspects of organizational culture affect workforce diversity and inclusion: meritocracy and multiculturalism.[39] Meritocracy focuses on ensuring equitable, unbiased treatment of employees. Multiculturalism emphasizes acknowledging, respecting, and valuing different groups. Multiculturalism is about how we socially interact, and meritocracy is about how we make decisions. Making a difference in diversity and inclusion requires both.

Meritocracy is about reducing bias in decisions associated with individual characteristics that are irrelevant to work performance, for example, assuming someone is more or less qualified for a job based on their perceived gender or ethnic characteristics associated with their first or last name.[40] The best way to create meritocracy is to build structured processes that base talent decisions on clearly defined, job-relevant criteria. Creating diverse workforces requires reducing bias in decision-making at every step of the employment life cycle starting with job design and continuing through recruiting, selecting, managing, rewarding, developing, and promoting employees (see Figure 8.1). This is because bias at one step can create bias in others. For example, bias in leadership promotion processes will decrease diversity among senior leaders. Lack of diversity of senior leaders will decrease attraction of diverse candidates, which will lead to fewer diverse employees. And fewer diverse employees will ultimately decrease the number of diverse leaders. It is not enough to eliminate bias at one area. Companies must root out bias everywhere that it occurs.

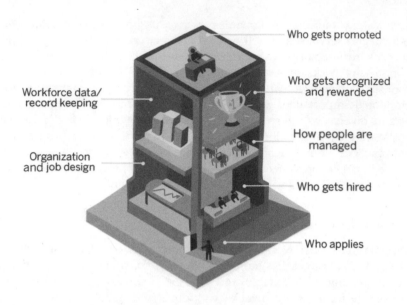

Who gets promoted

Who gets recognized and rewarded

Workforce data/ record keeping

How people are managed

Organization and job design

Who gets hired

Who applies

FIGURE 8.1 Decisions and actions that influence diversity and inclusion.

Multiculturalism is about creating inclusive cultures. The experience of work can be very different for someone with a different demographic and cultural background compared to their colleagues. People who do not belong to the majority demographic group in a company often feel less comfortable and less accepted. Promoting multicultural awareness helps overcome this problem by creating inclusive cultures where differences in backgrounds, values, and behavioral norms are recognized, accepted, and even celebrated. Multiculturalism promotes diversity and inclusion by distinguishing between organizational norms that are critical to supporting the company's strategy and mission versus cultural norms where diversity of thought and expression is expected, encouraged, and welcomed. An example is the shift in attitudes toward the presence of children in the workplace. In the past, many company cultures conveyed an implicit assumption that children should not "interfere" with work—that having childcare responsibilities made a person less productive. This created significant bias against women who tend to have primary childcare responsibility in most societies.[41] In recent years there has been a significant change in this attitude. Companies celebrate and support employees in taking care of their children and communicate that it is possible to be both a highly productive employee and a highly involved parent.

Solving a problem as complex as diversity and inclusion requires both multiculturalism and meritocracy. Technology influences meritocracy by shaping how companies recruit, select, manage, develop, and compensate employees.

It also shapes multiculturalism by influencing how employees communicate and interact with each other. The design and use of technology can help in creating more meritocratic and multicultural organizations. Examples include solutions that help companies find candidates from different demographic backgrounds, reduce bias in the methods companies used to recruit and select candidates, help create a greater sense of belonging by bringing together employees based on common interests, or that automatically identify patterns in staffing or compensation data that suggest the presence of bias.

Supporting Remote Work Models

The 2020 pandemic forced companies to adopt remote work to protect employee health. This shift challenged long-standing assumptions about work including the belief that employees need to be in an office to do a good job. Supporting remote work opens up career opportunities for employees who historically were prevented from working due to family care obligations, physical disabilities, or economic constraints that make traveling to the workplace every day difficult if not impossible.[42] Companies that support remote work can recruit from talent pools less constrained by candidates' geographic location or ability to commute. Companies that discourage remote work will also find it increasingly difficult to attract and retain talent.[43]

Employees' desire for remote work varies based on their home office environment, commute time, job type, manager relationships, and individual personalities. But there are two things all employees want. First, they want flexibility to determine when they need to come to the office given their job, life situation, and personal preferences. Second, they want transparency in how use of remote work will affect their career at the company. Remote work does not mean working from anywhere at any time. Effective remote work cultures clarify when employees are expected to be working and not working. Employees should know when they are expected to be available for meetings and requests but should also feel comfortable turning off their computers and phones and detaching from work. Remote workers usually put in longer hours than in-office employees, and the risk of burnout among remote workers is even higher if companies do not encourage workers to set boundaries and take breaks.[44]

Part of effective remote work involves periodically meeting in person. Remote work is often referred to as hybrid work because it involves a mixture of remote and onsite work. Remote work strategies should define when and why people are expected to get together. There are many reasons for in-person meetings, including new hire onboarding, team and relationship building, and problem-solving sessions that require collaboration over multiple hours or days. At the same time, companies should not require people to be together without having a clear purpose for getting together. Meeting in person comes with a cost in terms of travel and meeting spaces that require money and time from both employees and the organization.

Effective talent management practices are particularly critical to remote work. Remote workers tend to be more productive and engaged than in-office employees when they are well managed, but more stressed when their manager is not effective.[45] Onsite work environments are more forgiving toward poor managerial skills, perhaps because employees can use visual cues to guess what their manager is thinking. By contrast, remote workers need ongoing communication about goals, clarity on how their contributions will be evaluated, and more intentional activities to help them advance their careers. It is also important to ensure remote workers are not punished for having less face time with leaders in an office than in-person workers.

We do not know how the move to remote work will change the future of organizations, cities, labor markets, and societies, but there are things we can be certain of. First, remote work will be much more common. There is no value in returning to a past characterized by unprecedented levels of commuter traffic.[46] Second, companies have an opportunity to rethink the nature of work to create the world we want instead of accepting the world as it was. Technology plays a central role in creating an engaging and inclusive remote world of work, but this is not just about remote work technology. It is also about using technology to support and enhance the value of in-person meetings that bring together typically remote employees.

Improving Employee Health and Well-being

Work is a major source of stress for many employees.[47] This stress damages employee well-being, hurts performance, and increases absenteeism and health care expenses.[48] Stressed out employees are unhealthy employees, and unhealthy employees are not fully productive employees.[49] They also are unhappy employees who are more likely to quit. If companies value the happiness, well-being, and retention of employees, then they need to create healthier work environments. The term *healthy workplace* is often associated with things such as safe work practices, ergonomically correct office furniture, nutritious cafeteria food, and on-site fitness centers. Although these are valuable, they are not the primary factors that affect employee well-being in most jobs. What makes work unhealthy in most jobs are things that cause mental and physical stress:

- Poor quality relationships with managers or coworkers
- Working with customers or coworkers who are upset, angry, or abusive
- Concerns over employment security and access to career opportunities

- Financial worries and work-family conflict
- Working long and/or irregular hours
- Intrusion of work activities (e.g., e-mails and phone calls) into off-work hours
- Lacking clear job goals and role ambiguity
- Performing monotonous and highly repetitive tasks
- Being assigned tasks or goals that seem unattainable given existing resources and time
- Frequent organizational restructuring and job reassignments

Supporting employee well-being starts with designing jobs in a way that lessens the physical and mental stress placed on employees, for example, giving employees regular schedules that promote effective sleep patterns, ensuring they have clear achievable goals, and providing interesting work assignments. Actively listening and working to address employee concerns also decreases stress levels.[50] Companies can also provide employees with self-management technology solutions to help cope with work-related stress in a healthy manner. Examples include solutions that help employees improve sleep hygiene or that guide employees in the use of cognitive behavioral therapy techniques to reduce the impact stressful situations have on well-being. Perhaps most important of all is ensuring managers and leaders in the organization show empathy, sensitivity, and support toward the stresses employees face in their roles.[51]

Building Environmentally Sustainable Work Practices

The impact of climate change and carbon emissions has become a major social concern around the world. As a result, how companies approach environmental sustainability is having a growing impact on their ability to attract and retain talent.[52] Most discussions of sustainability emphasize moving toward more sustainable manufacturing and transportation methods. But employee actions also significantly influence a company's overall environmental impact. Employees are often the main source of carbon emissions in less capital-intensive industries such as technology and professional services. The following are some ways employee behavior affects environmental sustainability:

- **Commuting.** Commuting is a major source of greenhouse gas emission. The recent shift to remote work models presents companies with an opportunity to rethink the use of office space and its impact on commuting. Companies can also provide incentives that encourage employees to commute using mass transit and other more environmentally sustainable methods.

- **Travel.** Business trips, particularly those involving air travel, represent a significant source of carbon emissions. Norms and assumptions about business travel influence whether employees conduct face-to-face meetings or use remote technology. When employees do need to travel, they should be encouraged to use more sustainable options such as trains instead of planes or electric instead of combustion cars.
- **Workplace habits.** Companies can encourage habits and patterns of behavior that decrease energy consumption and waste. This includes actions as simple as turning off lights and computers when not in use or using reusable cups and utensils instead of disposable ones.
- **Purchasing decisions.** Employees can be encouraged to consider the environmental impact of the vendors they employ, whether it is staying at more environmentally conscious hotel chains or procuring supplies from more environmentally sensitive providers.
- **Job locations.** Deciding where to locate offices and plants has a significant impact on the environment. Choosing locations that minimize commuting times, allow for reuse of existing facilities, and decrease use of resources to transport materials and products can reduce a company's overall environmental footprint.

Creating a more environmentally sustainable workforce requires leadership role modeling combined with employee awareness and enablement. For example, the best way to get employees to choose train travel over air travel is to have leaders visibly opt for train tickets instead of plane tickets. Most employees would probably think twice before paying to fly on a jet when their CEO took a more environmentally friendly train for the same trip. Leaders should also track and regularly discuss company sustainability goals and recognize employees for making progress against them. Employees can be educated on ways to be more sustainable and be given data and recognition that call attention to their environmental impact. They can also be given tools to support more environmentally sustainable actions. This can take a variety of forms ranging from putting reusable utensils in the cafeteria to using technology that encourages employees to purchase materials from more environmentally sustainable providers. Changing the culture of a company to encourage sustainable decisions and behaviors is one of the least expensive and most impactful ways to increase environmental sustainability. It does not require redesigning manufacturing systems, retooling processing plants, or shifting supply lines. It just requires changing the employee experience in a way that gets to act differently in the future from how they acted in the past.

Applying These Concepts to the World You Live In

Companies need to be financially sound to survive, and the best employee experiences tend to happen when organizations are achieving their financial targets. However, money is not the only thing of value that drives employee experience. Companies that show they value peoples' time, rights, and communities can more effectively attract, engage, and retain employees. It is one thing to say these values are important but quite another to actually make them a priority when designing jobs, filling roles, developing people, and managing performance. Employees have negative reactions when corporate social responsibility programs come across as false marketing and leadership hypocrisy.[53] Much can be gained when companies sincerely commit themselves to values that go beyond making money, but committing to such lofty goals without meaningful action is a formula for losing employee trust. To quote an old saying, "Don't talk the talk unless you are willing to walk the walk."

Exploring the following questions can help in thinking about the concepts discussed in this chapter within the context of the company or companies you work with.

What It Means for an Organization to Value Something

- Does your company have strategic goals tied to nonmonetary objectives such as employee well-being, workforce diversity, and environmental sustainability? Are any of these goals associated with metrics that are reported to the board?
- In most companies, the chief financial officer is responsible for guiding corporate actions to ensure the company meets its financial goals. Does your company have equivalent roles or functions for leaders focused on non-financial factors that affect employee experience (e.g., chief diversity officer, chief security officer)? If yes, what influence do they have on business decisions, policies, and processes?

Increasing Efficiency: Valuing Employees' Time

- What functions or processes does your company have in place to ensure employees' time is focused on things that matter the most given their roles and objectives? How does it protect employees from having to spend a lot of time on noncritical administrative tasks and activities?

- What activities or processes create the greatest level of frustration among employees in terms of being a "waste of their time"? How could you address these challenges either through process redesign or technology?

Managing Risks: Valuing and Protecting Employees' Legal Rights, Security, and Privacy

- What are the greatest risks to employee security and safety in your company? Are employees aware of these risks? What actions can you take to manage and reduce these risks?
- Imagine your company had to suddenly change the structure of the organization to react to a sudden shift in the market, a divestiture, or a merger. How would the solutions currently used to support compliance topics such as payroll, compensation, security access, or job certifications be affected by this sort of shift? What aspects of these solutions enable the organization to quickly change and which aspect constrain or make change difficult?

Building Socially Responsible Cultures: Valuing the Well-being of Employees and Their Communities.

- How diverse is your company's workforce? Where are you achieving or failing to achieve diversity targets and expectations? What methods does your company use to ensure meritocratic decision-making and promote multicultural work environments?
- How effectively does your company support the use of remote work models? Do you have clear guidelines and norms for the use of remote work? How does the design and use of office space and online communication technology affect the use of remote work in your organization?
- How do you measure the well-being of employees? What are the greatest sources of stress for employees? What programs, solutions, and activities do you have in place that help support employee well-being? What other actions might you take?
- How important is environmental sustainability to your employees? What actions are you taking to create a more environmentally sustainable company? What is the carbon footprint of your organization?

CHAPTER 9

Using Employee Data to Guide Business Decisions

Talent Pipelines and Oil Refineries

An oil company was struggling to achieve production objectives due to work stoppages in its refineries caused by a series of safety incidents. No one had been injured, but each incident resulted in a delay in production. The initial reaction was to increase safety training and reinforce the importance of following safety protocol. But analysis of employee experience data indicated the problems were due to operator error resulting from fatigue. A staff shortage combined with high production targets had resulted in operators working large amounts of overtime. Plant operators wanted to hire more employees, but there was a lack of qualified job candidates. Analysis of labor market data showed a shortage of qualified candidates in the local community. Further analysis of candidate experience data revealed the pay offered by the company was not high enough to draw qualified candidates from other regions of the country. When the company used data to calculate the cost of paying higher wages to attract qualified candidates against the loss in revenue caused by work stoppages in refineries, it became apparent the best way to keep the oil flowing was to invest in building a stronger talent pipeline of qualified candidates.

Many business leaders have a limited appreciation toward the value of employee data. These leaders pay attention to salary costs, attendance, and productivity metrics that directly affect profit and loss, but they glaze over when shown data such as skills inventories, engagement levels, and talent pools. They may ask for help when turnover increases or productivity declines but show little interest in the metrics that predict why employees quit or lose their motivation. This needs to change if companies are to unlock the full value of people to drive business results. Taking advantage of employee data leads to better use of employee capabilities. It also prevents spending money on solutions that do not address actual problems. Imagine if the oil refinery in the previous story had acted on its initial intuition to invest in safety training. Not only would it have been ineffective, but the failure to address the real problem might have made employees more frustrated. They didn't need training; they needed rest and reduced overtime. It could have even led them to quit, further compounding the actual problem, which was a shortage of qualified candidates.

Employees are the most expensive, most important, and most variable factor in business operations. Employees can be extremely productive, but they can also be extremely *counter* productive. The difference depends on the capabilities employees bring to the job and the experiences they have at work. As people become more important to business performance, business leaders need to change their attitude toward the importance and value of employee data. This change might be compared to how business leaders embraced the importance of quality management data in the 1980s and customer service data in 1990s. There was a time when many business leaders paid little attention to quality and customer satisfaction metrics. Now, board meetings regularly include discussion of process improvement and customer satisfaction measures. It is time for business leaders to undergo a similar mindset change toward employee data.

The expanding use of work technology is generating masses of valuable employee data, but relatively little gets used to guide business decisions that have a major impact on the employee experience. This chapter explores why employee data are not used more extensively and provides guidance on how to change this by examining six challenges that often limit the use of employee data to guide business decisions.

- **Understanding the value of employee data.** People will not use data to make decisions if they do not think they need it. One step to increasing the use of employee data is to make leaders aware of what they do not know about their workforce and their employee experience.
- **Having useful employee data.** Companies often lack tools to collect detailed data about the people they employ. Advances in technology are making it easier to collect employee data, but companies must effectively leverage this technology to realize its benefits.
- **Being aware of employee data.** Historically employee data were often locked in files and databases not easily available to business leaders. Fortunately, advances in cloud-based mobile technology are making employee data easier to access.
- **Interpreting employee data.** The value of employee data comes from using it to understand, predict, and influence business-relevant outcomes. Part of making employee data meaningful is helping leaders interpret it in the right context.

- **Managing employee data risks.** Employee data do not always put companies or leaders in the best light. Leaders must be confident that analyzing data will not put the organization at risk.
- **Linking employee data to business results.** Companies employ people to drive business outcomes related to sales, service, and productivity. But data about these outcomes are not contained in the same technology systems used to manage employee data. To truly understand the impact of workforce management decisions and methods, companies need to analyze relationships between employee data and business operations data.

Employee data can fuel more effective business decisions, actions, and conversations about people, but companies need to use the data for this to happen and need to interpret the information in the right way.

Understanding the Value of Employee Data

Expenses related to employee salary, development, and benefits frequently account for 50% or more of a company's operating costs. Given how much people cost, one might expect business leaders to be obsessive about ensuring people-related decisions are as accurate as possible. But they aren't. One can find many examples of smart business leaders making seemingly stupid decisions when it comes to people.[1] Why is this and how can we change it?

There are two basic ways people make decisions: based on data or based on intuition. The advantage of intuition is that it is quick, free, and easy to understand. The disadvantage of intuition is it is frequently biased and inaccurate.[2] Data-based decisions tend to be more accurate and less biased than intuition, but they typically take longer, require some level of cost, and may require using mathematical concepts that are harder to understand. If we want business leaders to invest the time and resources needed to make data-based employee decisions, we must make them aware of what they are losing by over-relying on intuition and underusing employee data, in other words, making leaders aware of how bad their intuitions can be when making decisions about people. Here are just a few examples that show how business leaders' decisions and assumptions about people are often flawed:

- **Staffing decisions.** The decision to hire someone is the most important decision companies make about employees. Every other decision or action is a consequence of this initial decision. Yet intuitive hiring and promotion decisions are influenced by characteristics that have nothing to do with job qualifications, including qualities as trivial as an employee's height.[3]
- **Job performance.** People often think high-performing employees are like average-performing employees but just more effective. From

a mathematical perspective, this can be described as viewing performance as a linear variable. But in many jobs, performance is distributed in a nonlinear, exponential fashion where the highest performing employees may contribute 10 times or more than their peers.[4] Problems arise when leaders assume high-performing employees are just a better version of solid-performing employees. At best, leaders fail to recognize and use the capabilities these individuals bring to the organization. At worst, high performers become frustrated at being constrained by management methods that fail to appreciate their value and they quit.

- **Employee experience.** Leaders' view of what it is like to work in the organization can be very different from those of other employees. Leaders' roles are relatively unique compared to other employees. They receive resources other employees do not get and are treated differently by coworkers and customers because of their status and position. Leaders also tend to be motivated by different facets than many employees. As a result, leaders are often wrong when they try to guess what employees are thinking or feeling based on their personal perceptions and intuition.[5]
- **Organizational decisions.** Many leaders incorrectly assume organizational decisions that make sense from a financial perspective will work out from a people perspective. For example, most acquisitions and restructurings fail to deliver expected financial results, and one of the main reasons they fail is employees affected by the change did not act the way leaders intuitively assumed they would.[6] This is less likely to happen if leaders consider employee data as well as financial data when making organizational decisions.[7]

The more leaders are aware of the dangers of relying solely on intuition to make people decisions, the more open they will be to supporting use of employee data. The role of employee data is not to replace leadership intuition but to augment it. Leaders did not become leaders by making bad decisions. Leaders' intuition about people, although often flawed, can also be highly accurate and insightful. The goal is to find the ideal balance between intuition and data.

Having Useful Employee Data

There is an old joke told in statistics classes about a man standing under a streetlight at night looking for his car keys. A passerby asks, "Where did you drop them?" and he responds, "Over there in the alley." The passerby then asks, "Then why are you looking for them here?" to which the man responds, "Because it is too dark to see in the alley so I'm looking where the light is." The point of this joke is that our ability to solve problems using statistics is limited by the data we have available. This can be a major challenge when it comes to analyzing employee data. Companies often fail to collect meaningful data about employees, and when information is collected it is often stored in inconsistent and inaccessible databases.

Table 9.1 summarizes different types of employee data, why it can be difficult to collect, and technology solutions that can help provide this data. Two particular advances in work in technology are making it much easier to collect employee data. Electronic profile solutions are enabling companies

TABLE 9.1 Using Technology to Collect Employee Data

Data Category	Common Data Collection Challenges	Technology Solutions That Can Help Provide This Data
Workforce Characteristics: data describing workforce characteristics such as job codes, salary and benefits, tenure, demographic characteristics (age, gender), work location, and reporting structures	Data are either never collected or are stored on hard-to-access files and spreadsheets using different databases and structures	Workforce design, compensation, payroll and benefits management, work scheduling, contractor management, certification management, facilities and system access, electronic profiles, role and goal management, interoperable data management
Employee interests and capabilities: data describing individual employee attributes such as skills, qualifications, works styles, and career interests	If collected at all, these data are often stored using unstructured forms such as résumés or placed in difficult-to-access files and stand-alone recruiting and career development systems	Electronic profiles, certification management, recruiting management, talent assessments, learning management
Employee experience and attitude: data measuring aspects of job satisfaction, engagement, inclusion, and confidence	Data are collected through time-intensive annual or periodic surveys and often stored on stand-alone databases	Experience measurement, electronic profiles

(Continued)

TABLE 9.1 *(Continued)*

Data Category	Common Data Collection Challenges	Technology Solutions That Can Help Provide This Data
Subjective performance: data such as ratings of performance or potential, peer ratings and other data about how employees are perceived by people they work with	Data are primarily collected through individual manager performance reviews and tended to be of questionable accuracy; peer feedback data tends not to be captured at all	Talent management, talent assessments, role and goal management
Objective performance: data such as attendance, productivity, sales, customer service, and other performance metrics that do not depend on ratings or subjective evaluations	Data are stored in multiple systems and databases that are difficult to access, lack standardization, or are not easily linked to other types of employee data	Role and goal management, interoperable data platforms
Work environment: data such as job schedules, work relationships, team composition, and work locations that reflect how, when, and where a person is working and whom they are working with	Data are not collected at all or are stored in multiple systems and databases that were difficult to access and lack data standardization	Workforce design, work scheduling, work experience platforms, team management, electronic communication, collaboration spaces, role and goal management, facilities and system access, relationship analysis, wearable and biometrics, interoperable data platforms
Financial outcome: business unit revenue, operating costs, and revenue per employee	Financial and business operations data are stored in systems that are neither linked nor aligned to employee data	Interoperable data platforms

to collect and consolidate a range of personal data about employees in one, easy-to-access system that can be managed to ensure data confidentiality and privacy. Interoperable data management solutions are enabling companies to integrate and analyze data from across a range of technology systems including business operations solutions. As will be discussed later in this chapter, having this ability to link employee data with business data can transform how organizations design and manage their workforce. Another area enhancing the availability of employee data is the growing use of experience measurement and relationship analysis solutions. This is generating data about how candidate and employee attitudes and relationships impact hiring, performance, engagement, retention, and development. Looking forward, we can also expect to see increasing use of wearable and biometric data to understand interactions among employee capabilities, work schedules, job locations, attitudes, well-being, and performance.

As the use of technology grows, the amount of employee data available will only increase. We have already reached a point where the challenge is frequently not about getting data but learning how to manage and use it. The more companies leverage employee data the more business leaders will come to appreciate its value, provided the data are used to address meaningful questions. Revisiting the joke from the start of this section, we are reaching a point when we can shine the data "streetlight" wherever we want, but now we have to know where to look.

Being Aware of Employee Data

People must be able to see data if they are to use it to guide decisions. Historically, employee data were often kept in reports, databases, and systems that were not easily accessible to business leaders. Many leaders did not know the data existed, or if they did, they had to ask someone to run a report that might take several days to return. When the data finally arrived, it might not be presented in an easily interpretable format and may already be out of date. Advances in technology are increasing accessibility and interpretability of employee data, providing functions that pull data from complex reports and present it on dashboards using interactive, easy-to-interpret tables, graphs, and charts. The following are examples of how this technology is increasing visibility and use of employee data.

Displaying Employee Data When Leaders Are Making Decisions

The best time to show leaders employee data is when they are making decisions relevant to that data. Workforce decisions can be broken into two categories: tactical decisions guiding day-to-day operations and strategic decisions guiding the direction of the group or company overall. Technology enables use of data for tactical decisions by embedding data analytics and reports into the systems used to make these decisions. For example, addressing implicit bias is a challenge to making equitable compensation decisions.[8] Unconscious biases lead people to base decisions on employee characteristics such as gender that are not relevant to actual job performance. One way to reduce bias is to embed data about employee performance into tools used for compensation decisions. This focuses leaders on criteria relevant to the decision and decreases the influence of implicit biases. Another example is showing compensation data in a way that highlights potential bias for one group over another, for example, detecting and visibly displaying current and future gender pay gaps to managers that might reflect biased compensation decisions. Making this information visible in the moment when leaders are making decisions helps improve decision quality.

Technology is improving the use of data for strategic workforce decisions through the creation of integrated executive dashboards. For example, one company created an interactive touch screen in their corporate boardroom that displays employee data alongside finance, operations, sales, and marketing data. The data can be organized by business functions, geographic regions, cost centers, or leadership reporting structures. Leaders can drill down to look at data based on specific regions, functions, or departments. Having employee data displayed alongside operational data provides a comprehensive picture of the organization. It also changes the nature of leadership meetings. Historically the agenda for executive-level meetings was often split based on function. Finance would present their data, followed by sales, followed by HR, and so forth. Consolidating all this data into one interactive display supports moving from talking about each function in isolation and toward talking about how the functions can collaborate to address broader business issues. For example, instead of HR leaders talking about turnover, finance leaders talking about revenue, and sales leaders talking about account opportunities, all three leaders can jointly discuss the impact of employee turnover on sales account opportunities and its subsequent impact on revenue. Having the data in one system also accelerates leadership decision-making. When different functions bring their own data reports, inevitably certain data will not align, leading to discussions over whose data are most accurate. Having the data in one system helps reconcile data irregularities so all leaders operate from a single source of truth.

Making Employee Data Readily Accessible When Leaders Are Interested in It

Business leaders who have little inherent interest in employee data can become very interested if the data affect the business operations they oversee. The challenge is how to get employee data in front of leaders at the precise time when it is relevant to their interests. Technology is helping address this challenge as illustrated by a story shared by an HR leader. Shortly after the company implemented a mobile-enabled workforce analytics solution, a sales leader complained about missing revenue targets because salespeople were quitting. When the sales leader commented, "I just lost two reps this quarter. We clearly have a turnover problem," the HR leader showed him turnover data for his region using a reporting tool accessible on their smartphone. After a few minutes looking at the data, the sales leader realized that turnover in their region had actually decreased over the past year and the two reps leaving was an anomaly. The ability to present employee data in real time during the conversation quickly redirected the sales leader's thinking. Imagine how this might have played out if the HR leader had said, "Let me file a request to get a report with turnover data in your region and we can schedule a meeting in two weeks to review it" or even worse if they had no way to access turnover data at all.

Calling Attention to Changes in Employee Data That Affect Leadership Actions

Employee data are useful for calling attention to critical issues such as sudden increases in turnover, shortages of critical staff, or rapid drops in employee engagement. In the past, HR departments would analyze employee data to spot changes and then schedule meetings with leaders to discuss the data. This method is time-consuming, can lead to long presentations going over lots of different data fields, and increases the risk of failing to address changes before they affect business performance. Technology can be used to keep business leaders informed of relevant changes in employee data without overwhelming them with information. These solutions can set triggers that automatically inform managers if employee data reach certain thresholds. For example, a global airline is required to have two certified safety experts on-site in every location, so they built a system that automatically informs regional leaders if there is a risk of falling below that level.

To be useful, business leaders must be able to access employee data at the right time without being overwhelmed by it. Technology can help display the right data at the right time to the right leader. As a result, increasingly the challenge is not about accessing and sharing employee data, it is educating leaders on how to use it.

Interpreting Employee Data

An expert in employee data analytics once told me that limited data in the wrong context are worse than no data at all because it gives people confidence to make bad decisions. This is a risk when sharing employee data with business leaders. Consider the following story. A division of a large company had grown significantly through acquisition but was not achieving its revenue goals. The ratio of workforce costs to revenue was well below the company's profit targets. Company leaders needed to streamline the workforce, so they collected data showing people's job titles, functions, and salaries. Based on this data, the leaders felt they could reduce costs by laying off people in several roles that appeared to be noncritical to business operations. After the layoffs were communicated, the sales team informed these leaders they had fired several people with specialized knowledge critical to winning deals. In an effort to increase profitability the company fired people who were central to driving profit. The decision to get rid of these people made sense based on data the leaders had about job titles and salaries. But what the leaders did not have were data showing how these people actually affected sales performance.

It might look like the leaders in this story made a stupid decision, but these leaders were not stupid people. They were smart people who made a confident decision based on accurate data interpreted the wrong way. What they lacked were the data needed to fully understand the context of their decision and its impact, both positive and negative. A critical part of using employee data is presenting it in a way that leads people to draw appropriate insights and conclusions. This is about providing data in the right context coupled with effective analytical interpretation. To illustrate this concept, consider the following five stories that demonstrate going from ineffective to effective use of employee data.

Interpreting Employee Data Without Any Business Context

A management consulting firm convinced the CEO of a large company that the best way to limit bureaucracy was to ensure every manager had at least five direct reports. The goal was to create a flatter, more agile organization. Department leaders were held accountable for creating organizational structures that met this rule regardless of the nature of their teams. This created problems for leaders who had given high-potential employees teams of two or three people so they could develop managerial skills before assuming roles with larger spans of control. The company looked at reporting structure data and forced the leaders to comply with the "five or more direct reports" rule without considering why they had smaller teams. This lowered the morale of the groups, hindered development of future leaders, and increased turnover of high-potential employees.

Interpreting Employee Data Without Enough Business Context

Hiring freezes are a common method used to control costs. Stopping hiring halts growth in operating costs caused by salary. What leaders implementing hiring freezes do not see is the financial losses they create. It starts with wasting the time spent recruiting skilled candidates, only to tell them they cannot be hired. The best candidates usually have multiple offers, so when a company implements a hiring freeze it is giving many of its top candidates to other companies. In many cases these are direct competitors. Employees are also hired to generate revenue and run efficient operations. When a hiring freeze goes into effect, the financial gains achieved by hiring employees is delayed and potentially lost forever. The problem with hiring freezes is not that they never make sense. The problem is they are often implemented based solely on data showing the costs saved by eliminating new hires, without considering data showing the financial gains that new hires generate. If the logic of using hiring freezes to improve financial performance was totally sound, then companies could become infinitely profitable by getting rid of their entire workforce.

Interpreting Employee Data with the Right Amount of Context

A major challenge for business operations is determining the optimal number of employees to hire to maximize profit and growth without generating excessive workforce costs. This is particularly important in low-margin industries where small differences in operating costs can make the difference between profit and loss. One retail organization made creative use of employee data to determine the optimal number of store managers to hire in a region. Historically the company strove to keep costs low by only hiring a new store manager when an existing store manager left. An HR leader observed that when a store manager left the engagement of employees in the store suffered, turnover increased, and sales declined. Pressure was placed on adjacent store managers to cover the store until a replacement manager was hired, and consequently the performance of adjacent stores suffered as well. He used store sales and turnover data to demonstrate that the cost incurred by waiting to hire store managers until after an existing manager quit was greater than the cost of employing an extra "floating" store manager in each region who could immediately step in and run a store when a manager left. This story illustrates the benefits of looking beyond simple employee data such as staffing and salary and incorporating contextual data that illustrate how people affect business operations.

Interpreting Employee Data with the Right Amount of Context Plus Analytical Insights

Some employee data need no explanation. Business leaders do not need guidance to understand the impact of results such as "high performers are quitting at twice the rate of low performers." As one statistician told me, the best data have interocular significance—its meaning hits you right between the eyes. But not all employee data provide such easy interpretation. This is why there has been rapid growth in the use of machine learning and other non-linear mathematical modeling solutions to draw insights from employee data that might otherwise be overlooked.[9] Analytical methods such as machine learning do not magically turn employee data into meaningful information. The data must meet certain conditions related to data quality and sample size. The information must also be tied to business metrics and presented in the right way. Advanced analytical methods can greatly enhance the value of employee data when these conditions exist. For example, a company wanted to develop staffing assessments to predict sales performance. The company had observed that better salespeople tend to be socially confident (e.g., they initiate conversations) and personable (e.g., they are interested in learning about others). Based on this, the company favored hiring candidates who were socially confident and personable. The company decided to test this assumption using nonlinear mathematical models to determine the relationship between candidate characteristics and sales based on several thousand employees. The analysis confirmed that good salespeople do tend to be socially confident and personable. However, the best salespeople were socially confident but not highly personable. These individuals sold the most because they were task focused. They were not starting conversations with customers just to talk; they were starting conversations to sell products. This insight made total sense to the sales managers once it was called out. But without advanced analytics the company would not have made this realization and modified its hiring profile.

Interpreting Employee Data with the Right Amount of Context Plus Analytical Insights Combined with Expert Interpretation

The highest level of data interpretation combines multiple sources of data, mathematical modeling methods, and the skills, intuition, and knowledge of subject matter experts. Analytical techniques such as machine learning can identify patterns in data that people could never see. However, people can make inferences based on data that no machine learning algorithm could ever consider. This point was made in an analysis of turnover data for a chain of hotels. The turnover in one hotel suddenly increased over a very short amount of time. A range of employee data was examined to explore whether something had changed in terms of how employees were being hired and managed. The analysis failed to provide any clear insights. At this point, the data experts working on the project asked to talk with the hotel staff. One of the hotel managers commented that the local bus company had changed its routes. A bus that used to stop in front of the hotel now stopped a half mile down the street in front of another competing hotel.

The turnover had nothing to do with what the hotel was doing. It was a result of an external change in the commuting time of hotel employees who relied on public transportation to get to work. No amount of advanced data analysis would have led to a simple insight that was immediately obvious to any person familiar with the actual hotel and its employees.

Employee data can provide valuable insights that improve business operations, but data can also mislead leaders into making bad decisions. The key lies not in the data itself, but in ensuring the data are interpreted in the right way at the right time in the right context and remembering that the most insightful interpretations of data tend to combine advanced mathematical analysis with old-fashioned human knowledge and experience.

Managing Employee Data Risks

Employee data often contain sensitive information about employees and organizations. For example, employee data may suggest that a company has a history of inequitable treatment toward certain demographic groups. It may highlight things about employee performance and compensation that can trigger emotional responses and difficult conversations. Or it may cast doubt on the leadership skills of company executives by surfacing issues related to employee trust. Part of using employee data is managing risks related to its sensitive nature. These risks tend to fall into three categories.

- **Data privacy.** Employee data contains information that could be misused if it fell into the wrong hands. Many countries have strict requirements about how and where employee data must be stored, who can access it, and when it must be destroyed. Anyone working with employee data should pay careful attention lest they violate regulations that can result in significant financial penalties and undermine the trust of employees.
- **Cultural concerns.** Increasing the transparency of employee data may reveal organizational characteristics that could create difficult conversations within the company. Foremost is the potential to uncover inequitable trends related to compensation and staffing. Leaders must be educated on how to appropriately respond to data that may suggest unfair employee treatment.
- **Legal exposure.** Employee data may surface patterns that could put the company at legal risk such as evidence of potential discrimination based on gender, age, or ethnicity. When dealing with such data, it is wise to consult corporate counsel and take precautions that minimize the potential of becoming a target of legal actions.

The risks associated with employee data are real, but they are also manageable. This starts by educating the people handling employee data on how to properly protect its confidentiality and security. It continues by controlling who sees employee data and ensuring the information is used only for appropriate purposes. Finally, it is important to educate leaders in the company on how to effectively discuss patterns in the data so they lead to constructive change and avoid destructive criticism. Some companies are so afraid of the risks inherent in employee data that they only use it for minimally required reporting. This fear of exposing sensitive data serves to perpetuate inappropriate practices rather than identifying and addressing them. When it comes to employee data, companies have two choices. One is to hide data in hope that any inconvenient truths will never come to light. The number of corporate scandals occurring in the media suggest this strategy is ultimately bound to fail. The other is to use employee data to better understand the world as it is, problems and all, and leverage the data to develop methods to improve the world for the better. This approach requires more active risk management upfront but leads to more positive outcomes over the long term.

Linking Employee Data to Business Results

The primary reason a company employs people is to deliver business results, but relatively few companies seriously analyze the link between workforce management practices, operating costs, and business outcomes. Even large companies with considerable resources may not be able to determine the financial value associated with investments used to recruit, hire, develop, manage, and pay employees. Consider this story: a compensation director of a large organization told me their company spent over $500 million annually on merit increases and bonuses. When I asked what the return on investment was on those millions of dollars, he replied, "To be honest, the only thing we know for sure is employees don't quit too often and don't complain too much." Imagine how a Chief Financial Officer would react if someone proposed spending millions of dollars per year on a project in which the criteria for success was "People won't quit or complain." But when it comes to investing money in people, that is what companies do every year.

The reason companies rarely look at the impact HR methods have on business results such as market growth, profitability, or customer satisfaction is largely because business results data are not stored in the same systems used to collect and manage employee data. Figure 9.1 illustrates the state of most companies' employee data and business data. Determining the

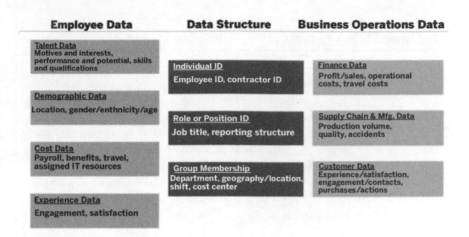

FIGURE 9.1 Relationship of employee data to business operations data.

business value of HR methods requires linking employee data (the left of the figure) to operational data (the right of the figure). The business operations data that leaders care the most about, such as financial performance, operational efficiency, and customer service metrics, are not stored in HR and work technology solutions; they are stored in business operations solutions. Furthermore, business data are often stored using data structures that are different from those used to organize employee data. As a result, it can be challenging to link these different types of data together. The primary problem of linking HR to business operations is not about having data. It is about being able to link the data companies already have. This is why the development of interoperable data management technology is so valuable. It enables companies to link employee data that describe a company's workforce with business operations data that show how the workforce is affecting profit, growth, and other key business outcomes.

Employees must be engaged and not quit if they are to provide value to a company, but companies do not pay employees to be engaged and not quit. The value of a company is not measured based on employee staffing, engagement, and retention levels. Companies pay people because the contributions employees make to the organization's value outweigh the cost of employing them. These contributions typically involve improving profit, growth, efficiency, brand image, and customer satisfaction. These factors are not measured by employee data. The only way to truly measure the business value of employees is to link data about employees to the data that is used to measure company value.

Applying These Concepts to the World You Live In

A common question companies ask about employee data analytics is, "What should we do first?" The answer to this question depends on where the company currently is in terms of analytical expertise, technological resources, and leadership culture. It is much easier to create momentum on the use of employee data if you work in a company that puts a strong emphasis on data and analytics in general. Such companies are more likely to have leaders who are receptive to the use of data, as well as technology and expertise that can collect and analyze data. But regardless of whether your company is analytically oriented, you can still benefit from starting in one of the following ways.

Examine an Existing Business Problem That Can Be Addressed Using Employee Data

This is a way to build credibility for employee data as a tool for business leaders. Begin by looking at strategic objectives the company's business leaders are trying to accomplish. For example, how is the company planning to drive profit and growth over the next year? Then ask the business leaders responsible for these objectives how much they will require hiring new talent, retaining critical talent, or getting people to do things in the future that are different from what they did in the past. Virtually every major strategic objective depends on getting people to do new things. This sort of change always has some impact on employee staffing, retention, engagement, or development. Once you make this connection, you can explore how the use of employee data could inform how the company addresses these changes. For example, companies focused on growth often struggle with finding, developing, and retaining talent to support expanding business operations. Employee data can be used to understand what sort of talent is needed, where to find it, and how to engage and develop it. Conversely, companies focused on cost control may be interested in employee data looking at reducing turnover costs or increasing employee productivity. Every major business operation can be supported by employee data, provided you can collect the data and show links between the data and business outcomes.

Draw Insights from Existing Employee Data

This approach starts by identifying what employee data are readily available, then conducting analyses to find insights in these data that will be interesting to business leaders. Examples include relationships between workforce costs and financial performance, trends in employee turnover or time to hire, or employee development and workforce productivity. If done right, this analysis can enlighten business leaders to the value of including employee data when managing business operations.

Build a Business Case for Collecting Better Employee Data

The most difficult spot to start from is when the organization lacks technology to effectively collect employee data. You cannot analyze data you do not have. Companies in this situation may benefit by calling attention to things they do not know that could be addressed by employee data, for example, asking leaders whether the turnover of high-performing employees is greater than the turnover of average employees, or asking if the money spent on training and compensation is generating positive results in terms of employee engagement, performance, and retention. The goal is to get leaders to appreciate what they do not know now but could know in the future if the company invested in tools to collect better employee data.

Implementing employee data also requires having people who understand how to collect, analyze, and use it to draw meaningful conclusions and recommendations. Many HR organizations employ analytically minded individuals, even though they may not always be in analytically oriented roles. These people may treat the request to work on an analytical project as a development opportunity. Alternatively, it may make sense to partner with other analytically minded functions. Most financial departments employ data analysts of one sort or another. The same is true for many sales operations, marketing, and IT functions. Reach out to these departments and explore whether they might be willing to collaborate to make better use of employee data. A benefit of this approach is it can facilitate linking employee data to operational business data from these other functional areas. A third option is to work with vendors who specialize in employee data analytics. The level of expertise of consultants who specialize in employee data analytics is likely to exceed expertise that might be available within your company. Additionally, external partners have a vested interest to demonstrate the value of employee data to business leaders because this often leads to more work for them.

If your first foray into employee data analytics is successful, then it will be far easier to get resources and support for additional projects. The opposite is true as well. An interesting article called "How to Fail at HR Analytics in 7 Easy Steps" describes several major pitfalls to avoid.[10] A general theme is start small and grow with demand. Another bit of advice on what not to do is even simpler. Do not do nothing at all. Companies who do not embrace the use of employee data will soon fall behind in a world where the success and failure of organizations increasingly depend on the accuracy of decisions made about whom to hire, how to develop them, and how to keep them engaged.

Exploring the following questions can help in thinking about the concepts discussed in this chapter within the context of the company or companies you work with.

Understanding the Value of Employee Data

- What employee-related decisions do business leaders tend to struggle with?
- What workforce decisions are made based more on intuition and assumptions than actual data?

Having Adequate Employee Data

- Ask business leaders, "If you had the ability to know anything you wanted about the company's employees, their potential, interests, and performance, what would it be?" What data could help provide this information?
- How does the company ensure it is making effective staffing, development, and management decisions? How can you tell if the workforce has the capabilities to execute on the company's long-term strategy?

Using Employee Data

- What employee data do operations leaders have access to? How do they use this information? Is it used effectively? What would make it more valuable?
- What employee data are kept hidden from business leaders? What are the reasons for hiding the information? Is there a way this data could be shown to leaders that would help them make more effective decisions?

Understanding Employee Data

- What are the most important business operation metrics in the company? How are these influenced by the capabilities of the workforce? What employee data are likely to predict or influence these metrics?
- List all the employee data currently available in the company. What insights might be gained from analyzing these data? Does it make sense to link this information together or to other business metrics to better understand the capabilities and impact of the workforce on company success?

CHAPTER 10

Changing the Employee Experience

Technology and the 12 Talent Reports

A large insurance company had built a highly structured process to identify, evaluate, and develop leadership talent. Each year a series of steps were conducted to produce 12 detailed reports providing different views of the talent across the company. The reports were works of art from a design perspective, using colors and shapes to convey different relationships among the data. The reports were part of an extensive talent review process culminating in a day-long leadership board session discussing current and future leaders. So, it was no surprise when the HR leadership team reacted negatively to learning that a new HR technology system implemented by the IT department could not replicate the reports. An emergency session with the technology vendor was called to figure out how to retain these critical 12 talent reports.

"We need your system to duplicate these reports before the review process starts next month!", the HR team stated. The vendor replied, "We cannot create these exact reports in such a short time frame without extensive and costly custom development." The company's IT team then said, "We do not have a budget for this; surely there must be a workaround." "No," said the HR team. "The board expects to see these reports just as they are!" The vendor offered a suggestion, "We cannot create the exact reports but perhaps we can create something that still supports how the reports are used to guide talent decisions." The HR team was skeptical but agreed to bring in a few senior business leaders for a conversation.

*The business leaders were asked to talk through their experience
with using each of the 12 reports. What data did they look at, how
did they talk about the information, and what decisions did it influence? To the shock of the HR team, the leaders shared, "We really
only look at three of the reports." When asked about the others, they
said, "We almost never use them." When the HR leaders asked, "Why
didn't you tell us?", they answered, "You never asked and the reports
don't bother us since we just ignore them." When the vendor outlined how the technology could present the data from three reports
they did use into a single dashboard, the leaders answered, "Thanks,
that will be a lot easier." They then thanked the HR and IT teams for
simplifying a complicated process.*

This story illustrates two important points. First, improving employee experience is not just about designing and deploying processes and tools. It
is about understanding how employees use processes and tools. Elegant
processes and impressive technology mean little if employees do not use
them or feel they are difficult and inefficient. Second, the biggest barrier to
change is people. This is not because people cannot change. As discussed
in Chapter 3, people are really good at change. It is because people may
not see the value in change. The talent tectonic forces of digitalization
and demographics are increasing pressure on companies to rethink the
employee experience in their organizations. Technology enables companies
to radically reshape employee experience. But having access to technology
does not guarantee companies will make the changes necessary to effectively adapt to a future that will be different from the past.

Before organizations will use technology to do things differently, leaders in the organization must understand the value of changing what they are
doing now. This requires that the people leading an employee experience
change effort meet four conditions:

- **Knowing where to focus.** Changing what matters most and not being
  distracted by things that are nice but not necessary.
- **Possessing expertise and influence.** Having the knowledge to effectively guide the change process and enough credibility as an expert in
  employee experience so that others listen to their advice.
- **Understanding available technology.** Knowing how to use work
  technology to implement and support the change.
- **Gaining Support and Cooperation.** Getting positive participation
  from leaders, managers, and employees who play a role in supporting,
  creating, and adapting to new forms of employee experience.

Knowing What to Change

Making meaningful improvements to employee experiences can require significant time and resources. It is important to focus on areas that will deliver the greatest positive returns on investment. Three things should be considered when deciding where to focus efforts: the nature of challenges facing the company, the relative impact of employee experience for different jobs, and the current level of employee experience associated with different events.

Focusing Efforts Based on Company Challenges

The following is a list of the perennial workforce challenges discussed in the previous chapters. Every company must address each of these at some level, but the relative importance of the challenges will change in response to external market pressures and internal business needs. Knowing which challenges are most critical to the company's current needs helps focus attention on improving the employee experiences that matter the most right now. One way to focus employee experience strategies is to meet with business leaders and rank order the challenges based on issues currently affecting the business. It is best to start this conversation by reviewing the company's business objectives, and then ask, "Which of these perennial challenges has the biggest impact on our ability to achieve our strategic goals?" Note, a low ranking does not mean a challenge is not important but merely that it is less of an issue for the company relative to the others.

- **Designing organizations.** Defining roles including pay structures and benefits and increasing, reallocating, or decreasing the size and structure of the workforce due to operational realignment, growth, mergers, or other forms of reorganization.
- **Filling jobs and roles.** Hiring, onboarding, and retaining talent (including contractors and internal candidates) to support the organization's growth and operations.
- **Developing capabilities.** Expanding or changing the skills of the workforce through learning, job design, reskilling, upskilling, internal movement, managed succession, and career development.
- **Engaging performance.** Focusing employee energy and supporting productivity and adaptability through job design, goals, coaching, development, learning, recognition, compensation, promotions, and job transfers.
- **Maximizing efficiency.** Reducing the time and money spent on operational workforce activities and processes through use of simpler or more intuitive and automated methods and technology solutions.

- **Ensuring compliance.** Complying with employment regulations related to payroll, time keeping, benefits, safety, data protection, hiring, staffing, training, and other workplace policies, rules, and laws.
- **Building culture.** Working in ways that support specific values and behavior associated with things such as inclusion, well-being, collaboration, customer service, safety, security, quality, global operations, and/or virtual work.

Focusing Efforts Based on Job Impact

All jobs are important, but some jobs have more influence on company performance than others. Pivotal roles are positions in a company that have an outsized impact on company success relative to other jobs.[1] Roles can be pivotal because of criticality, talent scarcity, scope, and performance impact:

- **Criticality.** How would business operations be affected if this role was unfilled? How important is it to engage and retain employees in these roles?
- **Talent scarcity.** How easy is it to hire qualified candidates for this role? How important is creating employee experiences that will attract and retain talent in these roles?
- **Scope.** How many people are employed in this job across the company? How many individuals would be affected by improving the employee experience in this role?
- **Performance impact.** How much difference is there in the value generated by an exceptionally high-performing individual in this role compared to the value generated by a solid performer? How important is it to engage and retain high-performing people in this role?

It often makes sense to initially focus on improving employee experience for pivotal roles and then expand the changes into other positions. For example, line workers are a pivotal role in utility companies given the number of people in these positions, the critical impact they have on operations, and the technical qualifications needed to perform the job. These jobs require working with powerlines, transmission towers, and underground cables with little access to offices or desks. A utility company adopted a philosophy of designing work methods based on improving the experience of its line workers for two reasons. First, making even small improvements in employee experience for these positions has significant benefits for the organization. Second, any method that works for line workers given their challenging work environment is likely to work for employees in the corporate office. One note of caution, if you focus on improving employee experience for specific jobs take care that employees in other less pivotal but still important jobs do not feel treated as second-class citizens.

Focusing Efforts Based on Current Levels of the Employee Experience

Employee experiences tend to create three broad emotional states: 1) *frustration, despair, and resentment* caused by unpleasant or disrespectful experiences that fall well below expectations, 2) *flat affect* caused by experiences that meet basic expectations, and 3) *engagement, enthusiasm, and enjoyment* caused by experiences that are inspiring and exhilarating. Employees do not expect every element of work to create an engaging and exhilarating experience. In fact, such an environment would be exhausting. There are some things at work such as completing expense reports or scheduling meetings where we just want the experience to be smooth and efficient. However, there are some activities in which it is important to create highly engaging experiences, for example, when starting a new job or when talking with a manager about one's role and career.

It would be unrealistic and potentially distracting to create highly engaging employee experiences across every aspect of work. But it is reasonable for employees to expect their company to try to eliminate or at least minimize the number of unpleasant experiences they encounter on the job. People often remember unpleasant experiences more acutely than pleasant ones.[2] Given the outsized impact bad employee experiences have on employee attitudes,[3] one method for focusing efforts to improve employee experience is to ask employees what activities they find frustrating or time-consuming and then address those first. These experiences do not have to become exhilarating, but they should not be annoying. When it comes to employee experience, sometimes good enough is good enough. But if it is not good enough, it is bad.

Expertise and Influence

Managing employee experience requires using a combination of expertise related to employee psychology, work technology, business strategy, and employment regulations to create agile and effective organizations. This is the domain of HR in most organizations, but in many companies HR professionals suffer from a lack of leadership credibility. This reflects a broader issue plaguing the field of HR: HR struggles to get respect as a profession.[4] The lack of respect for HR expertise extends to the most senior levels with a significant number of companies appointing people to the role of chief human resource officer (CHRO) who have no prior HR experience. By contrast, virtually no company appoints people to the CFO or CIO roles without deep financial or IT experience.[5] The practice of hiring CHROs without HR backgrounds appears to be declining, but the fact it happens shows how little some CEOs and corporate boards value the importance of HR knowledge. Why is this and how can it be changed? The answer requires understanding why HR expertise matters and why it is perceived as being unimportant.

Throughout my career I have heard people say things like "I don't care about HR" or "HR is irrelevant." Whenever I hear this, I wonder, "Do you care whether employees execute on your business strategies?" HR is about a lot more than following employment regulations and paying employees on time. It is about creating methods to predict and change human behavior to support business goals. This requires addressing highly complicated problems such as the following:

- Restructuring organizations to account for shifting skill requirements, labor markets, and technologies that are transforming the nature of work.
- Finding ways to attract highly specialized talent from diverse sources around the world.
- Predicting how people will perform in jobs that involve doing things they have never done before.
- Recognizing high-performing employees without making lower-performing employees feel underappreciated.
- Helping people change their behavior and develop skills to meet new business demands.
- Overcoming implicit cultural stereotypes to create inclusive, supportive organizations.
- Finding ways to effectively manage talent while complying with a constantly changing set of complex employment regulations.

Doing these sorts of things in an efficient, effective, and sustainable manner requires a combination of business insight, technological savvy, psychological knowledge, administrative excellence, legal awareness, and change management savoir faire. Many people do not realize how much knowledge goes into creating HR practices that deliver positive employee experiences and support business objectives. Nor do they appreciate what it takes to stay on top of the technological, cultural, and economic forces that constantly reshape the nature of HR. The problem is that HR professionals struggle to communicate their expertise in an effective manner. As a result, many people think HR is simpler than it actually is. HR professionals must be bolder in owning their professional expertise. This is not about overwhelming people with HR theories and minutia. It is about engaging business leaders in a collaborative manner that clearly conveys, "I know a lot more about attracting, developing, motivating, and retaining people than you." This includes constructively educating leaders when their actions indicate a lack of understanding related to creating effective employee experiences.

The reasons we need HR departments are similar to the reasons we need financial departments. If someone asked why companies force leaders to track budgets and money under the guidance of a centralized finance department, people might respond that finance is a specialized area of expertise. It is unrealistic to expect leaders to create effective accounting and budgeting processes on their own. Furthermore, financial resources aren't owned by leaders. They are owned by the company. Leaders are just allowed to use them. As such, the organization needs centralized processes to ensure managers are using financial resources appropriately. These are the same reasons why companies need HR departments. HR is a specialized area of expertise. Most leaders do not fully understand how to effectively hire, evaluate, motivate, and develop employees. Nor do leaders own the talent in their departments. They are just allowed to manage them. At one level, human resources are the same as financial resources: an expensive, highly flexible, powerful resource that is critical to supporting business needs, but also a highly sensitive resource that must be managed appropriately to be effective.

When it is done well, the role of HR involves engaging business leaders to define and implement methods that balance the needs of the company, and the experiences employees want and in many cases demand. Many HR professionals in the past failed to take ownership for this role. Instead of focusing on effective use of people, they focused on tasks associated with meeting employment requirements and regulations. In their defense, before we had modern payroll and compliance technology these things took a lot of work and very bad things happen when they go wrong. But as a result of these past practices, HR is often seen as being more about managing administrative processes and avoiding risks, and less about addressing business needs through creating better employee experiences. This view of HR as an administrative function also permeates the self-identity of many HR professionals. This was illustrated when I worked with a company that was automating its hiring processes. During a project meeting, the CHRO was informed that some HR professionals were worried about losing their jobs as a result of the technology. They wondered what they would do when they no longer had to manually screen candidates, process new hire paperwork, and enroll employees in the payroll system. The CHRO was surprised people were clinging to tasks that she viewed as somewhat mundane parts of HR.[i] In response, she asked how often these HR people had conversations with the employees they supported. She was told that HR talked to employees only when there were problems that needed to be fixed. This led to expanding the project to include changing the role expectations of HR professionals. Going forward, each HR professional was expected to talk to every employee they supported at least once a year about how the company could help them be more successful. These proactive conversations led to a variety of positive changes, including retaining several high-performing employees who were about to leave the organization because of work issues that no one had ever asked them about.

The best way the field of HR can earn respect as a strategic profession is to develop expertise in techniques for creating effective employee experiences and use this expertise to drive demonstrable business results.[6] This requires overcoming perceptions of HR as a profession of administrative experts focused on compliance. When necessary, HR professionals must constructively challenge business leaders to stop managing people based on outdated or misguided beliefs and assumptions. Gaining respect also requires showing how the company can improve business outcomes by shaping and changing employee experiences. It is easy to show the costs associated with employees but difficult to quantify the value they provide. Nevertheless, HR professionals must find ways to demonstrate the financial value of their work if they want to be recognized as being business relevant.

Understanding Available Technology

Early in my career a senior HR practitioner advised that technology should not drive process design. Work processes, he said, should reflect what makes sense for employees and the organization regardless of the features found in work technology systems. After years designing technology-enabled processes and witnessing how internet, mobile, and social technology have changed work, I can confidently state this advice was wrong. In fact, it is not even possible to follow. Designing a work process without considering the technology that will support it is like designing a building without considering what materials will be used to build it. As the fable of the three little pigs tells us, the technology we use to build things—whether it is straw, sticks, bricks, or bytes—has significant long-term consequences on the ultimate

---

[i]Payroll processing is sometimes referred to as the "plumbing of HR." When it fails to work it creates massive employee experience problems, but it is not something most people like to think about every day. As one payroll administer put it, "a good day in payroll is a day when no one talks about it."

outcome of our efforts. Technology places constraints on process design, but technology also enables creating processes that were not previously possible. Consider the inter-relationship between technology and performance management. For years people complained about the ineffectiveness of annual performance appraisals. Given how much people disliked annual reviews, one might ask why these processes were ever created in the first place? Did someone think it was a good idea to design a process that encouraged managers and employees to try to fit a year's worth of assessment, feedback, and development discussion into a single conversation? The reason companies created the traditional annual performance appraisal was probably because it was all they could do given the technology available at the time. Imagine this conversation occurring in the late 20th century:

Business leader: We need a method to communicate job objectives, coach employee performance, and guide decisions related to development and compensation. This method must be applied across thousands of employees located in multiple regions. It cannot take too much time, and the only technology you have to do it is paper and pencils. What process do you recommend?

HR professional: Given these constraints, the best we can do is this annual performance appraisal rating form. Everyone will hate it, but it is all we can do with the technology we have.

It seems unlikely anyone would have created the old annual performance appraisal process if they had access to online, mobile, and social technology. Now that these technologies are readily available, companies are redesigning performance management to emphasize ongoing conversations instead of annual reviews. Similar examples can be found for virtually every aspect of work. Advances in staffing technology have replaced time-intensive, manual, résumé-review processes with automated methods that find and screen candidates using online data collection and scoring algorithms. Advances in online social learning and simulation technology are leading companies to radically modify or totally eliminate costly classroom training courses that many employees viewed as a poor use of time. Advances in mobile technology are reshaping how we communicate to employees, provide feedback, and hold coaching conversations. The question is not whether you will use technology to improve employee experience. The question is which technology will you use and how can you maximize its capabilities to support the needs of your company. We design processes based on what we believe is possible and technology defines what we believe is possible. The more we understand the capabilities of work technology the more effective we become at finding new ways to improve employee experience.

Work technology is a powerful tool for improving employee experience, but like all tools it only works if used in the right way. The best technology applications that help people do things that are difficult or tedious or that enable people to do things in line with our natural preferences. Staffing technology[ii] is a great example of automating tedious and often difficult tasks associated with searching for jobs and sorting through applications. Social learning technology[iii] is an example of technology supporting people's natural preferences. The most natural way for people to learn is through apprenticeship-type learning relationships where novice employees work with more skilled employees. The problem with the apprenticeship approach is it does not scale very well. By contrast, classroom type training courses can be scaled across a large number of people. But there is nothing natural about sitting through classes to learn things. What we want is more knowledgeable people to coach us on what to do so we can do it ourselves. This is what social learning technology enables. A reason staffing and social learning technology have been so successful is they leverage strengths and mitigate weaknesses that are inherent to being human. Once people understand what this technology does, they want to use it. And once they use it, they don't want to go back to the old way of doing things.

The worst technologies force us to do things that feel inefficient or impersonal. You have experienced this feeling if you have ever been stuck on hold pressing numbers on phone routing system when what you want is to talk to an actual person. Automation implemented to save administrative support costs for companies often does it at the expense of employee experience. I refer to this technology as "solutions that raise the blood pressure of thousands of employees at scale." Automation is not efficient if it makes the people who are required to use it feel like they are wasting their time. Technology also becomes problematic when it does things that should be done by people. Despite advances in AI, technology will never be more human than actual humans. Machines cannot care about people's emotional needs or take moral responsibility for decisions that affect people's lives such as

---

[ii]If you want to see an example of staffing technology visit the career site of any Fortune 1000 company and go through the steps involved to find employment opportunities and apply for a job. If you visit several websites, you will soon come to appreciate how technology affects the candidate experience.

[iii]Perhaps the most widely used application of social learning technology are the millions of instructional videos found on YouTube.

eliminating jobs, hiring candidates, or allocating compensation. Technology is a poor substitute for humans when it comes to treating people with compassion, understanding, sensitivity, and empathy. A lot of critical moments that affect employee experience involve these sorts of interactions (e.g., hiring decisions, coaching conversations, providing recognition and support). Technology can and should play a role in supporting these conversations and decisions, but they must be performed by people to be fully effective.

The work technology used to improve the employee experience should also be viewed as something that constantly evolves. Managing work technology is more like tending a garden than building a house. It continuously grows or it decays. Technology either evolves to support the changing needs of the companies and employees it serves, or it becomes outdated and constraining to the very people it is intended to help. As a general rule, any work process designed more than three years ago is out of date simply because there are things that are technologically possible now that were not possible when the process was designed. That does not mean every process needs to be changed every three years, but every process should be critically examined on a regular basis considering recent technological innovations. It helps to have people in the organization who have a strong understanding of work technology and can spot technological innovations that can be used to improve the employee experience in the company. In a hyper digitalized world, technology also becomes a major tool for driving change. Consider the example set by consumer technology. When consumer application providers such as Apple, Google, or Microsoft change their technology they don't put users through a change management program. They simply change the apps and users adapt. Similarly, if work technology is easy to use and performs a function that employees understand and believe is valuable then employees will simply use it. The technology creates the change.

Despite all this technological progress, the perennial workforce challenges companies were facing 50 years ago are the same challenges they face today. Technology has given us the ability to find, hire and collaborate with colleagues on the other side of the world, but managers still struggle to fill positions and employees still complain about managers who do not set clear goals and provide supportive feedback. The technology available to address these perennial challenges is steadily improving, but getting to the next level of employee experience requires asking the right questions about how to use new technology applications. This is not about asking technology-centric questions such as "How can we use work experience platforms or machine learning technologies in our company?" It is about asking employee-centric questions such as "Is there a way to conduct organizational restructurings so they do not negatively affect employee productivity by making better use of work experience platforms?" or "Could we reduce gender inequity in pay practices by leveraging the capabilities of machine learning technology?" Only by asking the right questions will we succeed in building technology-enabled solutions that solve the employee experience challenges that matter the most to companies and the people who work in them.

Gaining Support and Cooperation

One of my favorite cartoons about work shows an executive looking at a downtrodden employee and telling them, "You do have good ideas, but we don't do things in this company just because they happen to be a good idea." This cartoon is funny because many of us can relate to being that employee. The talent tectonic forces of digitization and demographics are creating multiple reasons and many ways for companies to improve the nature of work. But the fact something is possible and valuable to do does not mean companies will do it. Technological advances rarely lead to large-scale innovation in work practices without some sort of triggering event (e.g., most companies did not adopt remote work until it was forced upon them by a pandemic). Efforts to improve employee experiences in companies tend to occur in a somewhat reactive manner in response to external threats. React and respond is one way to change, but it is rarely the most efficient and effective. A better approach is to proactively use technology to improve the employee experience by enlisting cooperation from senior leaders, middle managers, and frontline employees. Each of these groups has a different perspective on change and each plays a different role in transforming employee experience. But what they all have in common is the human tendency to view change more in terms of avoiding risks than realizing opportunities.[7]

Senior Leaders Fear Change Will Waste Resources

The tendency to stick with familiar technology and existing work practices is often strongest among senior leaders.[8] The reluctance of senior leaders to change is related to their seniority. Leading organizations requires complex skills that are acquired through job experience.[9] Because it takes time to gain this experience, most senior leaders have worked for at least 20 years before achieving executive status.[10] The ability to learn new technology stays relatively constant as we age, but what does change are the reasons why people choose to adopt technology.[11] Older workers tend to focus on the value the technology will provide, whereas younger workers are often more interested in the technology itself. Older workers have seen a lot of technological innovation over their careers and are aware that just because something is new does not mean it is valuable. Younger employees have typically been far more immersed in modern technology during their formative years than their older peers. As a result, they are often frustrated when they encounter work practices based on outdated technology.[12] But that does not mean using technology to change existing work practices is always worth the effort. Older employees may have a better sense of what changes are valuable but may not realize what is possible with modern technology. The result is a disconnect where no one fully considers both what is possible and what makes sense. This problem is compounded by the fact that the people with the greatest capacity to drive change in existing work methods are senior leaders. The behavior of senior leaders largely defines the culture of a company. Because leaders set the culture, they tend to be comfortable with "the way we do things." They have little incentive to try new work methods. And there may be no one else in the company positioned to drive them to change. As a result, companies persist in doing things the way they've always been done simply because its leaders have always done it that way.

Convincing senior leaders to invest in improving employee experience requires connecting the change to things they care about. Part of this is showing how improvements in employee experience can positively affect the growth, profitability, and agility of companies. Another approach is linking changes in employee experiences to issues that are personally meaningful to leaders. For example, one factor that has lead companies to invest resources to create more equitable employee experiences for women are concerns senior male executives have for the career experiences of their daughters.[13] A third approach is making leaders more aware of how their employees are experiencing work. Making effective business decisions depend on having accurate information about the workforce. One reason leaders are often accused of being out of touch with workers is because they have little visibility into who works for them. Many leaders cannot even answer this simple question, "How many people are employed in your company, including contractors, and what goals are they focused on achieving?" It is difficult for leaders to inspire the people in their company if they do not have a good sense of who these employees are, how they are feeling, what they are currently doing, and what they are capable of doing in the future. One benefit of improving employee experience methods is enabling leaders to better understand, appreciate, and lead the people who work for them. It is not uncommon for leaders, when shown employee experience data, to respond by saying "I didn't realize people felt this way or understand the impact it was having on our company."

Middle Managers Fear Being Overwhelmed by Change

One of the most critical, challenging, and underrated roles in a company is that of the middle manager. Managers are the link between senior leaders who set strategies and employees who execute them. They are responsible for creating alignment between the goals of the company and the actions of employees. The role of leaders is to define the business results the company expects to achieve. The role of employees is to achieve results. The role of employees is to ensure that the results employees achieve align with the things leaders expect. The job of a manager is fundamentally about two activities: (1) making staffing decisions to build a team capable of executing the company's strategic goals and (2) aligning company business objectives with what employees want to do, can do, and are actually doing. However, few people are employed solely to be managers. Most managers are also expected to perform individual contributor tasks and activities that have nothing to do with managing others. Given the scope of their job responsibilities, managers tend to work longer hours than other employees.[14] They are highly sensitive to any changes that might make it more difficult to perform their work or take time away from core job duties.[15]

Managers play a critical role in improving the employee experience given the influence they have on employees' job expectations, recognition, development, and career growth.[16] However, managers often receive little training on how to do these things well.[17] Managers are frequently criticized and even ridiculed for being ineffective and insensitive at managing people. But it is not the managers who are responsible. It is the companies that put people in manager roles without equipping them with the knowledge and tools they need to be successful, who do not reward managers who create positive employee experiences, and who tolerate ineffective manager behavior instead of addressing and correcting it. The old saying that "employees don't quit companies, they quit managers" is not true. Employees quit companies that employ lousy managers. The majority of managers know they should be actively building their teams and coaching their employees, but many lack the time to do it, are not rewarded for doing it, and do not know how to do it well.

Enlisting manager support to improve the employee experience involves showing how the change will help them be more effective managers. This includes being sensitive to the time pressure managers are under. Avoid presenting the change as a new initiative or program that will take managers away from their ongoing work responsibilities. Instead, present the change as a way to improve things managers are already doing to run their teams. If you really want to get support from managers, show that the change will require less time than what they are already doing. Also make sure they have access to training if they need it and recognize and reward them for doing it. One of the most effective deployments of work technology I have seen started with the CEO standing in front of the company's managers and saying, "This new solution is not asking you to do anything you should not already be doing. We expect managers to regularly talk with employees about their goals, recognize their progress, and proactively help them with challenges. This just makes it easier to have these conversations and reminds us if we forget to do it" He then closed by showing how he was using the system, commenting that "if your CEO can find time to do it then so can you."

Frontline Employees Fear Change Will Make Their Jobs Worse

Most full-time employees devote at least 35% of their waking hours to work, potentially much more if they have long commutes. People literally give over a third of their conscious life to the organization. What employees want from work is to know that this is time well spent. That they are spending their lives doing something meaningful that allows them to achieve their personal and professional goals. Based on the data and experiences I have seen working with thousands of companies over my career, I believe the vast majority of employees want to do a good job. They show up with a desire to do effective work, help others, and achieve their career goals. Yet companies often make it difficult for employees to do these things. Work should be about getting important stuff done. But for many employees, work is about showing up and waiting to be told what to do, trying to track down the people, tools, and resources needed to do it, and then learning that what they were doing didn't matter that much anyway. Employees tend to see changes as either requiring them to spend time on something they do not want to do or taking away resources and freedoms that they value. To get employees excited about improving the employee experience, focus on things that demonstrate that the company values and appreciates their time, skills, and potential. What employees want are things that reduce time spent on repetitive or administrative tasks, help them do their jobs more effectively, build and strengthen their relationships with others, support their career objectives, and enable them to achieve their work and nonwork goals. These things don't just help employees to be successful, they also help companies to be successful.

Applying These Concepts to the World You Live In

Much of the $350 billion global health and wellbeing industry is driven by the fact that people struggle to do things that are good for them.[18] It can be very difficult for people to change even when they know it is in their best interest. Because organizations are groups of people, and people are naturally skeptical toward change, resistance to change tends to get stronger as companies grow in size. The forces of talent tectonics are increasing the value of creating positive employee experiences, and the advances in work technology are making it easier to improve employee experience. But it is the employees in organizations, whether senior leaders, middle managers, frontline employees, or HR professionals, who ultimately create and support the changes that lead to better employee experience. The following questions can help in thinking about the concepts discussed in this chapter within the context of the company or companies you work with.

Knowing Where to Focus

- Review the perennial workforce challenges listed in the "Company Challenges" section of this chapter. Which of these will have the greatest impact on the company's ability to achieve its strategic goals? What things would make the company more successful in addressing these challenges?
- What are the most pivotal roles in your company? How would you rank the perennial workforce challenges in terms of the quality of people's employee experience in these jobs? How could you improve the employee experience in these roles?
- What activities or processes in your company create the greatest level of frustration for employees? What can be done to make these less annoying or time-consuming?

Expertise and Influence

- What are the strengths of the company's HR function in terms of expertise on improving the employee experience? What capabilities or skills does the company need to develop?
- What objectives is HR expected to achieve? How do these affect the profit, growth, and agility of the company? How does the company measure the value of creating effective employee experiences?

Understanding Available Technology

- What is the company's plan or strategy for using technology to increase the employee experience? How is this plan determined and modified over time? Who is responsible for its execution?
- How does the HR function partner with the IT function in the company? Are there people in the company who actively look for developments in technology that the company can use to improve the employee experience?

Support and Cooperation

- What improvements in the employee experience would be most valuable to senior leaders? What changes would best support the company's performance, growth, and key cultural values?
- What improvements in the employee experience would be most valuable to middle managers? How could changes in the employee experience save managers time and/or increase their ability to staff, manage, develop, and engage their teams? What skills do managers need to improve the employee experience? How are they rewarded for creating better employee experiences?
- What improvements in the employee experience would be most interesting to frontline employees? How can the company help employees be more successful in achieving their career goals? What changes would strengthen employees' perception of the company as a great place to work?

CHAPTER 11

The Employee Experience and the External Environment

Manufacturing Cars and Shaping Societies

Henry Ford was one of the most successful business leaders in history. Although some things he said and did would be repugnant to modern social values, his actions reshaped the nature of work and organizations.[1] Ford is often associated with the development of automobile mass-manufacturing technology, but what is less known is that many of his most innovative leadership decisions focused on the employee experience.[i]

Ford is widely remembered for using assembly lines to transform the auto industry. The idea of using assembly lines actually came from Ransom Olds, who created the Oldsmobile. Ford's genius was creating an organization that could use assembly lines to mass-manufacture affordable cars at a global scale. Ford devoted much of his attention and resources to develop a workforce able to sustain new high-volume methods of production. This led to paying workers well above market wages, providing health care and education benefits, supporting employee safety and well-being, building housing and schools close to the factories and plants, and taking other steps to support employees and their families. One could argue that Ford's greatest accomplishment was not developing mass-production technology that made cars. It was building a workforce that could use this technology to create a global manufacturing company at a scale never before seen in history. What is impressive about Henry

---

[i] The term *employee experience* was not actually in use when Ford was alive.

Ford's leadership is not just what he did, but his willingness to chal-
lenge traditions and prevailing assumptions that existed in the early
20th century about the relationship between employees and employ-
ers. Ford's reasons for improving employee experience were far from
altruistic.[2] Nevertheless, many things about work we now take for
granted, including eight-hour workdays, livable wages, and worker
safety programs, can be traced to decisions made by Henry Ford to
improve the employee experience at the Ford Motor Company.

Ford realized his company could not achieve its vision of creating mass-
manufactured, affordable automobiles without increasing the invest-
ment made in its employees. His decision to invest in people was not
just a reaction to external labor market pressures or shifting employee
expectations. He did it because he believed the investment would pay
off in increased employee commitment, performance, and loyalty. He
also did it despite criticism from internal stakeholders and external
business leaders that it would ruin the Ford Company and hurt the
local economy. And what is perhaps most interesting, he did it in part
to change the nature of the entire automotive economy, asserting that
"unless an industry can so manage itself as to keep wages high and
prices low it destroys itself, for otherwise it limits the number of its cus-
tomers. One's own employees ought to be one's own best customers."[3,ii]

This chapter looks at the future of the employee experience by considering how it is affected by broader socioeconomic conditions. Companies do
not work in a vacuum. National and local social services, laws, and infrastructure investments have a massive impact on the availability of talent in the
labor market and the expectations and needs of employees. The experiences
that companies are able to create for their employees are enabled or constrained by the experiences people have outside of work. It can be difficult
to talk about issues such as education, health care, and workforce regulations
without sounding political. But these observations are not about politics. It is
an examination of things in society that directly affect how companies must
manage the employee experience to build successful organizations.

In this chapter—and in this book, generally—I have tried to steer clear of
ideological beliefs, with one exception. I believe work should positively affect
the quality of people's lives. Though one can make economic arguments to

---

[ii] This statement was viewed as controversial when Ford said it in 1926. A century
later many employees still cannot afford to buy the products and services they create. This is perhaps neither good nor bad, but it is interesting to think about when
one considers the relationship of people to their work.

support this view, I hold this belief for moral reasons. Economic arguments are amoral in the sense they can and have been used to justify highly exploitive work arrangements, including slavery, which is the polar opposite of this belief.[4] I believe the ability to pursue happiness is a fundamental right of all humans. Because most people have to work given economic realities, people should be able to find happiness in their work. It is ethically wrong to exploit positions of power to enrich oneself by restricting the ability of others to pursue happiness. Creating high-quality work environments positively influences the lives of employees, their families, their managers, their customers, and society at large. Higher-quality work environments create better world environments.[5] Happiness is not about everyone getting the same level of rewards from work (if you question this, reread Chapter 7). Nor does it come from living a life of leisure free from any responsibility or obligations to others (see Chapter 2). Happiness comes from work that provides a sense of fulfillment, purpose, accomplishment, belonging, respect, and meaning. This is what a good employee experience is all about.

The reason I wrote this book is to help people create higher-quality work environments, recognizing that the only way to create positive and sustainable employee experiences is by creating successful and adaptable companies. Achieving this vision depends on how companies treat employees, but it also depends on the external social and economic environments where companies operate. These environments are shaped by cultural beliefs and government policies that reflect how societies view the nature of employment, what it means to not work, and the support people should receive to find meaningful work and pursue successful careers. The following are four areas where societal values and attributes significantly influence the future of work, the adaptability of organizations, and the quality of the employee experience.

- **Blending learning and working.** Digitalization is accelerating the speed at which existing jobs are automated and new jobs are created. Societies must rethink the concepts of education and working so that people can adapt to a changing economy through lifelong learning.
- **Maximizing labor force potential.** The changes caused by talent tectonics increase the importance of fully leveraging the capabilities of a society's labor force. This involves removing economic barriers that prevent people from working, making it easier to move into new jobs, and allowing people to structure jobs based on their particular needs.
- **Technological accessibility.** In a hyper digitalized world, providing people with safe, efficient, affordable, and reliable access to the internet is critical to the infrastructure of a functioning economy. Having access to the internet is in some ways as important to finding gainful employment and effectively performing work as having access to energy, safe transportation, and clean water.

■ **Corporate social advocacy.** In a world where work and life inter-
twine, companies must play a greater role in supporting communities
and addressing societal issues that employees care about. This creates
a virtuous cycle where companies support communities, communities
support people, and people support companies.

This chapter explores each of these areas, why they matter to the employee
experience, and how social values, resources, and regulations affect them.

Blending Education and Work

Digitalization is predicted to automate as much as 50% of the work currently
performed by people over the next 10 years.[6] Although there is debate
about the accuracy and economic impact of these predictions,[7] what is
certain is much of the work currently done by people will soon be done
by machines. At the same time, technology is predicted to create millions
of new jobs.[8] The skills that people will need to perform these new jobs
are likely to be significantly different from the skills used to perform past
jobs eliminated by automation. This creates a challenge for companies and
societies in general: how can we help people develop the skills to transition
into new jobs and careers throughout the entire course of their lives?

When technology eliminates jobs, it does more than just affect the people
who were performing those jobs; it also increases the anxiety of other people
in the organization about the future of their jobs.[9] It is important to position
automation as a tool for transforming work and not as a method to eliminate
employees. The goal of technology should never be to replace employees simply to replace employees. The goal should be to enable people to focus their
time and energy on the kind of work that humans are good at and enjoy, and
that machines tend to do poorly. Chapter 2 discussed this concept and how
it relates to the employee experience. Companies can support this by finding
ways to bring employees along in the digital transformation through development and training. This was much of the focus of Chapter 6. An important part
of this is giving people confidence that they can acquire the skills needed to
adapt to the changing nature of work. At a certain point, the gap between an
employee's existing skills and the skills they need for their next job becomes
too great to be addressed by their current employer. This is when society can
either help this person transition to their next role or simply let them fend for
themselves as an unemployed person with skills that no longer matter.

Companies provide extensive learning resources, but they are not educational institutions. It is unrealistic to expect companies to provide the
level of training that people will need to make the large-scale career transitions necessary to adapt to the digitalization of work. For example, a
hospital might provide development support so that a medical assistant

can move into a new job as a x-ray technician, but it may be unrealistic for the company to train them to be a medical imaging technician.[10] And it would be extremely unlikely for the company to provide the training necessary to pursue a career building and installing x-ray machines. This is why we have schools, colleges, and universities. There are some skills that are hard to acquire without investing significant amounts of dedicated time and resources solely to the practice of learning.

As digitalization accelerates the pace of job disruption, societies need to rethink the nature of schools, work, and education. The concepts of school and work as they are used today are rooted in social and political changes that took shape in the 1800s. The industrial revolution created a demand for more skilled labor, which led to a rise in public education. From a cynical viewpoint, the purpose of this education was not to better the lives of people. It was to graduate skilled workers to staff factories.[iii] Our society has historically thought about education and work based on a mindset that most of us will go to school to learn for roughly the first 25 years of our lives. We then graduate and work until we retire about 40 years later. This model does not make sense in a rapidly changing, digitalized economy that depends on a workforce committed to lifelong learning. In particular, it implies that learning and working are separate activities, that people are not ready to work until they graduate, and that most students are under the age of 30.

False Assumption 1: Learning and Working Are Distinct

The concept of "graduation" suggests a demarcation between being a student and being an employee. This demarcation may have made sense when educational resources such as books and teachers were physically located in schools, jobs involved repetitive tasks that did not require constantly learning new things, and work was tied to specific geographic locations. In the digitalized world, educational resources can be accessed anywhere at any time, jobs constantly change and require constant learning, a lot of work can be done remotely, and schools can be attended online. In this world, people do not have to choose between learning and working. They can and should do both throughout their entire lives. Every employee can be a student and every student can be an employee.

False Assumption 2: We Finish School Before We Start Working

There is value in certifying that people have mastered job-relevant skills before being allowed to perform different roles. But students do not need to formally

---

[iii] Like most commentaries about history, this is only partially true. Providing public education was also fueled by altruism and the belief that democracies cannot effectively function without an educated citizenry.

graduate from a school to effectively use their skills. In fact, students may be more motivated to learn skills when they can apply them to solve real-world issues. This does not mean we should abolish diplomas or formal education, but students should not wait to graduate before they start exploring how to apply their knowledge and skills. Schools, companies, and societies should collaborate to make working part of the learning process, and vice versa.[11] This includes companies creating job roles that emphasize the learning value of work so that students are not exploited as a cheap source of labor.

False Assumption 3: Most Students Are Young

Today's educational system is largely is built on the premise that most students will be attending school relatively early in their lives, before they have significant social and financial obligations (e.g., raising children, paying home mortgages). Many colleges and universities still refer to people who enroll after the age of about 25 and/or who have family care obligations as "nontraditional" students, even though these people make up the majority of students in many countries.[12] The assumption that most students are young and without significant financial and family care obligations leads to the creation of educational programs that are insensitive to the realities faced by older people who do not fit that profile. As a result, the ability to access education often decreases as we age.

The assumption that most students are young is not just wrong, it is harmful because it encourages designing and funding educational institutions based on an outdated model of work and employee experience. Consider the previous example comparing the skills required of medical assistants, x-ray technicians and x-ray machine manufacturers. Imagine a woman working as a medical assistant had taken advantage of company-sponsored training to build her skills to become an x-ray technician, only to see her job eliminated due to automation of x-ray processing methods as a result of innovations in the medical technology industry (a very real possibility).[13] Now assume that she is a working parent responsible for supporting the housing and care of small children (also a very real possibility).[14] In many societies, it would be extremely difficult for her to enroll in a full-time college program and get the technical skills required to pursue a new career in the growing medical technology industry—the very industry that built the technology that automated her old x-ray technician job. This might have been a viable option when she was younger and had no family care responsibilities and few existing financial obligations. Now, it would work only if she had some way to attend classes instead of working, still pay her rent, and provide care for her children without taking on unhealthy levels of debt. She has the desire to pursue a new career and companies in the growing medical technology industry need more qualified employees. But she has no path to get from where she is now to where she and potential future employers want her to go. This is not a problem that employees or companies can solve on their own, though it negatively affects both parties. It is something that requires changing how education is provided across the broader society.

In a digitalized world, learning and working should be viewed as a single continuum between acquiring knowledge and using knowledge. We focus more on one or the other at different times, but people should think of themselves as both students and employees throughout their lives. By contrast, many societies treat work and learning as mutually exclusive. People are either getting paid to work based on their skills or paying to learn skills so that they can get work. In reality, one of the main benefits people can get from working is learning. Furthermore, if people in a society do not continuously learn new skills, then companies will eventually run out of qualified candidates to hire. This is why companies consider the educational infrastructure of cities when deciding where to open or expand offices and facilities.[15] Companies need skilled people to grow their businesses, people need socially supported education to grow their skills, and societies need successful companies to grow their economies. This should create a virtuous circle among all three parties, but it requires societies to provide resources that ensure people can acquire education at all phases of their lives, regardless of their current economic status or family care obligations.

Maximizing Labor Force Potential

The health and resilience of a society's labor market is improved by increasing workforce involvement, movement, and flexibility. Involvement reflects the participation of members of a society in the workforce. It is affected by barriers such as affordable childcare that prevent capable candidates from securing meaningful employment.[16] Movement reflects the ease with which employees are able to change jobs to support career progression or in response to shifts in the economy. It comes from having a fluid labor market where companies must attract and retain talent based on providing good employee experiences and where employees can change jobs without being constrained by factors that are irrelevant to their capabilities or career interests. Flexibility reflects the ability of employees to collaborate with companies to design jobs that fit their particular interests. It is about removing regulations and other constraints that force people to work in ways that are unrelated to the actual requirements of their work. All of these are heavily influenced by a society's cultural norms, support systems, and employment regulations.

Enabling Involvement

A company's ability to adapt to increasing workforce diversity and growing skill shortages depends on engaging potential employees across the labor force regardless of their demographic background or current economic situation. Chapter 8 discussed ways that companies can create more inclusive and diverse workforces. But many things that prevent people from participating in the labor market are outside the control of organizations. Most countries have regulations that place restrictions on the ability to employ people based on their citizenship or immigration status. These regulations frequently date back to the 20th century and do not reflect the realities of the modern global labor market.[17] Many countries used to have discriminatory policies that specifically denied educational and career opportunities to certain demographic groups. Social policies of extreme discrimination have lasting repercussions that affect employment opportunities available to members of these groups decades after the policies have been abolished.[18] Another factor that limits many people's ability to work is access to family care services. The closure of schools caused by the COVID-19 pandemic illustrated how many families were using the public education system as a form of affordable childcare. When the schools were closed, millions of working parents were forced to quit their jobs so they could care for the families.[19] As skills shortages grow and demographic diversity increases, societies should strive to remove barriers that prevent people with the ability, skills, and desire to work from obtaining meaningful employment. This is not just about giving people jobs; it is also about providing companies with the talent they need to succeed.

Supporting Movement

The combination of growing skills shortages, accelerating rates of change, and more complicated career paths increases the importance of a highly fluid labor market where employees can easily change jobs. This enables companies to effectively compete for talent based on providing desirable career opportunities, gives employee greater career freedom, and encourages employees to proactively leave jobs that are likely to be eliminated due to automation or industry decline. The advent of online staffing has made it much easier for people to find new job opportunities. Employees are always just a few clicks of the mouse away from applying to another job. The move toward remote work is reducing the biggest historical barrier to labor market mobility, which is where an employee lives. The increasing willingness of companies to rehire former employees also makes the decision to change jobs less risky because people can return to their old employer if the change does not work out as planned.[20] However, there are two major barriers in some societies that significantly limit the ability of employees to make career changes: worker protection laws and affordable health care.

Worker protection laws found in many societies trace back to the highly transactional and adversarial nature of employee-employer relationships that existed in the mid-20th century. At that time, many people expected to spend most of their career with a single company. Rather than encouraging movement, these laws were designed to protect employee livelihoods by making it hard for companies to end employment relationships. Although well intended, strict worker protection laws can reduce the willingness of companies to hire people.[21] These regulations focus on protecting the jobs people already have rather than helping people move to new positions. This makes employees reluctant to give up existing protected positions for fear that they will be unable to get another position with similar benefits and protections. The problem is the jobs people have now may not exist in the future. Many existing workers protection laws do not reflect the realities of an increasingly dynamic world of work, and as a result they run the risk of limiting the success of the very workers they are designed to protect.

Having access to health care is a key factor affecting people's overall happiness and quality of life.[22] Some countries, most notably the United States, have laws and economic structures that create strong links between a person's employment status and their access to affordable health care.[23] Companies in these countries may be legally obligated to provide employees with health care insurance or some other method that ensures access to medical services. Making employers responsible for providing health care is a bit like making employers responsible for providing employees with family housing.[iv] It decreases labor mobility and prevents effective transfer of talent within the economy by hindering the ability of companies to hire employees and the ability of employees to change employers. People in many countries might find it odd to base career decisions on access to health care services, but this is a major factor in the job choices of US employees.[24] Unemployment also becomes more devastating as families lose both their income and their health care simultaneously. People can control much of their spending, but health care is a cost that people have little ability to control. If countries want to encourage a highly adaptable labor market, then they should seek to break links that tie access to health care to a person's employment status.[v]

[iv] This was a common practice in the industrial age when "company towns" were extremely common. These towns could have benefits but were also the source of highly exploitive work practices because they gave employers such extensive control over the lives of employees (see *The Company Town: The Industrial Eden's and Satanic Mills That Shaped the American Economy* by Hardy Green).

[v] This raises questions about who should be responsible for ensuring people have access to health care, which is an extremely politicized topic in the US that is well outside the focus of this book.

Supporting labor market movement is critical to building more resilient societies. Providing people with a basic level of economic security during job transitions enables employees to find better quality work and decreases health issues.[25] It also decreases the negative effects that fear of unemployment has on employees and their families.[26] This is good for employees and societies, and it is also good for companies. When employees feel supported in making job transitions, they are more likely to consider career changes. This enables companies to hire employees who might otherwise have remained in a less beneficial job for fear of what they could lose if they left their existing employer. It also increases confidence of existing employees to take risks to advance their careers knowing that losing one's job, although not desirable, is unlikely to devastate the lives of themselves and their families.

Allowing Flexibility

One rarely hears the words *regulation* and *flexible* in the same sentence. Job regulations and laws governing work processes and employee-employer relationships play an important role in societies, but many existing job regulations ignore the growing complexity between people and work. Chapters 4 and 5 discussed how companies are using flexible job design and job sculpting to create roles tailored to meet the unique interests of people. But I have yet to see a job regulation that can be shaped to fit the unique work preferences of individual employees. Job regulations force employees and companies to comply with standard policies regardless of whether they make sense or are even relevant to the job. To be clear, I am not against job regulations! The history of work provides countless examples illustrating why companies should be held accountable for treating employees fairly and creating safe and healthy work environments. The issue is that many existing regulations are based on assumptions that no longer make sense given how much technology has changed work. For example, mobile phones did not exist in 1938 when the United States created the Fair Labor Standards Act to govern how employees are paid for their time.[27] As a result, many companies do not allow employees to access work systems on their smartphones for fear that they will be held in violation of not paying employees for time spent on work-related activities.[28] Employees may want to access company smartphone apps from their homes but are prevented by a regulation that was written at a time when apps did not even exist. Other examples can be found that relate to one-size-fits-all laws applied to contract employment, part-time employment, and even use of e-mail on weekends.[29] Regulations are important to protect employees from exploitive work practices and unsafe work environments but should not prevent employees from creating beneficial work arrangements tailored to fit their unique needs.

Technological Accessibility

Several years ago, I had an opportunity to visit Tanzania. While driving through a small remote village, our guide commented that within the year the village would grow into a small town. When I asked what was driving this growth, he shared "they just ran a power line to this town. That store is the first building in this entire area to have access to reliable energy."[vi] His comment emphasized how much of an impact access to reliable infrastructure has on economic opportunities in a community. Reliable energy, clean water, and safe transportation were critical to the economic growth of communities during the manufacturing age. As we enter an age of work characterized by digitalization, an additional critical element of infrastructure is access to affordable and reliable internet connections.[30]

Almost every work practice and method discussed in this book involves online technology in one way or another. This includes solutions to find jobs, take training courses, collaborate via shared work platforms, or simply send an e-mail to a colleague. People cannot do these things if they cannot access the internet. The availability, bandwidth, and cost of internet access varies widely across societies, with the highest cost and lowest quality typically found in rural and/or poorer areas.[31] People without internet access are prevented from fully participating in the labor market. Companies cannot access talent in these communities because there is no way to connect with them. At the time I wrote this there were over 10 million open online job postings in the US[32] and about 25 million households in the US that did not have internet access.[33] How many people in those 25 million households might be qualified to perform one or more of those 10 million jobs?

Corporate Social Advocacy

Corporate social advocacy refers to companies taking a stance to influence social-political issues.[34] It is beyond the scope of this book to speculate how societies should solve issues as complex as providing access to health care, education, and technology, or rewriting employment regulation, but these issues matter to companies striving to improve the employee experience and create more agile, adaptable workforces. These are often viewed as political topics, but they affect the success, growth, and survival of companies, which is why companies should engage their communities around these broader social issues. Corporate social advocacy goes beyond making

---

[vi] Sub-Saharan Africa has some of the lowest levels of energy access in the world. Fewer than 50% of people have access to reliable energy in many countries (https://www.oecd.org/environment/cc/climate-futures/Achieving-clean-energy-access-Sub-Saharan-Africa.pdf).

pledges on corporate websites and launching internal initiatives to attract and engage talent. It involves companies using their economic power to drive positive change in the societies where they operate. This ranges from supporting local programs focused on education, health, or environmental improvement to exerting pressure on governments to create more equitable and sustainable societies.[35] The importance of corporate social advocacy was memorably explained during a conversation I had with several company leaders discussing social equity in the United States. The leaders noted that social equity is not just about creating better lives for those in the community. It is about creating better lives for employees and customers. Our employees and customers are part of our community. The community is us.

Applying These Concepts to the World You Live In

Creating positive employee experiences goes beyond what happens inside of companies. How employees experience life at work is affected by how they experience life outside of work. Work meetings often start with talk about things happening outside of work. Work and nonwork experiences cannot be balanced like two separate boxes hanging from opposite ends of a pole, as though what we experience outside of the workplace can be kept separate from the experiences we have at work. In reality, work, family, volunteer activities, hobbies, and all our other pursuits sit in one single box called life.[36] Some people prefer to keep them more separated than others, but they always interact. Trying to compartmentalize work from family or societal concerns is like trying to compartmentalize work from health. We can ignore an area for a while, but ultimately work and nonwork experiences interact and influence each other.

Creating great employee experiences at work involves supporting people with having good experiences outside of work. This does not mean meddling in employees' personal affairs, but it does mean being sensitive to nonwork issues that are affecting employees.[37] It also includes corporate social advocacy efforts that improve societies and communities so that employees can experience more fulfilling careers at work. The following questions can help in thinking about the concepts discussed in this chapter within the context of the company or companies you work with.

Blending Learning and Working

- How does or how could your company partner with schools in local communities to support people with developing their careers and adapting to the changing nature of work?

- What jobs in your company are likely to be eliminated, downsized, or radically changed due to automation or changes in the business market over the coming years? What can be done to help employees transition into new types of jobs and careers?

Maximizing Labor Force Potential

- Is your company able to effectively recruit employees across all segments of society? Are there certain demographic groups you struggle to recruit and employ? What makes it difficult to reach these groups and how might you reduce these barriers?
- What barriers lead employees in your industry to cling to existing jobs rather than seek new opportunities? How do these barriers limit your company's ability to attract new talent? What things could be done that would give people more confidence to change employers?
- How do work regulations negatively affect the employee experience in your company? Are there things employees would like to do and that would be safe to do, but that they are unable to do because of regulations? Is there any way to get around these restrictions without risking legal violations?

Technological Accessibility

- Could a person without internet access apply for a job at your company? How would they do it? When is this likely to happen (what sort of job or what work location)? Is there a way to help provide internet access to individuals in the communities where your company operates?
- Not all technology is equally accessible to all people. What steps do you take to ensure that the technology that candidates and employees use can accommodate people with different visual, auditory, or language needs and abilities?

Corporate Social Advocacy

- What are the most important social causes affecting your organization? What are you doing to support the communities and social causes your employees care about?
- Does your company or industry employ people to lobby for government change? Are they addressing issues related to labor market potential, educational opportunity, and technological accessibility that affect employees in your industry?

CHAPTER 12

Where Do We Go from Here?

Shaping the Future of the Employee Experience

We Do Not Want Another Employee Experience Revolution

A man born in the United States in 1870 was statistically likely to live to age 39. In 1970, this had increased to age 70. Many of these 31 additional years of life were due to improved working conditions.[1] Technology that enabled the shift from an agricultural to manufacturing economy vastly improved people's prosperity and well-being, but these gains did not come easily. The benefits of the industrial revolution were not shared equally across all segments of society. Benefits for the upper half of society often came at a cost of suffering for the lower "working classes." Early factories had horrific working conditions frequently likened to the pits of hell where worker injuries and fatalities were treated as an operational expense. This led to massive social unrest as workers demanded better treatment from employers. This unrest fueled class-based revolutions in several nations and resulted in widespread, violent confrontations among workers, employers, and government forces around the globe. It also led to positive developments such as outlawing use of child labor, ensuring workers had safe work environments and living wages, and the right to take time from work without losing their jobs. The nature of the employee experience fundamentally changed for the better over the course of the 20th century.[2] But it is not the kind of violent transition we want to repeat.

About 150 years ago, technology started to fundamentally transform the nature of work, which in turn transformed the nature of organizations and societies. We are in the midst of another such transformation. There are many reasons to believe this transformation will involve far less turmoil than the last one. The industrial revolution replaced complex craft jobs with more simplistic jobs focused on repetitive tasks that emphasized rule following and physical stamina. Because these jobs tended to be easy to learn, workers were easy to replace, and job security could be ensured only through contractual obligations backed by the threat of worker strikes. The current transformation is having the opposite effect. Repetitive jobs are being automated and replaced by jobs that require learning new skills and capabilities. Job security in the digital economy is not so much about what you can do as it is about what you can learn to do. Skilled workers are much harder to replace, which gives them the ability to demand better employee experiences. But jobs requiring their skills may still be eliminated due to advances in technology. What is certain is the nature of work will change over the coming years. What is yet to be determined is what work will look like for the majority of employees.

This last chapter does not talk about what the future of employee experience should look like because we know what it should look like. It should look like what a good employee experience looks like now: people collaborating and supporting one another in a healthy work environment doing meaningful things that matter to them. This last chapter is a more philosophical discussion about what it will take for us to share this future across all employees and not just a lucky few. When I was in graduate school, I kept a workers' rights poster from the early 20th century on my office wall. It showed an oil-covered worker laboring in a dimly lit factory under a massive, bone-crushing machine. The face of the worker had been replaced by a clock, and the bottom of the poster read "Work: a prison of measured time." That poster reminded me that I never wanted a job where my value was based more on my time instead of what I contributed. It shouldn't matter where I sit or how long I sit there, what should matter is what I get done. Second, it made me sensitive to how technology can be used to create inhuman work environments where people feel more trapped than enabled. The time clock is a great example. Companies need some way to measure the contributions of their employees. In an agrarian economy, this was based on what people produced. A worker was paid based on the fruits of their labor, often literally. But in the industrial age, development of technology resulted in work becoming divided into specific tasks. Workers became separated from the end products of their labor, so companies developed technology to track time as a proxy for contributions. The result was that work became more about "punching the clock" than achieving something meaningful. There are many jobs where it does make sense to pay people based on their time, but employees should not have to spend their large portions of their life stuck in a job doing something that is meaningless and unfulfilling just to get paid.

When technology vendors talk about the digitalization of work, they tend to focus on the benefits that come from work experience platforms, opportunity matching systems, collaboration spaces, virtual reality, and other technological innovations. Labor market economists often take a more dismal view, viewing technology as a tool for maximizing profits by reducing employee costs through automation or outsourcing jobs to countries with lower wages and standards of living. Depending on whom you talk to, contract management technology is either fueling the gig economy or creating the disposable worker economy, and chatbots are either artificially intelligent digital assistants that improve user experience or impersonal robots that replace people with machines. In my view, technology is neither good nor bad. What matters is how we choose to use it. Consider these two visions of the future of work:

- **The utopian future of work.** Imagine a world where there are no interviews, job applications, org charts, or paperwork. A world where work is efficient, engaging, and enjoyable. People can work when they want and where they want and engage colleagues around the world in ways that work best for them, whether it is video chats, in-person meetings, or virtual reality meetups. Finding a job is not about recruitment and selection but about matching interests to opportunities. Companies are not about reporting structures and contracts but about communities of people collaborating to achieve shared goals. In this world, layoffs and retirement no longer exist, having been replaced with ongoing career transitions and lifelong learning. People have a sense of stability and employment security because they are given resources that enable them to constantly develop new skills for the next generation of jobs.
- **The dystopian future of work.** Imagine a world where the labor market has split into two categories: highly skilled and everyone else. The highly skilled is composed of people who have mastered the art of lifelong learning. There is a constant shortage of these workers, which allows them to craft jobs so that they can do them when, how, and where they want, at a high level of pay. These professionals enjoy benefits associated with being in demand, but they work incessantly under the constant stress of knowing that their current skills may soon become irrelevant due to relentless technological innovation. The other labor market is composed of workers whose skills were rendered obsolete by technological advances. The supply of these workers greatly exceeds the number of jobs they are qualified to perform, so unemployment is rampant. Their world is a never-ending competition for low-paying semiskilled work. If they find a job, they know it is just a matter of time before it is eliminated with the next generation of cost-saving

automation technology. These workers long to be part of the highly skilled workforce, but family responsibilities and economic constraints prevent them from getting the education needed to enter the highly skilled labor market.

Technology is creating both the utopian and dystopian worlds. On the utopian side, companies are using technology to match people to work opportunities regardless of where they live or who they know, enabling people to structure jobs to fit their interests and lifestyles, and proactively identifying and training people on future skills they will need before they need them. We are also seeing the dystopian world emerge as evidenced by growing wage gaps and chronically unemployed and underemployed workers. What we do not know is which world is going to dominate our future. The future we get will depend on choices companies make about how to use technology to reshape employee experience and how societies choose to adapt to a much different world of work.

To create a more utopian future, we must invest in technology to maximize human potential and not just reduce workforce costs. Technology will always eliminate certain types of jobs and create new ones. It can also help workers transition to new types of work. Reductions in workforce costs gained by automating work tasks should be reinvested to help employees develop skills for the next generation of jobs. Societies must also update work regulations and social programs to reflect the changing nature of work. We cannot effectively transition to the future without letting go of the past. Technology has the potential to create a future in which people no longer worry about having to "work for a living" and instead focus on living a fulfilling, purposeful life that includes work. But as history shows, technology can also create horrific working conditions and punishing labor markets. Technology is going to change the world of work, that is certain. Whether technology leads to a future of work that is more utopian than dystopian depends entirely on how we choose to use it. Let us choose wisely.

One final thought about managing employee experience and the future of work. Many words used to talk about work depersonalize what it really is. Terms such as *human capital, surplus labor, headcount costs, applicant tracking, talent acquisition,* and *job shortages* give the impression that workforce management is some sort of supply chain activity involving commodities instead of people. At its most basic form, work is someone giving their life in the form of time and attention to a company, and a company is at its core when a group of people collaborating to accomplish something they could not do on their own. Those of us who are privileged with the opportunity to shape the nature of work have a responsibility to our fellow humans to give them the best employee experiences possible. Employee experience is life experience.

Applying These Concepts to the World You Live In

I regularly get asked what it is that companies that excel at managing employee experience and creating agile workforces do differently. The answer is they view things through a different mindset and often consider what others may overlook. Building organizations that will thrive in the future of work is not about knowing the best practices for improving the employee experience. It is about asking the right questions to create the best employee experiences for your company and embracing the use of technology to make it happen.

This book closes by revisiting the seven perennial workforce challenges first listed in Chapter 1: designing organizations, filling roles, developing capabilities, engaging performance, maximizing efficiency, ensuring compliance, and building culture. These challenges always exist and are never truly resolved. The term *perennial* was chosen to describe them because it is used by gardeners to describe plants that survive over multiple growing seasons. Perennials must be nurtured and shaped each year, or they become unhealthy or grow out of control. A perennial is pruned every spring, but each spring it might need a different type of pruning. Managing a workforce is somewhat like cultivating a garden of perennials. Technology changes how we address workforce challenges, but they are never fully solved because the nature of these challenges changes over time. The faster the world changes, the more quickly past solutions to these challenges grow out of date, and the more critical it is to revisit them on a regular basis. For example, it will always be important to have the right organizational design. But what defines the right design can change quickly based on changes in business markets, operating strategies, or workforce membership.

There is no one best way to address the seven perennial challenges; there is only what is best given the current situation and available technology. I have found that the companies that excel at managing these challenges tend to be the ones who never feel they are good enough. They constantly ask, how could we do this better, what do we need to improve, and how could technology enable us to do this differently from how it was done in the past? Listed next are questions related to each of these perennial challenges that company leaders should discuss at least once a year, keeping in mind that the best solutions to workforce challenges are usually ones that companies help to create for themselves.

Designing Organizations (Defining Roles and Reallocating, Incorporating, or Exiting Existing Talent Due to Growth, Mergers, Reorganizations, and Other Organizational Changes)

- How do we ensure our workforce is staffed at the right level? Is our company making effective use of contract labor and/or virtual workforces? Have we designed jobs that people actually want to do? Is the structure of our jobs and compensation levels aligned to the realities of the labor market?
- Does the design of our company reflect and support how people actually collaborate with each other? What can we do to replace traditional "command-and-control" hierarchical organizational structures with flatter, more agile, relationship-based team structures?
- Are we maximizing the return on investment we get from money spent to hire, pay, reward, develop, and retain people? What workforce investments will generate the greatest return in terms of workforce productivity, creativity, and adaptability?

Filling Jobs and Roles (Hiring, Onboarding, and Retaining Talent [Including Contractors and Internal Candidates] to Support the Organization's Growth and Operations)

- Is the company positioned to quickly scale the workforce in response to changing business needs, acquisitions, or market expansions? Do we have ways to quickly transition people internally based on shifting business requirements?
- Are we able to attract and hire employees quickly and efficiently? Are we making workforce decisions in a way that will create the kinds of leaders and skilled employees we need for the future? Are we effectively hiring qualified candidates with diverse backgrounds?
- Given our business strategy, what skills will we need to hire for in the future that we don't have now? How and where will we find this talent? How effective are we at hiring based on future learning potential and not just current qualifications?

Developing Capabilities (Expanding or Changing the Skills of the Workforce Through Learning, Job Design Reskilling, Upskilling, Internal Movement, Managed Succession, and Career Development)

- Do people have access to the knowledge, tools, and relationships they need to be successful in their jobs? Is it easy to track and complete required training? Are we taking advantage of technology to make learning fun, engaging, and effective?
- Are managers supported and rewarded for developing talent? Do we design and staff jobs to incorporate learning into work?

- How do we enable career development and progression? Do we make effective use of social learning and collaborative developmental relationships? How can people identify and work toward future career opportunities?

Engaging Performance (Focusing Employee Energy and Supporting Productivity and Adaptability Through Job Design, Goals, Coaching, Development, Learning, Compensation, Promotions, and Job Transfers)

- Are people focused, energized, and committed to doing what is needed to make the company successful? Can we quickly communicate changes in strategy so that employees understand what it means for their jobs and careers?
- When employees show up at work each day, how can we be sure they are focusing on the things that truly matter for our company's success? How do we recognize people for their contributions? How do we ensure employees feel valued in terms of informal recognition and tangible rewards and compensation?
- What are we doing to make sure that our managers are effective at managing? How do we hold managers accountable for inspiring, coaching, and retaining talent? What is the turnover rate of high performers versus low performers?

Maximizing Efficiency (Reducing the Time and Money Spent on Operational Workforce Activities and Processes Through Use of More Intuitive and Automated Technology Solutions)

- Are we effectively leveraging technology to control and manage the costs associated with workforce management?
- Can we effectively scale the methods we use to manage our workforce and create a productive environment to support our future growth?
- How are we using artificial intelligence, chatbots, and other forms of intelligent technology to make the employee experience more enjoyable, engaging, and efficient?

Ensuring Compliance (Complying with Employment Regulations Related to Payroll, Time Keeping, Benefits, Safety, Hiring, Staffing, Training, and Other Workplace Policies, Rules, and Laws)

- Do we have methods in place to ensure we are complying with changing localized laws and regulations governing human resource practices, data collection, security, and storage?

- Have we implemented adequate tools to ensure our data are effectively protected from cybersecurity threats? Do we have an effective security culture where employees are aware of security risks and take steps to prevent them? How do we manage physical security?
- Are the agility and flexibility of the company affected by the solutions used to manage payroll and other administrative processes? Is it easy to make changes to how jobs are designed and compensated?

Building Culture (Working in Ways That Support Specific Values and Behavior Associated with Attributes Such as Inclusion, Well-being, Collaboration, Customer Service, Safety, Quality, Global, and/or Virtual Work)

- Are we creating an environment where employees can manage the challenges of work and life in a healthy, productive, and sustainable manner?
- Are we instilling a culture of inclusion that fully leverages the talents of an increasingly diverse workforce?
- What actions are we taking to support the communities and social causes that matter most to our employees?

Appendix: The Peloton Model of Team Performance[i]

Figure A.1 illustrates a model I use when helping companies determine how to manage performance differences. It uses the analogy of the pelotons that form in a long bike race such as the Tour de France. Pelotons are the fastest form of long-distance bike riding because they allow riders to draft off each other. Riders take turns at the front similar to how geese take turns flying at the front of the flock to break the wind. It is not possible to form a peloton without having a group of riders, and the pace of the peloton is influenced by every member of the group. The same concept is true for the performance of groups in an organization. This makes the analogy of a peloton useful in understanding different levels of performance.[ii] The percentages provided in the following descriptions are general estimates and vary widely across groups.

- **Breaking away** riders have sprinted out in front of the larger group. The speed of these riders is driven by internal self-motivation, although they are also influenced by the speed of other breakaway riders. In a multiday race the breakaway riders change constantly. No person can achieve breakaway status in every single stage of the race.
  - **Breakaway performance** describes employees whose contributions are having a major impact on the overall performance of the group. These employees may have found ways to add value no one had considered before or have achieved phenomenal levels of results through a combination of motivation, skills and perhaps a bit of luck. The value created by breakaway performance in some jobs is more

---

[i] This model predates and has no relation to the exercise equipment company that shares the same name.

[ii] The purpose of the model is to understand the nature of different types of employee performance in a group context. This model does not accurately describe the behaviors of bike racers in the modern era of radio communication and complicated team-based race strategies. I have been told by a professional cyclist that it does reflect some general truths when applied to amateur level racing.

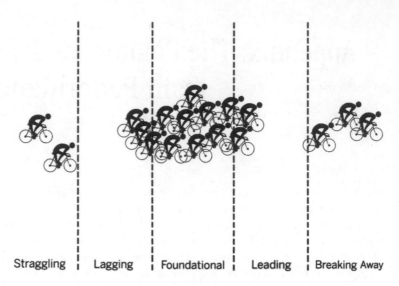

Straggling | Lagging | Foundational | Leading | Breaking Away

FIGURE A.1 The peloton model of performance differences.

than five times greater than the value of average performance.[1] One company I worked with referred to this category of performance as "legendary" because it inspired stories about what it was possible to achieve. People capable of performing at this level may quit an organization if the work environment is limiting their success. This includes having to work with low-performing people. Employees achieving breakaway performance want to be recognized for their outstanding contributions and given additional resources and opportunities to do even more. This category typically encompasses less than 10% of the workforce.

- **Leading riders** are at the front of the peloton. The speed of these riders is partially influenced by looking at the breakaway riders that they hope to catch. The other factor that influences their speed is how fast the people are riding in the peloton behind them. They may not catch the breakaway riders, but they want to stay at the head of the pack.

  - **Leading performance** describes employees whose contributions exceed expectations but that are not at breakaway performance levels. Employees often move back and forth between breakaway and leading-edge performance levels. Leading employees tend to set the pace in terms of defining what good performance looks like in the company. Managing leading performance is about letting employees know they are viewed as critical talent and investing to help them reach even higher levels of performance. This category tends to be about 25% to 35% of the workforce.

- **Foundational** riders are in the middle of the peloton. Some of these may be former breakaway or leading riders who have dropped back to rest and recover from the previous days' rides. Their speed is heavily influenced by the riders immediately in front of them and behind them.
  - **Foundational performance** describes employees whose contributions are valuable to the company but that are not considered exceptional. This group often contains long-tenured, loyal employees who are critical to supporting ongoing operations and service continuity. Employees often move back and forth between this category and leading performance. Some may have exhibited breakaway or leading performance in previous jobs before they were promoted to more challenging positions. Managing foundational performance is about showing meaningful appreciation for what these employees contribute and giving them access to development resources to achieve higher levels of performance. This category tends to be about 40% to 50% of the workforce.
- **Lagging** riders are at the back of the peloton. They may be intentionally going slow to save energy or may be struggling to keep up. The speed they ride influences the speed of the riders in front of them. This in turn influences the speed of the entire peloton.
  - **Lagging performance** reflects employees who are still effective in their role but are not effective enough. This could be a result of being in a role that does not play to their strengths or a consequence of trying to do the right things in the wrong way. It might also be caused by things outside of work distracting them from being fully effective. These are not bad employees. They are good employees who are failing to fulfill their role expectations. In many cases these employees possess critical skills that the organization needs. Managing people at this performance level is about increasing self-awareness about what they need to improve, providing a path for improvement, and giving them confidence in their ability to get back on track. This category is usually about 10% to 15% of any large workforce.
- **Straggling** riders have fallen well behind the peloton. Some stragglers may catch up with the peloton, but others may drop out of the race entirely.
  - **Straggling performance** is not just below expectations; it is counterproductive. Employees in this category may be in a job that does not align with their skills, be facing issues outside of work that are preventing them from doing a good job, or have beliefs that conflict with the values of the organization. Managing these employees requires being clear on what they need to improve and holding them accountable for improving within a set amount of time. It is unproductive and unfair to force other people to rely on them. If they do

not improve then they should be moved into another role or out of the organization entirely. These individuals should be shown respect even if they are being transitioned out of their jobs, both because it is the right thing to do and because other employees will form impressions of the organization based on how they are treated. Many work groups will not have any employees in this category, and it rarely includes more than 5% of an organization.

Most business leaders can sort employee performance into these five categories fairly easily. Providing five categories tends to provide enough range to distinguish among performance levels but is not overly complex. Overly simplistic models with two to three categories tend to overlook important performance differences between employees. Overly complex models with more than seven categories can lead to managers overemphasizing small performance differences between employees to justify placing them into different categories.

It is important to recognize that not every group will have the same distribution across categories. For example, occasionally more than 50% of a small team could be in the breakaway performance category, although such "all-star" teams rarely last, because members often move on to new roles.[2] It is also possible that in smaller teams all employees could perform at the same level. When assessing performance, managers should be challenged to critically compare the performance of team members through dialogue with their leaders and peers. But they should not be required to place specific percentages of employees into different groups. It is not effective nor fair to require managers to make evaluations that do not reflect their honest views.

References

Introduction

1. The Government of the Roman Empire Under early Principate. (n.d.). [Gif]. Fordham University. https://sourcebooks.fordham.edu/ancient /spqr-under-augustus.gif

2. Ribeiro, E., Macambira, M., & Neiva, E. R. (2017). Social network analysis in organizations as a management support tool. In E. R. Neiva, C. Vaz Torres, & H. Mendonça (Eds.), *Organizational psychology and evidence-based management: What science says about practice* (pp. 243–265). Springer International Publishing AG. https://doi.org/10.1007/978-3 -319-64304-5_13

3. Klerk, E., Kersely, R., Bhatti, M., & Vair, B. (2017). *Global equity themes*. Credit Suisse Equity Research Institute for Mergers, Acquisitions and Alliances. (2019). *Mergers and acquisitions statistics*. https://imaa-Institute. Org. https://imaa-institute.org/mergers-and-acquisitions-statistics/

4. Stall, R. (2020b, December 2). *How advancing mobility will disrupt the mining and metals sector*. https://www.Ey.Com. https://www.ey.com /en_us/mining-metals/how-advancing-mobility-will-disrupt-the -mining-and-metals-sector

5. Frey, C. B., & Osborne, M. A. (2013, September 17). *The future of employment*. https://www.Oxfordmartin.Ox.Ac.Uk

6. Indexmundi. (2019, December). United States: Life expectancy at birth. https://www.indexmundi.com/facts/united-states/life-expectancy-at -birth#:~:text=The%20value%20for%20Life%20expectancy%20at%20 birth%2C%20total%20(years),value%20of%2069.77%20in%201960

7. Gallagher, B. J. (2020, July 15). Fertility rate: "Jaw-dropping" global crash in children being born. BBC News. https://www.bbc.com/news /health-53409521

8. Levanon, G. (2021). Labor shortages are making a comeback. The Conference Board. https://www.conference-board.org/topics/labor-shortages /labor-shortages-comeback

9. Hodson, T., & Otten, I. W. (2014). The overwhelmed employee. Deloitte Insights. https://www2.deloitte.com/us/en/insights/focus/human-capital -trends/2014/hc-trends-2014-overwhelmed-employee.html

10. Rudolph, C. W., Rauvola, R. S., Costanza, D. P., & Zacher, H. (2020). Generations and generational differences: Debunking myths in organizational science and practice and paving new paths forward. *Journal of Business and Psychology, 36*(6), 945–967. https://doi.org/10.1007 /s10869-020-09715-2

11. Meyer, K.D. (2012, April)). Do values really differ by generation? A multi-assessment review. The Conference of the Society for Industrial & Organizational Psychology, San Diego, CA.

12. Derickson, A. (2014). *Black lung: Anatomy of a public health disaster*. Cornell University Press.

13. Seller, M. (1989). A history of women's education in the United States: Thomas Woody's classic—sixty years later. *History of Education Quarterly, 29*(1), 95–107. doi:10.2307/368607

14. Arthur, M. B. (1994). The boundaryless career: A new perspective for organizational inquiry. *Journal of Organizational Behavior, 15*(4), 295–306. http://www.jstor.org/stable/2488428

Chapter 1

1. Qualtrics. (2020). 2020 global employee experience trends. https:// success.qualtrics.com/rs/542-FMF-412/images/EX_Global_Trends _Report_Ebook.pdf

2. Barrero, J. M., Bloom, N., & Davis, S. J. (2021, April). Why working from home will stick. *Working Paper 0-174*. Becker Friedman Institute for Economics at University of Chicago.

3. Charlier, S. D., Greg, L. S., Lindsey, M. G., & Cody, J. R. (2016). Emergent leadership in virtual teams: A multilevel investigation of individual communication and team dispersion antecedents. *The Leadership Quarterly, 27*(5), 745–764. doi:10.1016/j.leaqua.2016.05.002

4. PopulationPyramid.net. (2019). *Population Pyramids of the World from 1950 to 2100*. https://www.populationpyramid.net/world/2019/

5. Passel, J. S., & Cohn, D. V. (2020). *U.S. population projections: 2005– 2050*. Pew Research Center's Social and Demographic Trends Project. https://www.pewresearch.org/social-trends/2008/02/11/us-population -projections-2005-2050/

6. Bulao, J. (2022). How fast is technology advancing in 2022? Techjury. https://techjury.net/blog/how-fast-is-technology-growing/#gref

7. Derks, D., van Mierlo, H., & Schmitz, E. B. (2014). A diary study on work-related smartphone use, psychological detachment and exhaustion: Examining the role of the perceived segmentation norm. *Journal of*

Occupational Health Psychology, 19(1), 74–84. https://doi.org/10.1037 /a0035076; Chiu, A. (2021, October 29). How to avoid "smartphone pinkie" and other pains and problems from being glued to your phone. *The Washington Post.* https://www.washingtonpost.com /lifestyle/2021/10/29/smartphone-pinky-hand-pain/

8. Grand View Research. (2022). mHealth apps market size, share & trends analysis report by type (fitness, medical), by region (North America, Europe, Asia Pacific, Latin America, Middle East & Africa), and segment forecasts, 2022–2030 (GVR-1-68038-555-7). https://www.grandviewresearch .com/industry-analysis/mhealth-app-market

9. Megginson, L. C. (1963). Lessons from Europe for American business. *The Southwestern Social Science Quarterly, 44,* 3–13. (Quote from p. 4.)

10. Anthony, S. D., Trotter, A., & Schwartz, E. I. (2019, September 4). The top 20 business transformations of the last decade. *Harvard Business Review.*

11. Hillenbrand, P., Kiewell, D., Miller-Cheevers, R., Ostojic, I., & Springer, G. (2019). Traditional company, new businesses: The pairing that can ensure an incumbent's survival. McKinsey & Company. https://www .mckinsey.com/industries/oil-and-gas/our-insights/traditional-company -new-businesses-the-pairing-that-can-ensure-an-incumbents-survival

12. Teachman, B. A. (2018). Finding new ways to calm the anxious mind: Using technology to train healthier interpretations and increase dissemination of evidence-based care. *Psychological Science Agenda, February.* https://www.apa.org/science/about/psa/2018/02/ anxious-mind

13. Granulo, A., Fuchs, C., & Puntoni, S. (2019). Psychological reactions to human versus robotic job replacement. *Nature Human Behavior, 3,* 1062–1069. https://doi.org/10.1038/s41562-019-0670-y

14. US Bureau of Labor Statistics. (2021). Number of jobs, labor market experience, marital status, and health: Results from a national longitudinal survey. https://www.bls.gov/news.release/pdf/nlsoy.pdf

15. Kelly, K. (2016). *The inevitable: Understanding the 12 technological forces that will shape our future.* Viking Press.

16. Urquhart, M. (1984). The employment shift to services: Where did it come from? US Bureau of Labor Statistics. https://stats.bls.gov/opub /mlr/1984/04/art2full.pdf; US Bureau of Labor Statistics. (2021). Employment by major industry sector. https://www.bls.gov/emp/tables/ employment-by-major-industry-sector.htm

17. Powell, W. W., & Snellman, K. (2004). The knowledge economy. *Annual Review of Sociology, 30,* 199–220. https://doi.org/10.1146/annurev.soc .29.010202.100037

18. United States Department of Labor. (1948). *Occupational outlook handbook: Employment information on major occupations for use in guidance.* US Government Printing Office.

19. Underwood, A. (2021). Most common jobs in America. Stacker. https://stacker.com/stories/3487/most-common-jobs-america

20. Rosling, H., Ronnlund, A. R., & Rosling, O. (2018). *Factfulness: Ten reasons why we're wrong about the world and why things are better than you think*. Flatiron Books.

21. Diener, E., & Seligman, M. E. P. (2002) Very happy people. *Psychological Science, 13*, 81–84. doi:10.1111/1467-9280.00415

22. Hunt, S.T. (2002). On the virtues of staying "inside of the box": Does organizational citizenship behavior detract from performance in Taylorist jobs? *International Journal of Selection and Assessment, 10*, 1–8.

23. Gonzalez-Mulé, E., & Cockburn, B. (2016). Worked to death: The relationships of job demands and job control with mortality. *Personnel Psychology, 70*(1), 73–112. https://doi.org/10.1111/peps.12206

24. Wright, T. A., & Cropanzano, R. (2000). Psychological well-being and job satisfaction as predictors of job performance. *Journal of Occupational Health Psychology, 5*(1), 84–94. https://doi.org/10.1037/1076-8998.5.1.84

25. Grandey, A. A., & Melloy, R. C. (2017). The state of the heart: Emotional labor as emotion regulation reviewed and revised. *Journal of Occupational Health Psychology, 22*(3), 407–422. https://doi.org/10.1037/ocp0000067

26. Lambert, L. S., Bingham, J. B., & Zabinski, A. (2020). Affective commitment, trust, and the psychological contract: Contributions matter, too. *European Journal of Work and Organizational Psychology, 29*(2), 294–314. https://doi.org/10.1080/1359432X.2019.1697743

27. Csikszentmihalyi, M. (2008). *Flow: The psychology of optimal experience*. Harper.

28. Evans, S. (2019, June 17). How technology is changing Australian mining jobs. *Mining Technology*.

29. AMD Telemedicine. (2016, February 22). How clinical telemedicine can help create new jobs. https://amdtelemedicine.com/how-clinical-telemedicine-can-help-create-new-jobs/

30. World Bank. (2018b, October). World development report 2019: The changing nature of work. https://doi.org/10.1596/978-1-4648-1328-3_ch1

31. Epstein, D. (2019). *Range: Why generalists triumph in a specialized world*. Riverhead Books.

32. Götmark, F., & Andersson, M. (2020). Human fertility in relation to education, economy, religion, contraception, and family planning programs. *BMC Public Health, 20*, 265. https://doi.org/10.1186/s12889-020-8331-7

33. Schwarz, J. (2021). *Work disrupted: Opportunity, resilience, and growth in the accelerated future of work*. Wiley.

34. Chand, M., & Tung, R. (2015). The aging of the world's population and its effects on global business. *Academy of Management Perspectives*, 28. https://doi.org/10.5465/amp.2012.0070

35. United Nations Department of Economic and Social Affairs. (2019). Growing at a slower pace, world population is expected to reach 9.7 billion in 2050 and could peak at nearly 11 billion around 2100. https://www.un.org/sustainabledevelopment/blog/2019/06/growing-at-a-slower-pace-world-population-is-expected-to-reach-9-7-billion-in-2050-and-could-peak-at-nearly-11-billion-around-2100-un-report/#:~:text=New%20York%2C%2017%20June%20%E2%80%93The,United%20Nations%20report%20launched%20today.

36. US Bureau of Labor Statistics. (2021). Employment projections: 2020–2030 summary https://www.bls.gov/emp/#:~:text=Employment%20is%20projected%20to%20increase%20by%2011.9%20million%20jobs%20from%202020%20to%202030&text=Employment%20is%20projected%20to%20grow,share%20of%20projected%20job%20growth

37. Adamcyzyk, A. (2019). 6 US cities and states that will pay you to move there. CNBC. https://www.cnbc.com/2019/08/31/6-us-cities-and-states-that-will-pay-you-to-move-there.html

38. US Bureau of Labor Statistics. (2021b, September). Fastest growing occupations. https://www.bls.gov/ooh/fastest-growing.htm

39. Jolles, D., Wassermann, D., Chokhani, R., et al. (2016). Plasticity of left perisylvian white-matter tracts is associated with individual differences in math learning. *Brain Structure and Function, 221*, 1337–1351. https://doi.org/10.1007/s00429-014-0975-6

40. Hunt, E. B. (1995). *Will we be smart enough? A cognitive analysis of the coming workforce.* Wiley.

41. International Labour Organization 2020. (2021). The future of work in the automotive industry: The need to invest in people's capabilities and decent and sustainable work. https://www.ilo.org/sector/Resources/publications/WCMS_741659/lang--en/index.htm

42. Silver, A., Kalloch, S., & Ton, Z. (2021). *A background note on "unskilled" jobs in the United States: Past, present, and future.* MIT Sloan School of Management.

43. Ton, Z. (2014). *The good jobs strategy: How the smartest companies invest in employees to lower costs and boost profits.* New Harvest.

44. World Bank. (2018b, October). World development report 2019: The changing nature of work. https://doi.org/10.1596/978-1-4648-1328-3_ch1

45. Hammond, C. (2004). Impacts of lifelong learning upon emotional resilience, psychological and mental health: Fieldwork evidence. *Oxford Review of Education, 30*(4), 551–568. https://doi.org/10.1080/0305498042000303008

46. Li, Y., Gong, Y., Burmeister, A., Wang, M., Alterman, V., Alonso, A., & Robinson, S. (2021). Leveraging age diversity for organizational performance: An intellectual capital perspective. *Journal of Applied Psychology, 106*(1), 71–91. https://doi.org/10.1037/apl0000497
47. Boehm, S. A., Kunze, F., & Bruch, H. (2013). Spotlight on age-diversity climate: The impact of age-inclusive HR practices on firm-level outcomes. *Personnel Psychology, 67*, 667–704.
48. Ng, T. W. H., & Feldman, D. C. (2012). Evaluating six common stereotypes about older workers with meta-analytical data. *Personnel Psychology, 65*, 821–858; Posthuma, R. A., & Campion, M. A. (2009). Age stereotypes in the workplace: Common stereotypes, moderators, and future research directions. *Journal of Management, 35*, 158–188.
49. Baugh, S. G., & Sullivan, S. E. (2009). *Maintaining focus, energy, and options over the career.* Information Age Publishing.
50. Harrison, D. A., Harrison, T., & Shaffer, M. A. (2019). Strangers in strained lands: Learning from workplace experiences of immigrant employees. *Journal of Management, 45*, 600–619. doi:10.1177/0149206318790648
51. Wartburg, R., & Pluss, J. D. (2021). Why Switzerland needs workers from abroad. *Workplace Switzerland.* https://www.swissinfo.ch/eng/why-switzerland-needs-workers-from-abroad/46694984
52. Levine, S. (2020). Diversity confirmed to boost innovation and financial results. *Forbes.* https://www.forbes.com/sites/forbesinsights/2020/01/15/diversity-confirmed-to-boost-innovation-and-financial-results/
53. HR Research Institute. (2019). The state of diversity and inclusion 2019: Improving D&I practices to boost organizational innovation and performance. https://www.hr.com/en/resources/free_research_white_papers/hrcom-state-of-diversity-inclusion-2019-feb2019_jrttnwuk.html54
54. Rapp, D. J., Hughey, J. M., & Kreiner, G. E. (2021). Boundary work as a buffer against burnout: Evidence from healthcare workers during the COVID-19 pandemic. *Journal of Applied Psychology, 106*(8), 1169–1187. https://doi.org/10.1037/apl0000951
55. Coughlin, J. F. (2017). *The longevity economy: Unlocking the world's fastest-growing, most misunderstood market. Public Affairs.*
56. Rockwood, K (2018, January). Hiring in the age of ageism. *HR Magazine.*

Chapter 2

1. Wikipedia contributors. (2021, December 2). Volatility, uncertainty, complexity and ambiguity. Wikipedia. https://en.wikipedia.org/wiki/Volatility,_uncertainty,_complexity_and_ambiguity
2. Koehn, N. F. (2011, December 25). Leadership lessons from the Shackleton expedition. *The New York Times.*

3. Stanek, K. C., & Ones, D. S. (2018). Taxonomies and compendia of cognitive ability and personality constructs and measures relevant to industrial, work and organizational psychology. In D. S. Ones, N. Anderson, C. Viswesvaran, & H. K. Sinangil (Eds.), *The SAGE handbook of industrial, work & organizational psychology: Personnel psychology and employee performance* (pp. 366–407). SAGE.

4. Meyer, K. D. (2012, April). Do values really differ by generation? A multi-assessment review. The Conference of the Society for Industrial & Organizational Psychology, San Diego, CA.

5. Whyte, W. H. (1956). *The organization man*. University of Pennsylvania Press.

6. Howard, A. (1995). *The changing nature of work*. Jossey-Bass.

7. Schultz, K., & Adams, G. (2007). *Aging and work in the 21st century*. Lawrence Erlbaum.

8. Costanza, D. P., & Finkelstein, L. M. (2015). Generationally based differences in the workplace: Is there a there there? *Industrial and Organizational Psychology, 8*(3), 308–323. https://doi.org/10.1017/iop.2015.15

9. Deal, J. (2006). *Retiring the generation gap: How employees young and old can find common ground*. John Wiley & Sons.

10. Wegman, L. A., Hoffman, B. J., Carter, N. T., Twenge, J. M., & Guenole, N. (2018). Placing job characteristics in context: Cross-temporal meta-analysis of changes in job characteristics since 1975. *Journal of Management, 44*(1), 352–386.

11. Morris, M. G., & Venkatesh, V. (2000). Age differences in technology adoption decisions: Implications for a changing work force. *Personnel Psychology, 53*(2), 375–403. https://doi.org/10.1111/j.1744-6570.2000.tb00206.x

12. Hunt, S. T. (2002). On the virtues of staying "inside of the box": Does organizational citizenship behavior detract from performance in Taylorist jobs? *International Journal of Selection and Assessment, 10*, 1–8.

13. Dweck, C. S. (2007). *Mindset: The new psychology of success*. Ballantine.

14. Butcher, K., VandenBerg, A., & Dodds, T. (2021, March 17). Why crawl? MSU Extension. https://www.canr.msu.edu/news/why_crawl

15. Duffy, R. D., Dik, B. J., Douglass, R. P., England, J. W., & Velez, B. L. (2018). Work as a calling: A theoretical model. *Journal of Counseling Psychology, 65*(4), 423–439. https://doi.org/10.1037/cou0000276

16. Caldwell, S. D., Herold, D. M., & Fedor, D. B. (2004). Toward an understanding of the relationships among organizational change, individual differences, and changes in person-environment fit: A cross-level study. *Journal of Applied Psychology, 89*(5) 868–882. https://doi.org/10.1037/0021-9010.89.5.868

17. Kanfer, R., Frese, M., & Johnson, R. E. (2017). Motivation related to work: A century of progress. *Journal of Applied Psychology, 102*(3), 338–355. https://doi.org/10.1037/apl0000133

18. Stajkovic, A. D., & Luthans, F. (1998). Self-efficacy and work-related performance: A meta-analysis. *Psychological Bulletin, 124*(2), 240–261. https://doi.org/10.1037/0033-2909.124.2.240

19. Zhang, Y., LePine, J. A., Buckman, B. R., & Wei, F. (2014). It's not fair . . . or is it? The role of justice and leadership in explaining work stressor– job performance relationships. *Academy of Management Journal, 57*(3), 675–697. https://doi.org/10.5465/amj.2011.1110

20. Ilies, R., Lanaj, K., Pluut, H., & Goh, Z. (2018). Intrapersonal and interpersonal need fulfillment at work: Differential antecedents and incremental validity in explaining job satisfaction and citizenship behavior. *Journal of Vocational Behavior, 108*, 151–164. https://doi .org/10.1016/j.jvb.2018.07.005; Lee, R. M., & Robbins, S. B. (1995). Measuring belongingness: The Social Connectedness and the Social Assurance scales. *Journal of Counseling Psychology, 42*(2), 232–241. doi:10.1037/0022-0167.42.2.232

21. McCarthy, J. M., Trougakos, J. P., & Cheng, B. H. (2016). Are anxious workers less productive workers? It depends on the quality of social exchange. *Journal of Applied Psychology, 101*(2), 279–291. https://doi .org/10.1037/apl0000044

22. Locke, E. A. (1976). The nature and causes of job satisfaction. In M. D. Dunnette (Ed.), *Handbook of industrial and organizational psychology* (pp. 1297–1349). Rand McNally. (Quote from page 1297.)

23. Ii, J. P. B., & Gilmore, J. H. (1999). *The experience economy* (updated ed.). Harvard Business Review Press.

24. Rose, T. (2016). *The end of average: How we succeed in a world that values sameness*. Harper Collins.

25. Human Resource Research Team. (2019). *Moments that matter in the employee experience*. Gartner.

26. Reichheld, F. F. (2001). *The loyalty effect: The hidden force behind growth, profits, and lasting value* (Revised ed.). Harvard Business Review Press.

27. Moreau, M. (2004). Occupational stress and incidence of sick leave in the Belgian workforce. *Journal of Epidemiology & Community Health, 58*(6), 507–516. https://doi.org/10.1136/jech.2003.007518

28. Hammer, L. B., Ernst Kossek, E., Bodner, T., & Crain, T. (2013). Measurement development and validation of the Family Supportive Supervisor Behavior Short-Form (FSSB-SF). *Journal of Occupational Health Psychology, 18*(3), 285–296. https://doi.org/10.1037/a0032612

29. Bormann, K. C., & Diebig, M. (2020). Following an uneven lead: Trickledown effects of differentiated transformational leadership. *Journal of Management, 47*(8), 2105–2134. https://doi.org/10.1177/0149206320931584

30. Kahn, W. A. (1990). Psychological conditions of personal engagement and disengagement at work. *Academy of Management Journal, 33*(4), 692–724. https://doi.org/10.5465/256287

31. Liu, D., Mitchell, T. R., Lee, T. W., Holtom, B. C., & Hinkin, T. R. (2012). When employees are out of step with coworkers: How job satisfaction trajectory and dispersion influence individual- and unit-level voluntary turnover. *Academy of Management Journal, 55*(6), 1360–1380. https://doi.org/10.5465/amj.2010.0920

Chapter 3

1. Wikipedia contributors. (2022, February 7). Nokia. Wikipedia. https://en.wikipedia.org/wiki/Nokia
2. Sulopuisto, O. (2013, November 12). Nokia: Where it all went wrong, by the man who made it the world's biggest mobile company. ZDNet. https://www.zdnet.com/article/nokia-where-it-all-went-wrong-by-the-man-who-made-it-the-worlds-biggest-mobile-company/
3. Gates, B. (1995). *The road ahead*. Viking Penguin.
4. Mauri, T. (2020). Want to think like Satya Nadella? Follow 3 simple rules. Inc.Com. https://www.inc.com/terence-mauri/how-satya-nadella-uses-learn-it-all-to-beat-know-it-all.html
5. Hernandez, B., Preimesberger, C., Kerravala, Z., & Rash, W. (2021). Why Microsoft selected SAP SuccessFactors HCM needs. eWEEK. https://www.eweek.com/enterprise-apps/why-microsoft-picked-sap-successfactors-for-its-hcm-needs/
6. Gulati, R. (2019, July–August). The soul of a start-up. *Harvard Business Review.* https://hbr.org/2019/07/the-soul-of-a-start-up
7. Sutton, R. I. (2007). *The no asshole rule: Building a civilized workplace and surviving one that isn't.* Business Plus.
8. Peterson, S. J., & Luthan, F. (2006). The impact of financial and non-financial incentives on business-unit outcomes over time. *Journal of Applied Psychology, 91*, 156–165.
9. Arena, M. (2018). *Adaptive space: How GM and other companies are positively disrupting themselves and transforming into agile organizations.* McGraw-Hill.
10. Mueller, J. S. (2012). Why individuals in larger teams perform worse. *Organizational Behavior and Human Decision Processes, 117*(1), 111–124. https://doi.org/10.1016/j.obhdp.2011.08.004
11. American Psychological Association. (n.d.). Social loafing. *APA dictionary of psychology.* https://dictionary.apa.org/social-loafing
12. Kuhl, J., & Goschke, T. (1994). A theory of action control: Mental subsystems, modes of control, and volitional conflict-resolution strategies. In J. Kuhl & J. Beckmann (Eds.), *Volition and personality: Action versus state orientation* (pp. 93–124). Hogrefe.

13. Edwards, B., Hofmeyr, S., & Forrest, S. (2016). Hype and heavy tails: A closer look at data breaches. *Journal of Cybersecurity, 2*(1), 3–14. https://doi.org/10.1093/cybsec/tyw003

14. Way, S. A., Tracey, J. B., Fay, C. H., Wright, P. M., Snell, S. A., Chang, S., & Gong, Y. (2015). Validation of a multidimensional HR flexibility measure. *Journal of Management, 41*, 1098–1131.

15. Charvat, J. (2003). *Project management methodologies: Selecting, implementing, and supporting methodologies and processes for projects.* Wiley.

16. Yue, C. A., Men, L. R., & Ferguson, M. A. (2020). Examining the effects of internal communication and emotional culture on employees' organizational identification. *International Journal of Business Communication, 58*(2), 169–195. https://doi.org/10.1177/2329488420914066

17. Morrison-Smith, S., & Ruiz, J. (2020). Challenges and barriers in virtual teams: A literature review. *SN Applied Sciences, 2*(6). https://doi .org/10.1007/s42452-020-2801-5

18. Hunt, S. T. (2014). *Common sense talent management: Using strategic human resources to improve company performance.* Pfeiffer.

19. Thaler, R. H., & Sunstein, C. R. (2021). *Nudge: Improving decisions about health, wealth, and happiness* (rev. ed.). Gildan Audio and Blackstone Publishing.

20. O'Neil, C. (2016). *Weapons of math destruction: How big data increases inequality and threatens democracy.* Crown.

21. Bersin, J. (2021). What is the metaverse? Facebook's strategy and how Microsoft, Disney, and Amazon could win. https://joshbersin .com/2021/11/what-is-the-metaverse-and-how-microsoft-disney-and -amazon-could-win/

22. Barakat, K. A., & Dabbous, A. (2019). Understanding the factors that affect the sustained use of chatbots within organizations. *International Association for Development of the Information Society, 17*, 71–84. https://doi.org/10.33965/ijwi_2019172106

23. Terblanche, N. (2020). Factors that influence users' adoption of being coached by an artificial intelligence coach. *Philosophy of Coaching: An International Journal, 5*, 61–70. https://doi.org/10.22316/poc/05.1.06

24. Warrenbrand, M. (2021). Applicant justice perceptions of machine learning algorithms in personnel selection. Masters Theses and Doctoral Dissertations, University of Tennessee at Chattanooga. https://scholar.utc .edu/theses/691

25. Ulrich, D. (1998). A new mandate for human resources. *Harvard Business Review.* https://hbr.org/1998/01/a-new-mandate-for-human-resources

26. Nieß, C., & Zacher, H. (2015). Openness to experience as a predictor and outcome of upward job changes into managerial and professional positions. *PLoS ONE, 10*(6), e0131115. https://doi.org/10.1371/journal .pone.0131115

27. Frazier, M. L., Fainshmidt, S., Klinger, R. L., Pezeshkan, A., & Vracheva, V. (2017). Psychological safety: A meta-analytic review and extension. *Management Faculty Publications*, 13. https://digitalcommons.odu.edu /management_fac_pubs/13

Chapter 4

1. Baltes, B., Rudolph, C. W., & Zacher, H. (2019). *Work across the lifespan*. Elsevier Gezondheidszorg.
2. Society for Human Capital Management. (2017). SHRM 2017 human capital benchmarking report. https://www.shrm.org/hr-today/trends -and-forecasting/research-and-surveys/Documents/2017-Human -Capital-Benchmarking.pdf
3. Pitts, F. H. (2017). Creative labor before and after going freelance: Contextual factors and coalition-building practices. In S. Taylor & S. Luckman (Eds.), *The new normal of working lives*. Palgrave Macmillan.
4. Grant, A. M., Berg, J. M., & Cable, D. M. (2014). Job titles as identity badges: How self-reflective titles can reduce emotional exhaustion. *Academy of Management Journal*, *57*, 1201–1225. http://dx.doi .org/10.5465/amj.2012.0338
5. Harter, J., Buckingham, M., & Organization, G. (2016). *First, break all the rules: What the world's greatest managers do differently*. Gallup Press.
6. Brannick, M. T., Levine, E. L., & Morgeson, F. P. (2007). *Job and work analysis*. SAGE Publications. https://doi.org/10.4135/9781483329505
7. Cerasoli, C. P., Nicklin, J. M., & Ford, M. T. (2014). Intrinsic motivation and extrinsic incentives jointly predict performance: A 40-year meta-analysis. *Psychological Bulletin*, *140*, 980–1008. https://doi .org/10.1037/a0035661
8. Hunter, E. M., & Wu, C. (2016). Give me a better break: Choosing workday break activities to maximize resource recovery. *Journal of Applied Psychology*, *101*, 302–311. https://doi.org/10.1037/apl0000045
9. Ward, D. (2015). Beyond the open office: The open office movement has sparked an important conversation about the role physical space plays in business outcomes. *HR Magazine*. https://www.shrm.org/hr -today/news/hr-magazine/pages/0415-open-office.aspx
10. Allen, T. J. (1997). Architecture and communication among product development engineers. Sloan WP #3983. Massachusetts Institute of Technology.
11. Robert Half. (2018). Nearly one-quarter of workers have left a job due to a bad commute. https://rh-us.mediaroom.com/2018-09-24-Nearly -One-Quarter-Of-Workers-Have-Left-A-Job-Due-To-A-Bad-Commute -According-To-Robert-Half-Survey

12. Hu, X., Barber, L., Park, Y., & Day, A. (2021). Defrag and reboot? Consolidating information and communication technology research in I-O psychology. *Industrial and Organizational Psychology, 14*(3), 371–396. doi:10.1017/iop.2021.3

13. Society of Human Resource Management (SHRM). (2020). Want your business to thrive? Cultivate your external talent. https://www.shrm.org/hr-today/trends-and-forecasting/research-and-surveys/Documents/SHRM%20SAP%20External%20Workforce%20Whitepaper.pdf

14. Chadwick, C., & Flinchbaugh, C. (2016). The effects of part-time workers on establishment financial performance. *Journal of Management, 42*(6), 1635–1662. https://doi.org/10.1177/0149206313511116

15. Rynes, S. L., Gerhart, B., & Minette, K. A. (2004). The importance of pay in employee motivation: Discrepancies between what people say and what they do. *Human Resource Management, 43*(4), 381–394. https://doi.org/10.1002/hrm.20031

16. LinkedIn. (2017). Get inside the mind of today's candidate' with new LinkedIn report. *LinkedIn News.* https://news.linkedin.com/2017/7/inside-the-mind-of-todays-candidate

17. Warren, A. M., & Zaklukiewicz, E. A. (2021, July 1). New wage range disclosure requirements in multiple states. *The National Law Review.* https://www.natlawreview.com/article/new-wage-range-disclosure-requirements-multiple-states

18. Connelly, B. L., Haynes, K. T., Tihanyi, L., Gamache, D. L., & Devers, C. E. (2016). Minding the gap: Antecedents and consequences of top management-to-worker pay dispersion. *Journal of Management, 42*(4), 862–885. https://doi.org/10.1177/0149206313503015

19. Donner, H., & Siciliano, F. D. (2021). The impact of earned wage access on household liquidity and financial well-being. *SSRN Electronic Journal.* https://doi.org/10.2139/ssrn.4007632

20. Chamberlain, A., Tian, G., Johnson, R., Zhao, D., & Thomas, L. (2020). *Which benefits drive employee satisfaction?* Glassdoor Economic Research. https://www.glassdoor.com/research/benefits-drive-employee-satisfaction/

21. Schminke, M., Ambrose, M. L., & Neubaum, D. O. (2005). The effect of leader moral development on ethical climate and employee attitudes. *Organizational Behavior and Human Decision Processes, 97*(2), 135–151. https://doi.org/10.1016/j.obhdp.2005.03.006

22. Pearsall, M. J., Christian, M. S., & Ellis, A. P. J. (2010). Motivating interdependent teams: Individual rewards, shared rewards, or something in between? *Journal of Applied Psychology, 95*(1), 183–191. https://doi.org/10.1037/a0017593

23. Reay, T., Golden-Biddle, K., & Germann, K. (2006). Legitimizing a new role: Small wins and microprocesses of change. *Academy of Management Journal, 49*(5), 977–998. https://doi.org/10.5465/amj.2006.22798178

24. Molenberghs, P., Prochilo, G., Steffens, N. K., Zacher, H., & Haslam, S. A. (2017). The neuroscience of inspirational leadership: The importance of collective-oriented language and shared group membership. *Journal of Management*, *43*(7), 2168–2194. https://doi.org/10.1177/0149206314565242

25. Cordery, J. L., Cripps, E., Gibson, C. B., Soo, C., Kirkman, B. L., & Mathieu, J. E. (2014). The operational impact of organizational communities of practice. *Journal of Management*, *41*(2), 644–664. https://doi.org/10.1177/0149206314545087

26. Kim, S. L., & Yun, S. (2015). The effect of coworker knowledge sharing on performance and its boundary conditions: An interactional perspective. *Journal of Applied Psychology*, *100*(2), 575–582. https://doi.org/10.1037/a0037834

27. Haslam, S. A., Jetten, J., O'Brien, A., & Jacobs, E. (2004). Social identity, social influence and reactions to potentially stressful tasks: Support for the self-categorization model of stress. *Stress and Health*, *20*(1), 3–9. https://doi.org/10.1002/smi.995

28. Eberly, M. B., Holley, E. C., Johnson, M. D., & Mitchell, T. R. (2017). It's not me, it's not you, it's us! An empirical examination of relational attributions. *Journal of Applied Psychology*, *102*(5), 711–731. https://doi.org/10.1037/apl0000187

29. Lam, C. F., Liang, J., Ashford, S. J., & Lee, C. (2015). Job insecurity and organizational citizenship behavior: Exploring curvilinear and moderated relationships. *Journal of Applied Psychology*, *100*(2), 499–510. https://doi.org/10.1037/a0038659

30. Frankel, S. (2016). Employers are using workplace wearables to find out how happy and productive we are. Quartz. https://qz.com/754989/employers-are-using-workplace-wearables-to-find-out-how-happy-and-productive-we-are/

31. Bennett, A. A., Campion, E. D., Keeler, K. R., & Keener, S. K. (2021). Videoconference fatigue? Exploring changes in fatigue after videoconference meetings during COVID-19. *Journal of Applied Psychology*, *106*(3), 330–344. https://doi.org/10.1037/apl0000906

32. Gonzalez-Mulé, E., Cockburn, B. S., McCormick, B. W., & Zhao, P. (2019). Team tenure and team performance: A meta-analysis and process model. *Personnel Psychology*, *73*(1), 151–198. https://doi.org/10.1111/peps.12319

33. Guillaume, Y. R., Dawson, J. F., Otaye-Ebede, L., Woods, S. A., & West, M. A. (2015). Harnessing demographic differences in organizations: What moderates the effects of workplace diversity? *Journal of Organizational Behavior*, *38*(2), 276–303. https://doi.org/10.1002/job.2040

34. Hollenbeck, J. R., & Jamieson, B. B. (2015). Human capital, social capital, and social network analysis: Implications for strategic human resource management. *Academy of Management Perspectives*, *29*(3), 370–385. https://doi.org/10.5465/amp.2014.0140

35. Buss, D. M. (2005). *The handbook of evolutionary psychology*. Wiley.
36. Thomas, G. E. (1999). Leaderless supervision and performance appraisal: A proposed research agenda. *Human Resource Development Quarterly, 10*, 91–94.
37. Friedrich, T. L., Vessey, W. B., Schuelke, M. J., Ruark, G. A., & Mumford, M. D. (2009). A framework for understanding collective leadership: The selective utilization of leader and team expertise within networks. *The Leadership Quarterly, 20*(6), 933–958. https://doi.org/10.1016/j.leaqua.2009.09.008
38. Bernstein, E., Bunch, J., Canner, N., & Lee, M. Y. (2016, June 20). Beyond the holacracy hype. *Harvard Business Review.* https://hbr.org/2016/07/beyond-the-holacracy-hype
39. Greer, L. L., de Jong, B. A., Schouten, M. E., & Dannals, J. E. (2018). Why and when hierarchy impacts team effectiveness: A meta-analytic integration. *Journal of Applied Psychology, 103*(6), 591–613. https://doi.org/10.1037/apl0000291
40. Kellerman, B. (2012). *The end of leadership*. Harper Business.
41. Waterman, R. H. (1990). *Adhocracy: The power to change (the larger agenda)*. Whittle Direct Books.
42. Cascio, W. F., Young, C. E., & Morris, J. R. (1999). Financial consequences of employment-change decisions in major US corporations. *Academy of Management Journal, 40*, 1175–1189.
43. Huang, G.-H., Wellman, N., Ashford, S. J., Lee, C., & Wang, L. (2017). Deviance and exit: The organizational costs of job insecurity and moral disengagement. *Journal of Applied Psychology, 102*(1), 26–42. https://doi.org/10.1037/apl0000158

Chapter 5

1. Hunt, S. T. (2007). *Hiring success: The art and science of staffing assessment and employee selection*. Jossey-Bass.
2. Hoffman, R., Casnocha, B., & Yeh, C. (2014, August 1). Tours of duty: The new employer-employee compact. *Harvard Business Review.* https://hbr.org/2013/06/tours-of-duty-the-new-employer-employee-compact
3. Adler, L. (2020, August 18). New survey reveals 85% of all jobs are filled via networking. LinkedIn. https://www.linkedin.com/pulse/new-survey-reveals-85-all-jobs-filled-via-networking-lou-adler/
4. Terjesen, S., Vinnicombe, S., & Freeman, C. (2007). Attracting generation Y graduates: Organisational attributes, likelihood to apply and sex difference. *Career Development International, 12*(6), 504–522. https://doi.org/10.1108/13620430710821994
5. Van Iddekinge, C. H., Aguinis, H., Mackey, J. D., & DeOrtentiis, P. S. (2017). A meta-analysis of the interactive, additive, and relative effects

of cognitive ability and motivation on performance. *Journal of Management, 44*(1), 249–279. https://doi.org/10.1177/0149206317702220

6. Alias, N. E., Noor, N. M., & Hassan, R. (2014). Examining the mediating effect of employee engagement on the relationship between talent management practices and employee retention in the information and technology (IT) organizations in Malaysia. *Journal of Human Resources Management and Labor Studies,. 2*(2), 227–242.

7. Kossek, E. E., Hammer, L. B., Thompson, R. J., & Burke, L. B. (2014). *Leveraging workplace flexibility for engagement and productivity.* SHRM Foundation.

8. Markus, H., & Nurius, P. (1986). Possible selves. *American Psychologist, 41*(9), 954–969. https://doi.org/10.1037/0003-066x.41.9.954

9. US Bureau of Labor Statistics. (2021, September). Fastest growing occupations. https://www.bls.gov/emp/tables/fastest-growing-occupations.htm

10. National Retail Federation. (1997). About retail jobs. https://nrf.com/insights/economy/about-retail-jobs; Bammant, H. (2022, January 7). A list of fashion industry jobs you didn't know existed (and how to get them). *Fashion Journal.* https://fashionjournal.com.au/fashion/translating-job-titles-in-fashion-industry/; Southard, J. (2021, November 10). 5 reasons to start a career in manufacturing. TERRA Staffing Group. https://www.terrastaffinggroup.com/resources/blog/5-reasons-to-start-a-manufacturing-career/

11. Campion, M. C., Ployhart, R. E., & Campion, M. A. (2017). Using recruitment source timing and diagnosticity to enhance applicants' occupation-specific human capital. *Journal of Applied Psychology, 102*(5), 764–781 https://doi.org/10.1037/apl0000190

12. Gardner, T. M., Erhardt, N. L., & Martin-Rios, C. (2011), Rebranding employment branding: Establishing a new research agenda to explore the attributes, antecedents, and consequences of workers' employment brand knowledge. In A. Joshi, H. Liao, H., & J. J. Martocchio (Eds.), *Research in personnel and human resources management* (Vol. 30, pp. 253–304). Emerald Group Publishing Limited. https://doi.org/10.1108/S0742-7301(2011)0000030008

13. For example, www.glassdoor.com.

14. Massachusetts Institute of Technology. (2013, March 19). How much does a company's reputation matter in recruiting? *MIT Sloan Management Review.* https://sloanreview.mit.edu/article/how-much-does-a-companys-reputation-matter-in-recruiting/

15. Avery, D. R., & Mckay, P. F. (2006). Target practice: An organizational impression management approach to attracting minority and female job applicants. *Personnel Psychology, 59*(1), 157–187. https://doi.org/10.1111/j.1744-6570.2006.00807.x

16. Walker, H. J., Feild, H. S., Bernerth, J. B., & Becton, J. B. (2012). Diversity cues on recruitment websites: Investigating the effects on job seekers' information processing. *Journal of Applied Psychology, 97*(1), 214–224.

17. Miller, S. (2019). Employers less transparent about pay, aspire to be more open. SHRM. https://www.shrm.org/resourcesandtools/hr-topics /compensation/pages/employers-less-transparent-about-pay.aspx

18. DeOrtentiis, P. S., Van Iddekinge, C. H., Ployhart, R. E., & Heetderks, T. D. (2018). Build or buy? The individual and unit-level performance of internally versus externally selected managers over time. *Journal of Applied Psychology, 103*(8), 916–928.

19. Pieper, J. R., Trevor, C. O., Weller, I., & Duchon, D. (2019). Refer-ral hire presence implications for referrer turnover and job perfor-mance. *Journal of Management, 45*(5), 1858–1888. https://doi.org /10.1177/0149206317739959

20. Newman, D. A., & Lyon, J. S. (2009). Recruitment efforts to reduce adverse impact: Targeted recruiting for personality, cognitive ability, and diversity. *Journal of Applied Psychology, 94*(2), 298–317. https:// doi.org/10.1037/a0013472

21. Zielinski, D. (2019, August 16). Study: Most job seekers abandon online job applications. SHRM. https://www.shrm.org/resourcesandtools/hr -topics/technology/pages/study-most-job-seekers-abandon-online-job -applications.aspx

22. Hardy, J. H., Gibson, C., Sloan, M., & Carr, A. (2017). Are applicants more likely to quit longer assessments? Examining the effect of assess-ment length on applicant attrition behavior. *Journal of Applied Psychol-ogy, 102*(7), 1148–1158. https://doi.org/10.1037/apl0000213

23. Handler, C. (2020, May 14). Talent assessment market overview. Rocket-Hire. https://rocket-hire.com/2018/02/02/talent-assessment-market -overview/

24. Hunt. S (2007). *Hiring success: The art and science of staffing assess-ment and employee selection*. Pfeiffer.

25. Walker, H. J., Bauer, T. N., Cole, M. S., Bernerth, J. B., Feild, H. S., & Short, J. C. (2013). Is this how I will be treated? Reducing uncertainty through recruitment interactions. *Academy of Management Journal, 56*(5), 1325–1347. https://doi.org/10.5465/amj.2011.0196.

26. Meglino, B. M., Denisi, A. S., & Ravlin, E. C. (1993). Effects of previous job exposure and subsequent job status on the functioning of a realistic job preview. *Personnel Psychology, 46*, 803–822.

27. Bal, P. M., & Boehm, S. A. (2019). How do I-deals influence client satisfaction? The role of exhaustion, collective commitment, and age diversity. *Journal of Management, 45*(4), 1461–1487. https://doi.org /10.1177/0149206317710722

28. Foulk, T. A., & Long, D. M. (2016). Impressed by impression management: Newcomer reactions to ingratiated supervisors. *Journal of Applied Psychology, 101*(10), 1487–1497. https://doi.org/10.1037/apl0000146

29. Bauer, T. N., & Erdogan, B. (2011). Organizational socialization: The effective onboarding of new employees. In S. Zedeck (Ed.), *APA handbook of industrial and organizational psychology: Maintaining, expanding, and contracting the organization* (Vol. 3, pp. 51–64). American Psychological Association. https://doi.org/10.1037/12171-002

30. Sertoglu, C., & Berkowitch, A. (2014, August 1). Cultivating ex-employees. *Harvard Business Review.* https://hbr.org/2002/06/cultivating-ex-employees

31. Rockmann, K. W., & Ballinger, G. A. (2017). Intrinsic motivation and organizational identification among on-demand workers. *Journal of Applied Psychology, 102*(9), 1305–1316. https://doi.org/10.1037/apl0000224

32. Rigby, D., Sutherland, J., & Takeuchi, H. (2021, August 27). Embracing agile. *Harvard Business Review.* https://hbr.org/2016/05/embracing-agile

33. McKinsey and Company. (2020). A new AI-powered network is helping workers displaced by the coronavirus crisis. https://www.mckinsey.com/about-us/new-at-mckinsey-blog/how-two-organizations-we-served-are-helping-workers-displaced-by-the-coronavirus-crisis-find-new-jobs

34. Truxillo, D. M., & Bauer, T. N. (2011). Applicant reactions to organizations and selection systems. In S. Zedeck (Ed.), *APA handbook of industrial and organizational psychology: Selecting and developing members for the organization* (Vol. 2, pp. 379–397). American Psychological Association. https://doi.org/10.1037/12170-012

35. Sydell, E., Hudy, M., & Ashley, M. (2022). *Decoding talent: How AI and big data can solve your company's people puzzle.* Fast Company Press.

Chapter 6

1. Van Hootegem, A., Niesen, W., & de Witte, H. (2018). Does job insecurity hinder innovative work behaviour? A threat rigidity perspective. *Creativity and Innovation Management, 28*(1), 19–29. https://doi.org/10.1111/caim.12271

2. Cheval, B., Tipura, E., Burra, N., Frossard, J., Chanal, J., Orsholits, D., Radel, R., & Boisgontier, M. P. (2018). Avoiding sedentary behaviors requires more cortical resources than avoiding physical activity: An EEG study. *Neuropsychologia, 119*, 68–80. https://doi.org/10.1016/j.neuropsychologia.2018.07.029

3. Kennard, J. (2017, October 17). Low completion rates of large open online courses force a rethink of effective executive training. *Training Journal*. https://www.trainingjournal.com/articles/partner_article/low-completion-rates-large-open-online-courses-force-rethink-effective

4. Ross, A. (2019, May 17). Why did Google abandon 20% time for innovation? HRZone. https://www.hrzone.com/lead/culture/why-did-google-abandon-20-time-for-innovation

5. McCall, M. W., Lombardo, M. M., & Morrison, A. M. (1988). *Lessons of experience: How successful executives develop on the job*. Amsterdam University Press.

6. Hernandez, M., & Guarana, C. L. (2018). An examination of the temporal intricacies of job engagement. *Journal of Management*, *44*(5), 1711–1735. https://doi.org/10.1177/0149206315622573

7. Jacobs, R., & Washington, C. (2003). Employee development and organizational performance: A review of literature and directions for future research, *Human Resource Development International*, *6*(3), 343–354. doi:10.1080/13678860110096211

8. Dearborn, J., & Swanson, D. (2017). *The data driven leader*. Wiley.

9. Livingston, S. (2016, February 18). Employees can learn resilience to stress. Business Insurance. https://www.businessinsurance.com/article/20160218/NEWS03/160219804/employees-can-learn-resilience-to-stress

10. Berson, Y., Oreg, S., & Dvir, T. (2008). CEO values, organizational culture and firm outcomes. *Journal of Organizational Behavior*, *29*(5), 615–633. https://doi.org/10.1002/job.499

11. Dweck, C. S. (2007). *Mindset: The new psychology of success*. Ballantine Books.

12. Pak, J., & Kim, S. (2018). Team manager's implementation, high performance work systems intensity, and performance: A multilevel investigation. *Journal of Management*, *44*(7), 2690–2715. https://doi.org/10.1177/0149206316646829

13. Wilkins, J. R. (2011). Construction workers' perceptions of health and safety training programmes. *Construction Management and Economics*, *29*(10), 1017–1026. https://doi.org/10.1080/01446193.2011.633538

14. Ricci, F., Chiesi, A., Bisio, C., Panari, C., & Pelosi, A. (2016). Effectiveness of occupational health and safety training. *Journal of Workplace Learning*, *28*(6), 355–377. https://doi.org/10.1108/jwl-11-2015-0087

15. Strivr Labs, Inc. (2021, May 29). The science behind learning in VR. https://www.strivr.com/resources/ebooks/science/

16. HR.com Limited. (2004, March). Avoiding "the sheep dip." https://www.hr.com/en/communities/training_and_development/avoiding-the-sheep-dip_ead0rt08.html

17. Kruger, J., & Dunning, D. (1999). Unskilled and unaware of it: How difficulties in recognizing one's own incompetence lead to inflated self-assessments. *Journal of Personality and Social Psychology, 77*(6), 1121–1134. https://doi.org/10.1037/0022-3514.77.6.1121
18. Allen, T. D., Eby, L. T., & Lentz, E. (2006). Mentorship behaviors and mentorship quality associated with formal mentoring programs: Closing the gap between research and practice. *Journal of Applied Psychology, 91*(3), 567–578. https://doi.org/10.1037/0021-9010.91.3.567
19. Kahn, W. A. (1990). Psychological conditions of personal engagement and disengagement at work. *Academy of Management Journal, 33*(4), 692–724. https://doi.org/10.5465/256287
20. Frazier, M. L., Fainshmidt, S., Klinger, R. L., Pezeshkan, A., & Vracheva, V. (2017). Psychological safety: A meta-analytic review and extension. *Personnel Psychology, 70*(1), 113–165. doi:http://dx.doi.org/10.1111/peps.12183
21. Chernyak-Hai, L., & Rabenu, E. (2018). The new era workplace relationships: Is social exchange theory still relevant? *Industrial and Organizational Psychology, 11*(3), 456–481. doi:10.1017/iop.2018.5
22. American Psychological Association. (n.d.). Belonging. *APA dictionary of psychology.* https://dictionary.apa.org/belonging
23. Fast, N. J., Burris, E. R., & Bartel, C. A. (2014). Managing to stay in the dark: Managerial self-efficacy, ego defensiveness, and the aversion to employee voice. *Academy of Management Journal, 57*(4), 1013–1034. https://doi.org/10.5465/amj.2012.0393

Chapter 7

1. Wiles, J. (2019). *The real impact on employees of removing performance ratings. Gartner.*
2. Torka, A. K., Mazei, J., & Hüffmeier, J. (2021). Together, everyone achieves more—or, less? An interdisciplinary meta-analysis on effort gains and losses in teams. *Psychological Bulletin, 147*(5), 504–534. https://doi.org/10.1037/bul0000251
3. Hunt, S. (2016). *Common sense talent management: Using strategic human resources to improve company performance* (p. 151). Wiley.
4. Locke, E. A., & Latham, G. P. (2002). Building a practically useful theory of goal setting and task motivation: A 35-year odyssey. *American Psychologist, 57*(9), 705–717. https://doi.org/10.1037/0003-066X.57.9.705 (Quote from p. 705.)
5. Dweck, C. S. (2007). *Mindset: The new psychology of success* (updated ed.). Ballantine Books.

6. Locke, E. A. & Latham, G. P. (Eds.). (2013). *New developments in goal setting and task performance*. Routledge/Taylor & Francis Group.

7. Mero, N. P., Guidice, R. M., & Werner, S. (2014). A field study of the antecedents and performance consequences of perceived accountability. *Journal of Management*, *40*(6), 1627–1652. https://doi.org/10.1177/0149206312441208

8. Kluger, A. N., & DeNisi, A. (1996). The effects of feedback interventions on performance: A historical review, a meta-analysis, and a preliminary feedback intervention theory. *Psychological Bulletin, 119*(2), 254–284. https://doi.org/10.1037/0033-2909.119.2.254
Harter, J. K. (2000). Managerial talent, employee engagement, and business-unit performance. *The Psychologist-Manager Journal, 4*(2), 215–224. https://doi.org/10.1037/h0095893

9. Wo, D. X., Schminke, M., & Ambrose, M. L. (2019). Trickle-down, trickle-out, trickle-up, trickle-in, and trickle-around effects: An integrative perspective on indirect social influence phenomena. *Journal of Management*, *45*(6), 2263–2292.

10. Zimmerman, B. J., & Schunk, D. H. (Eds.). (2011). *Handbook of self-regulation of learning and performance*. Routledge/Taylor & Francis Group.

11. Thaler, R. H., & Sunstein, C. R. (2009). *Nudge: Improving decisions about health, wealth, and happiness* (rev. and expanded ed.). Penguin Books.

12. Fleenor, J. W., Taylor, S., & Chappelow, C. (2009). Leveraging the impact of 360-degree feedback. *Personnel Psychology, 62*(1), 175–179. https://doi.org/10.1111/j.1744-6570.2008.01133_2.x

13. Beck, J. W., Beatty, A. S., & Sackett, P. R. (2014). On the distribution of job performance: The role of measurement characteristics in observed departures from normality. *Personnel Psychology, 67*(3), 531–566.

14. Dietz, B., van Knippenberg, D., Hirst, G., & Restubog, S. L. D. (2015). Outperforming whom? A multilevel study of performance-prove goal orientation, performance, and the moderating role of shared team identification. *Journal of Applied Psychology, 100*(6), 1811–1824. https://doi.org/10.1037/a0038888

15. Quade, M. J., Greenbaum, R. L., & Petrenko, O. V. (2017). "I don't want to be near you, unless . . .": The interactive effect of unethical behavior and performance onto relationship conflict and workplace ostracism. *Personnel Psychology, 70*(3), 675–709.

16. Botelho, E. L., Wright, B., & Powell, K. R. (2021, September 17). Research: When getting fired is good for your career. *Harvard Business Review*. https://hbr.org/2018/10/research-when-getting-fired-is-good-for-your-career

17. Bloom, N., & van Reenen, J. (2007). Measuring and explaining management practices across firms and countries. *The Quarterly Journal of Economics, 122*(4), 1351–1408. https://doi.org/10.1162/qjec.2007.122.4.1351

18. Folger, N., Brosi, P., & Stumpf-Wollersheim, J. (2021). Applicant reactions to digital selection methods: A signaling perspective on innovativeness and procedural justice. *Journal of Business Psychology*. https://doi.org/10.1007/s10869-021-09770-3

19. Pytel, L., & Hunt, S.T. (2017). *Total workforce management. SAP SuccessFactors.* https://www.successfactors.com/en_us/download.html?a=/content/dam/successfactors/en_us/resources/white-papers/wp-calibration-best-practices.pdf

20. Beugre, C. D., & Baron, R. A. (2006). Perceptions of systemic justice: The effects of distributive, procedural, and interactional justice. *Journal of Applied Social Psychology, 31*(2), 324–339. https://doi.org/10.1111/j.1559-1816.2001.tb00199.x

21. Deng, H., & Leung, K. (2014). Contingent punishment as a double-edged sword: A dual-pathway model from a sense-making perspective. *Personnel Psychology, 67*(4), 951–980.

22. Hunt, S. T. (2014). *Common sense talent management: Using strategic human resources to improve company performance.* Pfeiffer.

23. Smith, D. (2015). Most people have no idea if they are being paid fairly. *Harvard Business Review.* https://hbr.org/2015/10/most-people-have-no-idea-whether-theyre-paid-fairly

24. Gerhart, B., & Fang, M. (2015). Pay, intrinsic motivation, extrinsic motivation, performance, and creativity in the workplace: Revisiting long-held beliefs. *The Annual Review of Organizational Psychology & Organizational Behavior*, pp. 489–521. (Quote from p. 489.)

25. Kerr, S. (1975). On the folly of rewarding A, while hoping for B. *Academy of Management Journal, 18*(4), 769–783. https://doi.org/10.5465/255378

26. Schaubroeck, J., Shaw, J. D., Duffy, M. K., & Mitra, A. (2008). An under-met and over-met expectations model of employee reactions to merit raises. *Journal of Applied Psychology, 93(2),* 424-434.

27. Shaw, J. D. (2014). Pay dispersion. *The Annual Review of Organizational Psychology and Organizational Behavior*, pp. 521–44.

28. Trevor, C. O., Gerhart, B., & Boudreau, J. W. (1997). Voluntary turnover and job performance: Curvilinearity and the moderating influences of salary growth and promotions. *Journal of Applied Psychology, 82*(1), 44–61. https://doi.org/10.1037/0021-9010.82.1.44

29. Han, J. H., Bartol, K. M., & Kim, S. (2015). Tightening up the performance–pay linkage: Roles of contingent reward leadership and profit-sharing in the cross-level influence of individual pay-for-performance. *Journal of Applied Psychology, 100*(2), 417–430. https://doi.org/10.1037/a0038282

30. Trevor, C. O., Reilly, G., & Gerhart, B. (2012). Reconsidering pay dispersion's effect on the performance of interdependent work: Reconciling sorting and pay inequality. *Academy of Management Journal, 55*(3), 585–610. https://doi.org/10.5465/amj.2006.0127

31. Belogolovsky, E., & Bamberger, P. A. (2014). Signaling in secret: Pay for performance and the incentive and sorting effects of pay secrecy. *Academy of Management Journal, 57*(6), 1706–1733.

32. Scarpello, V., & Jones, F. F. (1996). Why justice matters in compensation decision making. *Journal of Organizational Behavior, 17*(3), 285–299. https://doi.org/10.1002/(SICI)1099-1379(199605)17:3<285::AID-JOB750>3.0.CO;2-0

33. Scheller, E. M., & Harrison, W. (2018). Ignorance is bliss, or is it? The effects of pay transparency, informational justice and distributive justice on pay satisfaction and affective commitment. *Compensation & Benefits Review, 50*(2), 65–81. https://doi.org/10.1177/0886368719833215

Chapter 8

1. STR. (2021, January 20). 2020 officially the worst year on record for U.S. hotels. https://str.com/press-release/str-2020-officially-worst-year-on-record-for-us-hotels

2. McMahon, A. M. (2011). Does workplace diversity matter? A survey of empirical studies on diversity and firm performance, 2000–09. *Journal of Diversity Management, 5*(2). https://doi.org/10.19030/jdm.v5i2.808

3. Merriam-Webster. (n.d.). Value. https://www.merriam-webster.com/dictionary/value

4. Walker, H. J., Feild, H. S., Bernerth, J. B., & Becton, J. B. (2012). Diversity cues on recruitment websites: Investigating the effects on job seekers' information processing. *Journal of Applied Psychology, 97*, 214–224. https://doi.org/10.1037/a0025847

5. King, E. B., Botsford, W., Hebl, M. R., Kazama, S., Dawson, J. F., & Perkins, A. (2012). Benevolent sexism at work: Gender differences in the distribution of challenging developmental experiences. *Journal of Management, 38*(6), 1835–1866. https://doi.org/10.1177/0149206310365902

6. Centers for Disease Prevention and Control. (2020). Key findings: CDC releases first estimates of the number of adults living with autism spectrum disorder in the United States. https://www.cdc.gov/ncbddd/autism/features/adults-living-with-autism-spectrum-disorder.html

7. Praslova, L. (2021, December 14). Autism doesn't hold people back at work. Discrimination does. *Harvard Business Review.* https://hbr.org/2021/12/autism-doesnt-hold-people-back-at-work-discrimination-does

8. Semmer, N. K., Jacobshagen, N., Meier, L. L., Elfering, A., Beehr, T. A., Kälin, W., & Tschan, F. (2015). Illegitimate tasks as a source of work stress. *Work & Stress, 29*(1), 32–56. https://doi.org/10.1080/02678373.2014.1003996

9. Eisenberger, R., Fasolo, P., & Davis-LaMastro, V. (1990). Perceived organizational support and employee diligence, commitment, and innovation. *Journal of Applied Psychology, 75*(1), 51–59. doi:10.1037/0021-9010.75.1.51

10. Fisher, S. L., & Howell, A. W. (2004). Beyond user acceptance: An examination of employee reactions to information technology systems. *Human Resource Management, 43*, 243–258.

11. Park, S., Jeong, S., & Chai, D. S. (2021). Remote e-workers' psychological well-being and career development in the era of COVID-19: Challenges, success factors, and the roles of HRD professionals. *Advances in Developing Human Resources, 23*(3), 222–236.

12. Lepine, J. A., Podsakoff, N. P., & Lepine, M. A. (2005). A meta-analytic test of the challenge stressor–hindrance stressor framework: An explanation for inconsistent relationships among stressors and performance. *Academy of Management Journal, 48*(5), 764–775. https://doi.org/10.5465/amj.2005.18803921; Wilson, C. A., & Britt, T. W. (2021). Living to work: The role of occupational calling in response to challenge and hindrance stressors. *Work & Stress, 35*(2), 111–131.

13. Byrne, Z. S., Peters, J. M., & Weston, J. W. (2016). The struggle with employee engagement: Measures and construct clarification using five samples. *Journal of Applied Psychology, 101*(9), 1201.

14. American Psychological Association. (2020, October). Stress in America™ 2020: A national mental health crisis. https://www.apa.org/news/press/releases/stress/2020/report-october#

15. Miner-Rubino, K., & Cortina, L. M. (2007). Beyond targets: Consequences of vicarious exposure to misogyny at work. *Journal of Applied Psychology, 92*(5), 1254–1269. https://doi.org/10.1037/0021-9010.92.5.1254

16. Kramer, R. M., & Cook, K. S. (2004). Trust and distrust in organizations: Dilemmas and approaches. In R. M. Kramer & K. S. Cook (Eds.), *Trust and distrust in organizations: Dilemmas and approaches* (pp. 1–18). Russell Sage Foundation.

17. MacDonald, H. A., Colotla, V., & Flamer, S. (2003) Posttraumatic stress disorder (PTSD) in the workplace: A descriptive study of workers experiencing PTSD resulting from work injury. *Journal of Occupational Rehabilitation, 13*, 63–77. https://doi.org/10.1023/A:1022563930482

18. Hagen, C. S., Bighash, L., Hollingshead, A. B., Shaikh, S. J., & Alexander, K. S. (2018). Why are you watching? Video surveillance in organizations. *Corporate Communications: An International Journal, 23*(2), 274–291. https://doi.org/10.1108/CCIJ-04-2017-0043

19. Auxier, B., Rainie, L., Anderson, M., Perrin, A., Kumar, M., & Turner, E. (2020, August 17). Americans and privacy: Concerned, confused and feeling lack of control over their personal information. Pew Research Center: Internet, Science & Tech. https://www.pewresearch.org/internet/2019/11/15/americans-and-privacy-concerned-confused-and-feeling-lack-of-control-over-their-personal-information/

20. Ikeda, S. (2019, May 28). Phishing attacks: Now more common than malware. *CPO Magazine*. https://www.cpomagazine.com/cyber-security /phishing-attacks-now-more-common-than-malware/

21. Guo, K. H., Yuan, Y., Archer, N. P., & Connelly, C. E. (2011). Understanding nonmalicious security violations in the workplace: A composite behavior model. *Journal of Management Information Systems*, *28*(2), 203–236. https://doi.org/10.2753/mis0742-1222280208

22. Jaafar, N. I., & Ajis, A. (2013). Organizational climate and individual factors effects on information security compliance behaviour. *International Journal of Business and Social Science*, *4*(10). https://doi.org /10.30845/ijbss

23. Wolford, B. (2019, February 13). What is GDPR, the EU's new data protection law? GDPR.Eu. https://gdpr.eu/what-is-gdpr/

24. Bhave, D. P., Teo, L. H., & Dalal, R. S. (2020). Privacy at work: A review and a research agenda for a contested terrain. *Journal of Management*, *46*(1), 127–164.

25. Alge, B. J., Ballinger, G. A., Tangirala, S., & Oakley, J. L. (2006). Information privacy in organizations: empowering creative and extrarole performance. *Journal of Applied Psychology*, *91*, 221.

26. Alge, B. J. (2001). Effects of computer surveillance on perceptions of privacy and procedural justice. *Journal of Applied Psychology*, *86*(4), 797.

27. Alder, G. S., & Ambrose, M. L. (2005). An examination of the effect of computerized performance monitoring feedback on monitoring fairness, performance, and satisfaction. *Organizational Behavior and Human Decision Processes*, *97*(2), 161–177.

28. Brynjolfsson, E., & McAfee, A. (2016). *The second machine age: Work, progress, and prosperity in a time of brilliant technologies*. W. W. Norton & Company.

29. Whitener, E. M. (1997). The impact of human resource activities on employee trust. *Human Resource Management Review*, *7*(4), 389–404. https://doi.org/10.1016/s1053-4822(97)90026-7

30. Casey, T., Griffin, M. A., Flatau Harrison, H., & Neal, A. (2017). Safety climate and culture: Integrating psychological and systems perspectives. *Journal of Occupational Health Psychology*, *22*(3), 341–353. http:// dx.doi.org/10.1037/ocp0000072.

31. Mearns, K., Hope, L., Ford, M. T., & Tetrick, L. E. (2010). Investment in workforce health: Exploring the implications for workforce safety climate and commitment. *Accident Analysis & Prevention*, *42*(5), 1445– 1454. https://doi.org/10.1016/j.aap.2009.08.009.

32. Wachter, J. K., & Yorio, P. L. (2014). A system of safety management practices and worker engagement for reducing and preventing accidents: An empirical and theoretical investigation. *Accident Analysis & Prevention*, *68*, 117–130. https://doi.org/10.1016/j.aap.2013.07.029

33. Weaver, G. R. (2004). Ethics and employees: Making the connection. *Academy of Management Perspectives, 18*(2), 121–125. https://doi .org/10.5465/ame.2004.13836241

34. Huang, L., & Paterson, T. A. (2016). Group ethical voice: Influence of ethical leadership and impact on ethical performance. *Journal of Management, 43*(4), 1157–1184. https://doi.org/10.1177/0149206314546195

35. Wang, H., Tong, L., Takeuchi, R., & George, G. (2016). Corporate social responsibility: An overview and new research directions. *Academy of Management Journal, 59*(2), 534–544. https://doi.org/10.5465 /amj.2016.5001

36. Ng, T. W., Yam, K. C., & Aguinis, H. (2019). Employee perceptions of corporate social responsibility: Effects on pride, embeddedness, and turnover. *Personnel Psychology, 72*(1), 107–137.

37. Levine, S. (2020, January 15). Diversity confirmed to boost innovation and financial results. *Forbes.*

38. HR.Research. (2019). The state of diversity and inclusion 2019: Improving D&I practices to boost organizational innovation and performance. https://www.hr.com/en/resources/free_research_white_papers/hrcom -state-of-diversity-inclusion-2019-feb2019_jrttnwuk.html

39. Leslie, L. M., et al. (2020). On melting pots and salad bowls: A meta-analysis of the effects of identify-blind and identity-conscious diversity ideologies. *Journal of Applied Psychology, 105*(5), 453–471.

40. King, E. B., Mendoza, S. A., Madera, J. M., Hebl, M. R., & Knight, J. L. (2006). What's in a name? A multiracial investigation of the role of occupational stereotypes in selection decisions. *Journal of Applied Social Psychology, 36*(5), 1145–1159. https://doi.org/10.1111/j.0021 -9029.2006.00035.x

41. Parker, K. (2015). Women more than men adjust their careers for family life. Pew Research Center. https://www.pewresearch.org/fact -tank/2015/10/01/women-more-than-men-adjust-their-careers-for -family-life/

42. Hunt, S. T. (2021, May 12). How hybrid remote work improves diversity and inclusion. *Forbes.* https://www.forbes.com/sites/sap/2021/05 /12/how-hybrid-remote-work-improves-diversity-and-inclusion /?sh=71d26222321f

43. Mayer, K. (2021, April 27). Requiring employees to return to the office? Get ready for them to quit. HR Executive. https://hrexecutive.com /requiring-employees-to-return-to-the-office-get-ready-for-the   Human Resources Research Team. (2021, March 4). 3 hybrid work challenges driving employee fatigue. Gartner. https://www.gartner.com /document/3998883?ref

45. Robinson, J., & Hickman, A. (2021, February 19). Leading teams forward, advised by Gallup remote work trends. Gallup.Com. https://

www.gallup.com/workplace/329726/leading-teams-forward-advised
-gallup-remote-work-trends.aspx

46. LeBeau, P. (2019, February 12). Traffic jams cost US $87 billion in lost productivity in 2018, and Boston and DC have the nation's worst. CNBC. https://www.cnbc.com/2019/02/11/americas-87-billion-traffic-jam -ranks-boston-and-dc-as-worst-in-us.html

47. Sonnentag, S., & Frese, M. (2003). Stress in organizations. In I. B. Weiner (Ed.), *Handbook of psychology*. Wiley. https://doi.org/10.1002/04712 64385.wei1218

48. Goetzel, R. Z., Jacobson, B. H., Aldana, S. G., Vardell, K., & Yee, L. (1998). Health care costs of worksite health promotion participants and non-participants. *Journal of Occupational & Environmental Medicine*, *40*(4), 341–346. https://doi.org/10.1097/00043764-199804000-00008

49. Moreau, M., Valente, F., Mak, R., et al. (2004). Occupational stress and incidence of sick leave in the Belgian workforce: The Belstress study. *Journal of Epidemiology & Community Health*, *58*(6), 507–516. https:// doi.org/10.1136/jech.2003.007518

50. Ng, T. W. H., & Feldman, D. C. (2011). Employee voice behavior: A meta-analytic test of the conservation of resources framework. *Journal of Organizational Behavior*, *33*(2), 216–234. https://doi.org /10.1002/job.754

51. Kossek, E. E., Pichler, S., Bodner, T., & Hammer, L. B. (2011). Workplace social support and work-family conflict: A meta-analysis clarifying the influence of general and work-family-specific supervisor and organizational support. *Personnel Psychology*, *64*(2), 289–313. https:// doi.org/10.1111/j.1744-6570.2011.01211.x

52. Jones, D. A., Willness, C. R., & Madey, S. (2013). Why are job seekers attracted by corporate social performance? Experimental and field tests of three signal-based mechanisms. *Academy of Management Journal*, *57*(2), 383–404. https://doi.org/10.5465/amj.2011.0848

53. Miao, Q., & Zhou, J. (2020). Corporate hypocrisy and counterproductive work behavior: A moderated mediation model of organizational identification and perceived importance of CSR. *Sustainability*, *12*(5), 1847. https://doi.org/10.3390/su12051847

Chapter 9

1. Hollon, J. (2008, April). The Stupidus Maximus award honoring bad management. *Workforce Management*.

2. Tsipursky, G. (2018). Why go with your gut is terrible advice: When it comes to making decisions at work, we're better off trusting our heads than our feelings. Fast Company. www.fastcompany.com/40575508 /why-go-with-your-gut-is-terrible-advice

3. Judge, T. A., & Cable, T. M. (2004). The effect of physical height on workplace success and income: Preliminary test of a theoretical model. *Journal of Applied Psychology, 89*, 428–441.
4. O'Boyle, E., & Aguinis, H. (2012). The best and the rest: Revisiting the norm of normality of individual performance. *Personnel Psychology, 65*, 79–118.
5. Jones, L., Watson, B., Hobman, E., Bordia, P., Gallois, C., & Callan, V. J. (2008). Employee perceptions of organizational change: Impact of hierarchical level. *Leadership & Organization Development Journal, 29*(4), 294–316. https://doi.org/10.1108/01437730810876122
6. Barkema, H. G., & Shchijven, M. (2008). Toward unlocking the full potential of acquisitions: The role of organizational restructuring. *Academy of Management Journal, 51*.
7. Cooper, C. L. (1993). The role of culture compatibility in successful organizational marriage. *Academy of Management Perspective, 7*.
8. Greenwald, A. G., Banaji, M. R., & Nosek, B. A. (2015). Statistically small effects of the Implicit Association Test can have societally large effects. *Journal of Personality and Social Psychology, 108*(4), 553–561. https://doi.org/10.1037/pspa0000016
9. Rosett, C. M., & Hagerty, A. (2021). *Introducing HR analytics with machine learning: Empowering practitioners, psychologists, and organizations*. Springer.
10. Berry, M. (2015, December). How to fail at HR analytics in 7 easy steps: A "leading loser" shares what he learned the hard way—so you won't have to. *HR Magazine*.

Chapter 10

1. Boudreau, J. W., & Ramstad, P. M. (2005). Talentship, talent segmentation, and sustainability: A new HR decision science paradigm for a new strategy definition. *Human Resource Management, 44*(2), 129–136. https://doi.org/10.1002/hrm.20054
2. Miron-Shatz, T., Stone, A., & Kahneman, D. (2009). Memories of yesterday's emotions: Does the valence of experience affect the memory-experience gap? *Emotion, 9*(6), 885–891. https://doi.org/10.1037/a0017823
3. Poncheri, R. M., Lindberg, J. T., Thompson, L. F., & Surface, E. A. (2008). A comment on employee surveys: Negativity bias in open-ended responses. *Organizational Research Methods, 11*(3), 614–630. https://doi.org/10.1177/1094428106295504
4. Cappelli, P. (2015, July 6). Why we love to hate HR . . . and what HR can do about it. *Harvard Business Review*. https://hbr.org/2015/07/why-we-love-to-hate-hr-and-what-hr-can-do-about-it

5. Upchurch, Z. (2020). CHRO trends report. Talent Strategy Group. https://talentstrategygroup.com/chro-trends-2020/

6. Ulrich, D., Younger, J., Brockbank, W., & Ulrich, M .(2012). *HR from the outside in: Six competencies for the future of human resources.* McGraw-Hill.

7. Slovic, P., Peters, E., Finucane, M. L., & MacGregor, D. G. (2005). Affect, risk, and decision making. *Health Psychology, 24*(4, Suppl), S35–S40. https://doi.org/10.1037/0278-6133.24.4.S35

8. Oreg, S., & Berson, Y. (2017). Leaders' characteristics and behaviors and employees' resistance to organizational change. *Academy of Management Proceedings.* https://journals.aom.org/doi/epdf/10.5465/ambpp .2009.44259813

9. Yukl, G. (2012). Effective leadership behavior: What we know and what questions need more attention. *Academy of Management Perspectives, 26*(4), 66–85. https://doi.org/10.5465/amp.2012.0088

10. Crist|Kolder. (2021). Volatility report. https://www.cristkolder.com /volatility-report/

11. Morris, M. G., & Venkatesh, V. (2006). Age differences in technology adoption decisions: Implications for a changing work force. *Personnel Psychology, 53*(2), 375–403. https://doi.org/10.1111/j.1744 -6570.2000.tb00206.x

12. York, J. (2017, March 8). The millennial expectation of technology in the workplace. *Forbes.* https://www.forbes.com/sites/paycom/2017 /03/08/the-millennial-expectation-of-technology-in-the-workplace /?sh=9e0df614a507

13. Dahl, M. S., Dezső, C. L., & Ross, D. G. (2012). Fatherhood and managerial style: How a male CEO's children affect the wages of his employees. *Administrative Science Quarterly, 57*(4), 669–693. https://doi .org/10.1177/0001839212466521

14. Brett, J. M., & Stroh, L. K. (2003). Working 61 plus hours a week: Why do managers do it? *Journal of Applied Psychology, 88*(1), 67–78. https:// doi.org/10.1037/0021-9010.88.1.67

15. Cavanaugh, M. A., Boswell, W. R., Roehling, M. V., & Boudreau, J. W. (2000). An empirical examination of self-reported work stress among U.S. managers. *Journal of Applied Psychology, 85*(1), 65–74. doi:10 .1037/0021-9010.85.1.65

16. Sikora, D. M., Ferris, G. R., & van Iddekinge, C. H. (2015). Line manager implementation perceptions as a mediator of relations between high-performance work practices and employee outcomes. *Journal of Applied Psychology, 100*(6), 1908–1918. https://doi.org/10.1037/apl0000024

17. Meinert, D. (2014, July 21). Five types of bad bosses: What HR can do to improve the performance of the most common types of problem managers. *HR Magazine.*

18. Ltd, RAM. (2021, July). Global weight loss products and services market 2021–2026. Research and Markets Ltd 2022. https://www.researchandmarkets .com/reports/5393446/global-weight-loss-products-and-services-market

Chapter 11

1. Grandin, G. (2010). *Fordlandia: The rise and fall of Henry Ford's forgotten jungle city*. Picador.
2. May, M. (1982). The historical problem of the family wage: The Ford Motor Company and the five dollar day. *Feminist Studies, 8*(2), 399–424. https://doi.org/10.2307/3177569
3. Nilsson, J. (2018, October 3). Why did Henry Ford double his minimum wage? *The Saturday Evening Post*. https://www.saturdayeveningpost .com/2014/01/ford-doubles-minimum-wage/
4. Wikipedia. Slavery as a positive good in the United States. https:// en.wikipedia.org/wiki/Slavery_as_a_positive_good_in_the_United _States#cite_note-1
5. Hunt, S. T. (2014). *Common sense talent management: Using strategic human resources to improve company performance*. Pfeiffer.
6. Halal, W., Kolber, J., & Davies, O. (2016). Forecasts of AI and future jobs in 2030: Muddling through likely, with two alternative scenarios. *Journal of Futures Studies, 21*(2), 83–96. https://doi.org/10.6531 /JFS.2016.21(2).R83
7. Coelli, M., & Borland, J. (2019). Behind the headline number: Why not to rely on Frey and Osborne's predictions of potential job loss from automation. Melbourne Institute Working Paper No. 10/19. Melbourne Institute Applied Economic & Social Research.
8. Lund, S., Madgavkar, A., Manyika, J., Smit, S., Ellingrud, K., & Robinson, O. (2021, September 9). The future of work after COVID-19. McKinsey & Company. https://www.mckinsey.com/featured-insights/future-of -work/the-future-of-work-after-covid-19
9. Schwabe H., & Castellacci, F. (2020) Automation, workers' skills and job satisfaction. *PLoS ONE, 15*(11), e0242929. https://doi.org/10.1371 /journal.pone.0242929
10. Radiology Schools. (2019, January 3). Medical assistant with limited x-ray training. Radiology-Schools.Com. https://www.radiology-schools .com/medical-assistant-x-ray.html
11. Chankseliani, M., & Anuar, A. M. (2019). Cross-country comparison of engagement in apprenticeships: A conceptual analysis of incentives for individuals and firms. *International Journal for Research in Vocational Education and Training, 6*(3), 261–283. https://doi.org/10.13152 /ijrvet.6.3.4

12. US Department of Education. (2015). Demographic and enrollment characteristics of nontraditional undergraduates: 2011–12. Institute of Education Sciences. https://nces.ed.gov/pubs2015/2015025.pdf

13. Leslie, A. G. W., Powell, H. R., Winter, G., Svensson, O., Spruce, D., McSweeney, S., Love, D., Kinder, S., Duke, E., & Nave, C. (2002). Automation of the collection and processing of x-ray diffraction data: A generic approach. *Acta Crystallographica Section D Biological Crystallography*, *58*(11), 1924–1928. https://doi.org/10.1107/s0907444902016864

14. Zippia. (n.d.). Registered medical assistant demographics and statistics in the US. https://www.zippia.com/registered-medical-assistant-jobs /demographics/

15. Porter, M. E. (2000). Location, competition, and economic development: Local clusters in a global economy. *Economic Development Quarterly*, *14*(1), 15–34. doi:10.1177/089124240001400105

16. Sweet, S. (Ed.). (2012). *Work and family policy international comparative perspectives*. Routledge.

17. Czaika, M., & de Haas, H. (2013). The effectiveness of immigration policies. *Population and Development Review*, *39*(3), 487–508. https://doi .org/10.1111/j.1728-4457.2013.00613.x

18. Gaskin, D. J., Headen, A. E., & White-Means, S. I. (2004). Racial disparities in health and wealth: The effects of slavery and past discrimination. *The Review of Black Political Economy*, *32*(3–4), 95–110. https://doi .org/10.1007/s12114-005-1007-9

19. Petts, R. J., Carlson, D. L., & Pepin, J. R. (2020). A gendered pandemic: Childcare, homeschooling, and parents' employment during COVID-19. *Gender, Work & Organization*, *28*(S2), 515–534. https://doi.org/10.1111 /gwao.12614

20. Snyder, D. G., Stewart, V. R., & Shea, C. T. (2020). Hello again: Managing talent with boomerang employees. *Human Resource Management*, *60*(2), 295–312. https://doi.org/10.1002/hrm.22051

21. Autor, D. H., Kerr, W. R., & Kugler, A. D. (2007). Does employment protection reduce productivity? Evidence from US states. *The Economic Journal*, *117*(521), F189–F217. https://doi.org/10.1111/j.1468 -0297.2007.02055.x

22. Graham, C. (2008). Happiness and health: Lessons and questions for public policy. *Health Affairs*, *27*(1), 72–87. 10.1377/hlthaff.27.1.72

23. Society of Human Resource Management. (2022). Complying with the Affordable Care Act. https://www.shrm.org/resourcesandtools/tools-and-samples/ toolkits/pages/complyingwithandleveragingtheaffordablecareact.aspx

24. Miller, S. C. (2021, August 19). Employees are more likely to stay if they like their health plan. SHRM. https://www.shrm.org/resourcesandtools /hr-topics/benefits/pages/health-benefits-foster-retention.aspx

25. van Hooft, E. A. J., Kammeyer-Mueller, J. D., Wanberg, C. R., Kanfer, R., & Basbug, G. (2021). Job search and employment success: A quantitative review and future research agenda. *Journal of Applied Psychology, 106*(5), 674–713. https://doi.org/10.1037/apl0000675

26. Bünnings, C., Kleibrink, J., & Weßling, J. (2015). Fear of unemployment and its effect on the mental health of spouses. *Health Economics, 26*(1), 104–117. https://doi.org/10.1002/hec.3279

27. US Department of Labor. (2022). History of the wage and hour division. https://www.dol.gov/agencies/whd/about/history

28. Nagale-Piazza, L (2018). Tips for managing workers' after-hours use of mobile devices. Society of Human Resource Management. https://www.shrm.org/resourcesandtools/legal-and-compliance/employment-law/pages/tips-for-managing-worker-after-hours-use-of-mobile-devices.aspx

29. Mankins, M. (2017). Why the French email law won't restore work-life balance. *Harvard Business Review.* https://hbr.org/2017/01/why-the-french-email-law-wont-restore-work-life-balance

30. Manyika, J. (2019, July 16). Technology, jobs, and the future of work. McKinsey & Company. https://www.mckinsey.com/featured-insights/employment-and-growth/technology-jobs-and-the-future-of-work

31. Lai, J., & Widmar, N. O. (2020). Revisiting the digital divide in the COVID-19 era. *Applied Economic Perspectives and Policy, 43*(1), 458–464. https://doi.org/10.1002/aepp.13104

32. US Bureau of Labor Statistics. (2021, December). Job openings and labor turnover summary. https://www.bls.gov/news.release/jolts.nr0.htm

33. McNally, C., McNally, C., Wheelwright, T., Archambault, M., Woodall, M., & Sandorf, B. (2021, October 18). Nearly 1 in 4 households don't have internet—and a quarter million still use dial-up. Reviews.Org. https://www.reviews.org/internet-service/how-many-us-households-are-without-internet-connection/

34. Dodd, M. D., & Supa, D. W. (2014). Conceptualizing and measuring "corporate social advocacy" communication: Examining the impact on corporate financial performance. *Public Relations Journal, 8*(3). http://www.prsa.org/Intelligence/PRJournal/Vol8/No3/

35. RippleMatch Team. (2020). 35 companies with powerful social impact initiatives. https://ripplematch.com/journal/article/companies-with-powerful-social-impact-initiatives-65f368a5/

36. Barber, L. K., Grawitch, M. J., & Maloney, P. W. (2016). Work-life balance: Contemporary perspectives. In M. J. Grawitch & D. W. Ballard (Eds.), *The psychologically healthy workplace: Building a win-win environment for organizations and employees* (pp. 111–133). American Psychological Association. https://doi.org/10.1037/14731-006

37. Hammer, L. B., Ernst Kossek, E., Bodner, T., & Crain, T. (2013). Measurement development and validation of the Family Supportive Supervisor Behavior Short-Form (FSSB-SF). *Journal of Occupational Health Psychology, 18*(3), 285–296. https://doi.org/10.1037/a0032612

Chapter 12

1. Luy, M., Wegner-Siegmundt, C., Wiedemann, A., & Spijker, J. (2015). Life expectancy by education, income and occupation in Germany: Estimations using the longitudinal survival method. *Comparative Population Studies, 40*(4), 339–436. https://doi.org/10.12765/cpos-2015-16
2. Rosling, H., Rönnlund, A. R., & Rosling, O. (2018). *Factfulness: Ten reasons we're wrong about the world—and why things are better than you think* (Later print. ed.). Flatiron Books.

Appendix

1. O'Boyle Jr., E., & Aguinis, H. (2012). The best and the rest: Revisiting the norm of normality of individual performance. *Personnel Psychology, 65*(1), 79–119. https://doi.org/10.1111/j.1744-6570.2011.01239.x
2. Szatmari, B. (2021). Young stars and red giants: The moderating effect of age diversity on the relationship between the proportion of high performers and team performance. *Journal of Applied Psychology.* https://doi.org/10.1037/apl0000971

Acknowledgments

This book is the result of insights, encouragement, and opportunities received from thousands of people I have had the good fortune to work with over the course of my career. If I ever worked with you as a colleague, customer, or coworker then you helped in some way to contribute to this book. Thank you! There are a few individuals that I must also thank by name, as without them this book would never have gotten past the idea stage. Jill Popelka made the project a reality with her unexpected phone call asking, "I hear you want to write a book. How can I help?" Courtney Kimbrough "penetrated the bureaucracy" to get the project underway, and Hayden Boshart, Marne Hermes-Newman, and Brandi Starks kept it moving down the track. My wonderful and talented nieces Sarah Hunt and Spenser Nickell-Hunt enthusiastically responded when I reached out for much needed assistance with illustrations and promotion materials. Haley Dominique, Christy Robinson, Andrew Postman, and Matt Hart provided valuable comments on the manuscript. And a super special thanks to Kelly Hamilton who did the painful work of reviewing my first drafts and highlighting improvements they desperately needed. Many others helped with encouragement and assistance in one form or another. Please know I am indebted for your support. I am acutely aware that I did not do this on my own.

About the Author

Steven T. Hunt, PhD, has published several previous books, including *Hiring Success: The Art and Science of Staffing Assessment and Employee Selection* and *Commonsense Talent Management: Using Strategic Human Resources to Improve Company Performance*. A prolific writer and keynote speaker, his work focuses on understanding the intersection of human psychology, work technology, and business performance. He has worked with over 1,000 companies spanning five continents across almost every industry. Dr. Hunt was awarded the honor of Fellow in the Society for Industrial-Organizational Psychology for advancing psychological science through creation and application of technology solutions that have positively influenced the employee experience for millions of people working around the globe. Dr. Hunt's career is devoted to the belief that better work environments create better world environments.

Index